Education on the Edge of Possibility

Renate Nummela Caine and Geoffrey Caine

Association for Supervision and Curriculum Development
Alexandria, Virginia

D0089250

Association for Supervision and Curriculum Development
1250 N. Pitt Street • Alexandria, Virginia 22314-1453 USA
Telephone: 1-800-933-2723 or 703-549-9110 • Fax: 703-299-8631

Gene R. Carter, *Executive Director*
Michelle Terry, *Assistant Executive Director, Program Development*
Ronald S. Brandt, *Assistant Executive Director*
Nancy Modrak, *Director, Publishing*
Julie Houtz, *Managing Editor of Books*
Carolyn R. Pool, *Associate Editor*
Margaret Oosterman, *Associate Editor*
John Somers, *Project Assistant*
Maritza Bourque, *Project Assistant*
Gary Bloom, *Director, Design, Editorial, and Production Services*
Karen Monaco, *Senior Designer*
Tracey A. Smith, *Production Coordinator*
Dina Murray, *Production Assistant*
Valerie Sprague, *Desktop Publisher*
Sarah Allen Smith, *Indexer*

Printed in the United States of America.

ASCD Stock No.: 197021   ASCD member price: $16.95; nonmember price: $20.95

April 1997 member book (pcr). ASCD Premium, Comprehensive, and Regular members periodically receive ASCD books as part of their membership benefits. No. FY97-6.

Library of Congress Cataloging-in-Publication Data

Caine, Renate Nummela.
    Education on the edge of possibility / Renate Nummela Caine and Geoffrey Caine.
        p.   cm.
    Includes bibliographical references and index.
    ISBN 0-87120-282-4 (pbk.)
    1. Educational change—United States—Case studies.   2. Teaching—United States—Case studies.   3. Learning—Case studies.
    I. Caine, Geoffrey.   II. Title.
    LA210.C286   1997
    370'.973—dc21   97-4604
                                                                CIP

01 00 99 98 97   5 4 3 2 1

Education on the Edge of Possibility

We dedicate this book to Arthur W. Combs.

Introduction

An old Jewish proverb goes something like, "May you live in exciting times." This wish has certainly come to pass for our generation and for those of us engaged in education. But for many of us who do not have the time or opportunity to step back and see the "big picture" or the larger whole, this time is like a perceptual trick picture. From one angle, we see exciting opportunities for change. Blink our eyes and we see the same image as a frightening roadblock. This book is intended to contribute to a bigger picture. We hope it lends direction and vision to our common work as educators.

Unlike our last book with ASCD (*Making Connections: Teaching and the Human Brain,* Caine and Caine 1991), this book is not about brain research. It is about what happened when we took our theory of learning, based on a wholistic interpretation of brain research, and attempted to implement it in two schools. From the outset, we knew that the theory represented a new way of looking at learning and change. Therefore, we did not begin with teaching strategies and techniques; we began by having teachers get together in what we call *process groups.* These groups provided the participants the support and freedom to question their deepest assumptions about learning and teaching. We expected this deep questioning to shift their mental models (beliefs that are often hidden even from themselves but that structure their moment-to-moment actions) and then to change what they did in the classroom.

The project has been both challenging and exciting, and ultimately, we have learned at least as much as our teachers. We share what we have learned in this book. Perhaps the most significant thing we have confirmed for ourselves is that, although actions are important, the thinking that influences and shapes what we do is far more critical. Changing our thinking is the first thing we have to do both individually and collectively, because without that change we cannot possibly change what we really do on a day-to-day basis. Regardless of what new "method" or latest technique is attempted, the mind/brain will always choose to reduce such practices to fit entrenched assumptions and beliefs. To really restructure anything means to restructure our thinking and shift deep connections in our psyche. We cannot just rearrange the pieces in the box; we need—collectively—to conceive of what we do in fundamentally different ways. As such, this book represents a process of coming to understand how systemic change takes place. It also frames the education dilemma in very broad terms. It is not a "how to" book, although we believe that it provides insights that can ultimately improve practice in significant ways.

The book also identifies three specific approaches to practice and the beliefs that drive them. In the course of our work with teachers, we discovered three models for teaching and practice—and they are, to some extent, at odds. It is as if the ship called "Education for the Future" has left the harbor and is already on the open seas. Some educators are still clinging to the belief that the ship hasn't left and are invested in business as usual. Some educators are enjoying the freedom of the open seas and are focusing on keeping the ship in good shape; and some are at the helm, excited about the foreign ports and places they are convinced they will visit. This journey of change, then, has many opinions, perspectives, and visions. It is no wonder that as educators and as a society we are having trouble communicating with each other about the best way to educate our children.

When we first submitted our book to ASCD, we knew that it was too long but did not know how to reduce the size. Fortunately for us, our collective editors suggested dividing the book into two. This meant more work but also made a great deal of sense. It gave us more "breathing room" to describe our research and emergent under-standings. This is therefore the first of two books.

Education on the Edge of Possibility draws a broad outline of where we see education to be, describes our work with schools, and discusses what we learned about implementing brain-based learning and teaching. The second book, entitled *Unleashing the Power of Perceptual Change: The Potential of Brain-Based Teaching,* focuses more closely on the three instructional approaches, the three perceptual orientations, and the entire change process.

We owe thank you's to a number too large to recognize here. Hundreds of teachers took part in our research efforts, some formally and many informally; and many chose to remain anonymous. We thank all of them.

We owe a special debt of gratitude to the teachers and administrators at Dry Creek Elementary School in Rio Linda, California, and Park View Middle School, in Yucaipa, California. In particular, we thank the teachers in D-track, who were with us from the beginning. They are the real heroes who continue to work with us and to learn along with us. We also thank their districts and school boards for allowing this new vision to emerge. Specifically, we thank Project LEARN and the Illinois Math and Science Academy for participating in our research. We also thank those at the California Department of Education for the insight and vision that created the restructuring grants, long-term (five-year) grants from the state of California awarded to individual schools on a competitive basis to finance school restructuring. Our thanks go to those who initiated the Title I programs at the federal level. Without both of these financial sources, this project would have been impossible.

We thank Donald and Peggy Caine and others for continually reminding us to be sensitive to the many issues and to make certain that we did not frighten people needlessly or raise barriers that could hurt any genuine progress. We thank our readers: Art Combs, Kris Halvorsen, Cindy Tucker, Melissa Proffitt, Roberta Parrott, Duncan Johnson, Carol Lawrence, Sharon Bannister, Randy Peters, Donna Orr, and Gareth Montgomery.

Special thanks go to our friend Art Combs, to whom we dedicate this book. Our long-term association and friendship goes back to Renate's years at the University of Florida. His insightful comments and generous help were necessary and deeply appreciated. We thank our dear friend Barbara Larrivee, a self-described "recovering behaviorist," for her suggestions on how to deal with our research without getting lost in the hermeneutic noosphere. We also owe much to Ron Brandt at ASCD, for his continuing faith in us, and to our excellent editor Carolyn Pool, for staying the journey.

Most important of all, we owe much to our friend and colleague Sam Crowell. Sam participated in our restructuring efforts from the beginning. He was unable to assist in the writing of this book because of other time commitments, including the writing of the process book to accompany this one, which has been titled *The Reenchantment of Learning* (Crowell, Caine, and Caine [in press]). Sam is mentioned throughout the book. We share many memories, from euphoria to moments of deep despair. We have definitely walked the road together.

And we both wish to thank our community of Idyllwild, that very special place deep within the last remaining forests of southern California. We thank our neighbors for their patience, we are grateful to the many little cafés and restaurants that provided meeting places and thinking room for our work, and we particularly thank our kindred spirits at the Uptown.

SECTION 1

Theory: The Foundation

Section 1 discusses the changes in our collective philosophy as the new sciences, systems thinking, and comparable developments in other fields come to replace a Newtonian frame of reference.

We introduce the new paradigm from the perspective of several new developments, the core of which is complexity theory. We explore ways in which complex adaptive systems self-organize. We suggest that the central issue with education is that, although the system is becoming more dynamical and is moving toward the edge of possibility, the fundamental ideas and purposes of traditional approaches to education still inhibit the appropriate type of change and adaptation.

The new paradigm requires a new type of person. The key to the emergence of that person—the possible human—is to better understand what "human potential" means in terms of brain research and other developments, and then to teach to actualize that potential.

Finally, in this section, we summarize a theory of learning that can guide new approaches to teaching and education. It is the theory that we previously spelled out in Making Connections: Teaching and the Human Brain *(Caine and Caine 1991, 1994).*

1

Cross Currents

One of the most fundamental problems in education today is that people do not have a clear, coherent sense of meaning about what educational change is for, and how it proceeds. Thus there is much faddism, superficiality, confusion, failure of change programs, unwarranted and misdirected resistance, and misunderstood reform. What we need is a more coherent picture that people who are involved in or affected by educational change can use to make sense of what they and others are doing. . . . Solutions must come through the development of shared meaning.

—Fullan and Stiegelbauer 1991, pp. 4, 5

Education Is Caught in Multiple Tensions

Everyone has an opinion about education. Newspapers, documentaries, teachers and administrators, businesspeople, and parents—all voice their opinions and concerns. Understandably, disagreements arise. But even within the turmoil and turbulence, certain patterns emerge concerning the nature of the tension and the way in which people address problems. These patterns of responses seem to produce paradoxical results: Despite a search for common viewpoints, multiple reforms, and many changes, *much stays the same!* The following patterns are illuminating:

● *Our collective pictures and visions don't match even when we use common terms.* We might agree, for instance, that all students need to master the basics. However, someone with a conservative bent might insist that discipline, including paddling, is the answer to making learning happen in schools. Learning the basics, in this view, requires students to sit at their desks and listen to the teacher. On the other hand, businesses with a futurist bent might mean something entirely different by discipline and the "basics." They want people with self-discipline. And although basics include the fundamentals of reading, writing, and computation, for many business leaders, such minimal standards are hardly worth their attention. They want individuals who can be in charge when left on their own, who can also be good team players, who can work with multiple cultures and languages, who are innovative and creative in their thinking, and who focus on possibilities rather than "right" answers or doing what they are told.

● *People hold fundamentally different views about who "owns" information and about how it reaches children.* Some people believe that schools and teachers select and control the flow of information in the form of facts and skills to be taught in a classroom setting. Others contend that in an age of information technology, relevant information can be found almost anywhere and that critical facts and skills can be acquired in an infinite variety of ways. The solutions that are offered for the salvation of education are bound up in the differences between these two sets of beliefs. Those who believe that schools are the appropriate disseminators of information, and therefore have control of it, argue for improvements in the delivery of this information to students. Those who see the walls between schools and the world of information being breached argue passionately for more student choice and control in learning. They believe that education is more a matter of organizing learning around complex and engaging experiences that motivate students to gather appropriate data and skills as needed.

● *With all the action and calls for reform, schools and the education system are notoriously resistant to change.* Although theorists and educators have collectively amassed an enormous amount of research on good teaching and on learning, our schools remain largely the same. By all indications, they are failing to make use of what we know. Indeed, Goodlad's work, particularly *A Place Called School* (1984), could lead to a sense of hopelessness. Multiple calls for change have occurred over the past 20 years, and we have elegant descriptions of what we need to change (e.g., Fullan and Stiegelbauer 1991; Perkins 1992; Sarason 1990, 1993b). Many of our elementary and middle schools and some, though fewer, high schools have taken a leap of faith and have "restructured." Calls for "strategies that work" are everywhere, both in schools and in the broader community.

Courageous educators and pioneering schools are making genuine breakthroughs in teaching and education (e.g., Wood 1992, Fiske 1992). Many of them have done so at tremendous personal and professional cost, only to be undermined by a new state budget or federal reform or local school board elections.

• *Even though the education system appears to resist change, it is enmeshed in an unprecedented degree of turmoil and turbulence.* Hardly a night goes by without some television piece on schools. The news is laden with debates about educational funding. Many political campaigns focus on education. Conflicts over values now regularly spill into the educational arena, drive school board activity, and influence curriculum and instruction. Computers are reaching into schools and classrooms at an astonishing rate and in many ways. And many initiatives for modifying the education system are being attempted or are in the pipeline. Examples include charter schools, proposals for a voucher system, business management of schools, distance learning, increasing numbers of home schoolers, and virtual schools on the Internet.

• *A jumble and clash of overlapping questions and issues all seem to run into each other.* Many parents are confused and disturbed as they begin to see that the "traditional" view of teaching that they experienced can severely handicap their children, who will live in a world filled with 500 TV channels to choose from, the Internet and e-mail, fax machines, virtual reality, and instant visual communication spanning the globe. At the same time, changes in assessment, grading, homework, and instruction become disconcerting and dissolve into a sea of mistrust when these innovations cannot be (or are not) appropriately explained to parents and the community by the educators implementing them.

School restructuring efforts have created new approaches to instruction and school organization, and some have tested the perceived limits of what change is possible; but most efforts at restructuring are still failing to give us a new, comprehensive view of where we are going. Here are some questions that have been surfacing:

    ◦ What should schools look like when information is loose and available everywhere in ways that are personally relevant and streamlined to individual students?

    ◦ Where will school be in the age of technology when some are arguing that our entire notion of place and space has shifted?

    ◦ Can school be in the home, with appropriate software approved by state boards and certified by common exams administered in "testing centers"?

    ◦ Can schools be housed in small local facilities run by an educated parent, where social skills are taught along with information and skills beamed in from a centralized "school"?

• ***Concerns about a teacher's role in using technology in classrooms have yet to be resolved.*** If teaching facts and skills is better done by computer and information is accessible everywhere, what is the teacher's role? What do teachers teach and how do they teach? In fact, who and what is the teacher?

Here is an enthusiastic response from a teacher whose children have access to computers for only one hour a day:

> My children used computers in school before, but not like this. Not an hour every day. . . . They're all doing better—in math, in English, in spelling (Letter to the Editor, *USA Today,* June 7, 1996, p. 3A).

We also have seen incredible, interactive software with choices, colorful examples, and instant feedback. What the teacher in the previous example doesn't yet understand is that she cannot compete if students are doing better on only one hour of technology a day. If teaching continues to be defined as providing information and teaching skills to students, then it will not take much before those with the purse strings will figure out that teachers are more expensive than software. Here is a quote from an article in the *L.A. Times* entitled "School's out—CD ROM's in." The article focuses on job training, but can schools be far behind?

> **Cost:** Training with CD-ROM's is cheap. Development and maintenance of computer-based training costs 64 percent less than conducting seminars, ASTD [American Society for Training and Development] says. Training one-on-one with a computer also eliminates the cost of traveling to a seminar (Kaplan, *L.A. Times,* April 8, 1996, p. D9).

As educators, we know that technology alone will never be enough. Education has always served to give a nation a shared social fabric. Education, for example, is partly where we acquire a common heritage, deeply steeped in democracy and democratic principles (Apple and Beane 1995). This is also the institution charged with developing common values through analysis and debate, and where identities, both personal and communal, are solidified. Yet across the United States, we have seen a parallel and deploring abandonment of education as the solution to the human dilemma. Prisons are replacing education as the solution to social problems. In California, the budget for prisons now exceeds that for postsecondary education (Rosen, *L.A. Times,* June 11, 1995, p. M5). On a per capita basis, the United States has the largest juvenile prison population among all developed countries (Fellmeth, *L.A. Times,* July 5, 1995, p. B7). We have our priorities in the wrong place.

• ***There is enormous teacher burnout, and yet much more is being demanded of teachers.*** The notion of improving the way the teacher delivers "stuff" permeates many efforts at restructuring, which is therefore seen as essentially providing more "add-ons," more programs, more things to do. There is a severe strain between what the system supports and advocates on a day-to-day basis and what restructuring seeks to accomplish. A high dropout rate among teachers with one to five years of experience may be an indication of this strain. They typically are the teachers who are given the most difficult class assignments. Teachers, particularly those engaged in restructuring, all too frequently speak of burnout as they attempt to accomplish more in a system that refuses to stretch and yet forces ever "new" techniques, methods, and solutions onto their already overcrowded responsibilities. This strain is particularly evident when teachers are not allowed to integrate such efforts at improved practice into a coherent sense of how these fit into their own understandings and assumptions about good learning and teaching.

In China and Japan, the average elementary school teacher spends approximately 40 percent of the day in planning and curriculum consultation, and rarely teaches more than three hours a day (Stevenson 1992, pp. 74–75). In the United States, that planning time translates into anything from a half hour to one or two hours per week in elementary schools. In high school, what is called preparation time amounts to one hour a day. Exceptions are relatively rare. How can teachers possibly integrate into practice the exploding knowledge base in the neurosciences, cognitive sciences, technology, individual disciplines, and what we now know about how to help children become healthier, more effective human beings, when all they have time for is to implement a predetermined lesson plan hour after hour with a 5- to 8-minute break in between?

Class size can also add to teacher burnout. In many states, elementary schools have at least 35 students per class.

• *Notwithstanding all the action and all the problems that we have described, some of the deep beliefs about how children actually learn have never been examined by many of those who are embroiled in the debate.* Even people who might have different views of what they want education to accomplish often share deep beliefs about "school" and teaching, which are not grounded in a coherent theory of learning. Their unarticulated beliefs are grounded in the experiences that they have had with their own education. Although the system is at the eye of a storm, the basic beliefs on which the whole edifice is built remain largely unexamined by the public and by vast numbers of educators. Many of the protagonists, therefore, don't know what they don't know.

Our Map in Outline

When so many well-intentioned and deeply invested people find themselves at loggerheads with each other in so many ways, the problem most likely runs deeper than we have collectively realized. In our examination of many issues—funding, phonics or whole language, site-based management, vouchers or charter schools, business partnerships and the privatization of school systems, demographics, technology, and parenting changes—we have asked a critical question:

Is there something functioning at an even deeper level that makes sense of the conflict and crisis, and that gives us a handle on how to approach the enormous problems we face?

In our research, we ventured into these waters with half a solution. We were, and continue to be, absolutely certain that a fundamental issue hinges on the understanding that stakeholders have of how human beings learn. We feel that many hold basic beliefs about learning that are far too limited; and the problems in and with education cannot be solved until these beliefs are changed. Thus, our approach is to work with the deeply held beliefs that educators have about learning, with the goal of changing those beliefs and so leading to changes in teaching.

In the course of our own work with schools, we began to explore even deeper issues. In the journey that we describe in this book, featuring two schools in particular, we were reacquainted with the fact that schools do not operate in a vacuum. Powerful forces keep traditional classroom teaching in place. We found that we could not describe our change process in isolation without looking at the broader "systems" question as well.

Ultimately, we believe that there is a coherent way to look at the problems; and there are ways to restructure education, renew educators, and significantly raise the standards of students. Accomplishing such renewal, however, requires a profound rethinking of much that we have taken for granted. For example, discoveries in biology and physics are making a new view of life and the universe explicit, while prolific uses of technology have enlarged and complicated our lives. At the same time, input from many fields is providing a new understanding of ourselves and the way we learn.

It seems to us that in evolutionary terms, education has worked well over the last 100 years. Although many people have fallen through the cracks and numerous inequities have occurred, the model of education has been a good "fit" for the industrial age. Large numbers of people have been equipped to function in industry. And education and industry have been perceived through the same larger lens.

What is now happening is that the world itself is changing, and the lenses through which we have peered are being replaced. As that happens in other larger spheres of life, a point is reached where education must follow suit.

We are leaving behind one way of looking at the world—a way that is built on a belief in stability and controlled change as ideal. In its place, we're moving toward an emerging understanding of the dynamism of life at every level. It is the understanding of change as natural to every facet of our existence and an embracing of continuing possibility that we have been keeping at bay. Four ideas can guide us in trying to understand change:

1. *Disequilibrium is everywhere, and we need to understand that.* All systems, including education, are caught up in the turbulence of extraordinary change. To understand and work effectively with any social system at this time, we have to come to terms with new ways of thinking, embodied in, but not limited to, what are being called the "new sciences." Among the new ideas that are helping us to rethink our basic assumptions are the notions of complex adaptive systems, self-organization, field effects, self-reference, and the edge of chaos. These ideas are examined in depth in later chapters. That thinking will help us grasp the ways in which the system is functioning and see how to guide and influence the directions we wish it to take.

2. The brain is equipped to deal with a turbulent world. But to understand this, we first need to come to terms with how the brain learns and to see how this knowledge translates into our everyday lives. Research from the neurosciences and many other fields is profoundly changing what we know about how people learn. Traditional approaches to learning and teaching sufficed in a stable and less turbulent world. Today, we have no choice but to ground our work with education in a thorough understanding of how the brain actually learns. The brain, and therefore we, are not limited to the learning of a digital computer. We are meant to learn from naturally complex and "messy" experiences. At the same time, our understanding of stress and the nature of anxiety and trauma is teaching us that we learn best when our emotional lives are orderly and coherent (when they make sense).

3. The change process is intrinsically transformational. Most of the work on school change, even when parents and other stakeholders have been included, has been directed at changing strategies, structures, and external behaviors. In a turbulent world, that approach cannot work. We are now finding out that the key is to assist systems to *self-organize* and transform themselves. This process can be influenced, but it simply cannot be controlled from the outside.

4. To function best in this new environment, we need to embrace a fundamentally different world view or perceptual orientation. In the course of our work with schools and business, we identified specific approaches to teaching. One favored control and a high degree of stability. Another favored fluid situations and students engaged in self-directed learning. Our greatest surprise was to find that these instructional approaches are grounded in intrinsically different ways of viewing reality. Because people have such differing perceptual orientations, some educators are more at home in the world of change and turbulence than others. It is therefore not simply a matter of changing strategies—it is a matter of seeing with different lenses.

We ultimately concluded that the most important step that we could take would be to come to understand these perceptual differences, and that the key to successfully transforming education lies in transforming ourselves.

The Bigger Picture:
The Paradigm Shift Is Real

Behind the frustration and the exhaustion, behind the recalcitrance of the overall system, lies an even bigger problem. In our journey—and we did not adequately appreciate this until we were well into it—we learned that the *paradigm shift* is real. That is, the basic model that we have of how the world works is itself being called into question. (The difference is described in depth in Chapters 2 and 3.)

The word *paradigm* is often used loosely and means different things to different people. A paradigm, for us, consists of all those deeply held beliefs and ideas that shape our grasp of reality. As such, it operates like a field. Fields are "unseen structures, occupying space and becoming known to us through their effects" (Wheatley 1992, p. 49). A field is an interactive, invisible web of relationships that permeates and is present in everything we do and say. As Garmston and Wellman note (1995), a field is as pervasive and omnipresent as gravity, and as taken for granted. For educators, a paradigm shift means that the basic ideas and beliefs that have governed education and the larger social system itself, and that penetrate into every nook and cranny of the system, are being called into question.

In essence, the prevailing paradigm is highly mechanistic. It is built on the idea that the world can be controlled like a big machine. The practical implication of this view is that we can change schools and restructure by working out what each part does and then changing the parts so that they work better. We can even redesign the parts, but the underlying belief is that we are in charge and can control the nature of change. All the reports on how difficult it has been to change education confirm the failure of this logic. It is as if our model of schools has always had a great deal in common with a model car—a car has a clear purpose; it has distinct and identifiable parts that make it run; and its performance can be quantifiably assessed. When parts break, they are fixed; and low performance can be enhanced by using better gasoline or higher-quality oil.

The problem is that schools are much more complex; in reality, they have more in common with the weather. When we think of a school as a weather system, our perspective changes.

The emergence of a new paradigm is illustrated by the idea that we live in times when "the ground itself is moving" (Emory, in Vail 1989). Sparked by changes in technology, rapid information flow, and other factors, every system is in, or moving toward, a state of disequilibrium, where change is constant and outcomes are often unpredictable. The problem is that when systems are moving toward "the edge of chaos," they can change radically; but the change cannot be controlled. The practical implication is that traditional procedures for solving problems do not work. One reason is that small actions can have large and unintended consequences, while large actions and interventions may have no impact whatsoever. In effect, we need to internalize a fundamentally new way of conceiving of and responding to the situation in which we find ourselves.

We Are All in This Together—And It Is Often Frightening

We experience the paradigm shift as uncertainty, not understanding what is expected of us on the job, with the real possibility that change can happen at any time and leave us behind. One teacher recently commented:

> Part of my fear is that I can't control the pace—I have always thought of myself as one of the "good" teachers—dedicated and willing to do what's best for my students. I have a reputation for successfully dealing with students other teachers have given up on. What if, during all these changes, I fall behind? What if I can't do it and fall behind? What if I can't stay up with the "good" teachers in this paradigm shift? There goes my sense of self (Letter from a teacher).

Educators are not the only ones experiencing a profound sense of loss of equilibrium. One of us recently looked up the prescribed treatment for a duodenal ulcer; the source was a book eight years old. The treatment spelled out in the book might as well have been written

50 years ago, because everything about the disease, from diagnosis to treatment, has changed in the past five years. The same holds true for accounting, where the picture of the accountant as the person adding up figures "after the fact" will soon describe an outdated trend (Egol 1994).

As noted previously, technology is a source of major disruption. For instance, in *The Road Ahead* (1995), Bill Gates talks about "Friction-Free Capitalism," which is essentially one cleared of intermediary agents. As Gary Chapman points out,

> This approach to the economy "may throw as many people out of work from services as were ejected from manufacturing 10 years ago. But there is no new sector to absorb these people, even at lower wages. What will they do?" . . . Beneath the celebratory rhetoric about the coming "friction-free" economy is a ticking time bomb: the explosive idea that tens of millions of workers can be summed up, and shunted aside, as mere friction (*L.A. Times,* January 11, 1996, D2).

These seem to be forbidding times, as our expectations, beliefs, and past training and abilities call for a stretch not all of us are prepared to make. Most particularly, many of us feel as though the old ship is being destroyed or taken away before the new ship is ready to sail. Sometimes we are bombarded by more information (in the form of solutions, for example) than we can integrate, and at other times there appear to be no answers at all. Angst seems to be widespread:

> Perhaps the most disturbing single piece of data in this book [*Emotional Intelligence*] comes from a massive survey of parents and teachers and shows a worldwide trend for the present generation of children to be more troubled emotionally than the last: more lonely and depressed, more angry, more nervous and prone to worry, more impulsive and aggressive (Goleman 1995, p. xiii).

Yet the mood is not one of universal despair. In the midst of a divisive election in the United States, for instance, a Knight-Ridder survey of U.S. attitudes revealed a significant degree of optimism, hope, and compassion (Cannon, *Austin American-Statesman,* February 4, 1996, p. D1). Many people have a sense of possibility, although they may be cynical at the same time about the institutions of government.

Perhaps society at large is intuitively beginning to sense that significant improvements are possible, but that something fundamental has to change. In any event, hanging on to the old beliefs and explanations compatible with the old paradigm ensures that many of the changes being introduced in education will have little beneficial effect. It is the equivalent of rearranging the proverbial deck chairs on the *Titanic.* That will no longer do. The collective field of knowledge is charged with new ideas, tumbling over themselves as they intrude into our awareness. They have been making themselves known for nearly a century, but in recent years have begun to take hold of thought and imagination in a much more compelling way, as evidenced by the interest generated by books such as *Leadership and the New Science* by Margaret Wheatley (1992).

One key idea of the new sciences is that many systems actually thrive when they are in a state of appropriate disequilibrium. This state is called "the edge of chaos," though we prefer to call it the "edge of possibility." Education as a whole is now moving in this direction. Although schools and schooling are slow to change, we will see massive changes in the nature of the education system itself; but these changes are essential for the continued success of the education enterprise. Much of this change, however, cannot be controlled or, indeed, adequately predicted.

Fortunately, even though change cannot be controlled, it can be influenced. The reason, as we discuss later, is that a social system on the edge of possibility tends to *self-organize* around a set of compelling beliefs. We suggest that the most potent impact on the shape the education system takes will be the meanings, purposes, and values that all of us decide are critical. As education reorganizes and redefines itself, it will give expression to the deep beliefs that prevail.

The Purpose of Education

Because dynamical systems organize around compelling beliefs, purposes, and meanings, the answer to the question "What is the purpose of education?" can no longer be taken for granted. Is there more to teaching than producing workers whose primary function in life is to support economic stability and growth? What do we teach our children that is not tied to how they will serve business? How can we tie democratic values, the works of Shakespeare and Plato, poetry, and the arts to education agendas focused on business functions? What of love? Of compassion? What of creativity and the arts? What of joy and feelings of connectedness to other human beings, animals, and nature? What happens to our "souls" as human beings and our soul as a nation?

In a century organized around materialistic science and industrial production, we have embraced the notion that what is worthwhile and real is limited to what we can touch, analyze, take apart, fix, and pay for. To what extent is that notion acceptable or accurate? The industrial paradigm has left much that is nonlinear and elusive undervalued or ignored. Why do we prepare people for a predictable, controllable world when in fact they will face a life filled with uncertainty and ambiguity?

If science teaches us that we are little more than machines whose lives can ultimately be reduced to brain functioning and the potential and proclivities programmed in our DNA, how do we answer young people when they choose to take drugs to make themselves feel better or create the illusion that they are smarter or more powerful?

The answers to such questions are far from simple, but they must be addressed—and not by educators alone. Society as a whole must become more intelligent. Too many of us are used to sound bites, simplistic explanations, and exposés and are experts in narrow fields or areas of focus. An understanding of systems thinking and how things are connected can help us reconceive the problems and the potential solutions.

First Steps: A Theory of How the Brain Learns

Peter Senge is reputed to have said that the problem with changing systems is that we have to do everything at once and yet we also have to find a place to begin. In our work, we needed a place to start, and it seemed to us that the best place was with a solid understanding of how people actually learn. It seemed to us that educators should be able to capitalize on what was being discovered about brain functioning. More specifically, we wanted to ground the understanding of learning in brain research.

How the Brain Learns

We explored research in the cognitive sciences and neurosciences and cross-checked it against advances in other fields, ranging from creativity and whole language to sports psychology and research on perceptual change. We explored the impact of stress on the immune system and the difference between helplessness and challenge. We examined traditional theories of memory and looked for guidance on the difference between memorization and the construction of meaning. We examined the ways in which people interpret experience, and at the difference between structured activities and experiences. We combed the research on reflection and metacognition. We explored the social construction of knowledge, the power of relationships, the nature of individual differences, and more.

The synthesis of our findings, and our theory of how people learn, were spelled out in *Making Connections: Teaching and the Human Brain* (1991, 1994a) and are summarized later in this book.

For want of a better label, we described what we do and advocate as "brain-based learning." The theory was an attempt to redefine the learner, moving our picture of the learner as an absorber of information to one who interacts dynamically with it. This theory also described teaching based on such a new understanding.

Brain-Based Learning

In *Making Connections,* we describe 12 "brain principles" of learning. Figure 1.1 (see p. 19) shows our revised principles; Chapter 5 provides a more detailed discussion. The brain principles make provision for the traditional model of teaching. They show, for instance, that every human being has a virtually unlimited set of memory systems that are designed for programming and for the memorization of meaningless information. But our minds also have the need to place memories and experience into a "whole"—and indeed our minds automatically do this. The "whole" is our autobiographical memory, which tells us how things in space relate and how ideas and experiences are connected. Without this type of memory, we could not find the bathroom twice without memorizing our route first, nor could we write a spontaneous sentence recalling an experience. Both memorization and integration are critical, and learning is best when information is embedded in rich, meaningful experiences. We also came to the conclusion that teaching for memorization of meaningless facts and procedures dictated by someone else usually induces *downshifting.* Downshifting is a psychophysiological response to threat associated with fatigue or perceived helplessness or both (Caine and Caine 1991, 1994a). Downshifted learners then bypass much of their capacity for higher-order functioning and creative thought.

In brain-based learning, educators see learners as active participants in the learning process. The teacher is not the deliverer of knowledge, but the facilitator and intelligent guide who engages student interest in learning. Students and teachers become partners in the pursuit of understanding. Traditional schooling assumes that children have to take on board lots of "stuff," and then someday they will know how to apply it when they go to work or have a profession. Brain-based learning makes this leap to the real world right from the start.

Brain-based instruction begins with the entire school and the child's whole being. The brain is not divided into individual segments marked "feelings" or "cognitive development" or "physical activity." Rather, active learners are totally immersed in their world and learn from their entire experience. "Children," the saying goes, "learn what they live." Instruction is correspondingly complex. Whereas short lectures and

---

FIGURE 1.1
BRAIN/MIND LEARNING PRINCIPLES

Principle 1: The brain is a complex adaptive system.

Principle 2: The brain is a social brain.

Principle 3: The search for meaning is innate.

Principle 4: The search for meaning occurs through "patterning."

Principle 5: Emotions are critical to patterning.

Principle 6: Every brain simultaneously perceives and creates parts and wholes.

Principle 7: Learning involves both focused attention and peripheral perception.

Principle 8: Learning always involves conscious and unconscious processes.

Principle 9: We have at least two ways of organizing memory.

Principle 10: Learning is developmental.

Principle 11: Complex learning is enhanced by challenge and inhibited by threat.

Principle 12: Every brain is uniquely organized.

---

memorization play a part, much more learning takes place when learners are constantly immersed in complex experience; when they process, analyze, and examine this experience for meaning and understanding; and when they constantly relate what they have learned to their own central purposes. When teachers assist students in engaging their own purposes, teachers may find that skill development, with its emphasis on practice, rehearsal, and refinement, becomes more effective. The challenge, therefore, is to fit skills and content to the learner, rather than fit the learner to the curriculum. We go in much greater depth on what this means later in the book. An example:

> I teach 4th and 5th graders all subjects. The thing that works most for me about Open Charter School is that I have moved away from standing in front of the classroom. I have become a learner along with my children. I work side by side with them in their learning rather than assuming that everything that comes from my mouth is the most important thing that is going to be important to them.

If you came into my classroom, you'd have a hard time finding a computer, and there are 30 of them in this room. We have them built inside the desks. We do not use "educational" software. The programming is taught in relation to where it fits in our [classes]. The computer is just one more step in the thinking and problem-solving process, and that's how it's used. It's just another tool. . . . We do not have an elitist group of children here. We have children from every socioeconomic background, from all ethnicities. We don't have behavior problems at this school. We trust the kids. (Comments are by Betty Jo Allen-Cohn, a teacher at Open Charter School, a magnet school in Los Angeles. Standardized test scores for 4th graders are more than twice the average in the L.A. School District and nearly twice the statewide scores) (Blair and Konley, *L.A. Times,* April 22, 1995, p. B7).

In a school or a classroom practicing brain-based learning, the importance of different intelligences (Gardner 1985, 1993) and learning styles is taken for granted. Assessment includes, but moves beyond, paper/pencil tests for surface knowledge. We expect to see authentic assessment of all types and students participating in the evaluation of their own learning process and progress. Assessment is also open to outside experts and expert panels. In such schools and classrooms, learning is driven by student purposes and meanings; and teachers facilitate and enhance student learning.

Our Approach:
Change Mental Models of Learning and Teaching

The overwhelming majority of teachers . . . are unable to name or describe a theory of learning that underlies what they do in the classroom, but what they do—what any of us does—is no less informed by theoretical assumptions just because these assumptions are invisible. Behind the practice of presenting a colorful dinosaur sticker to a 1st grader who stays silent on command is a theory that embodies distinct assumptions about the nature of knowledge, the possibility of choice, and what it means to be a human being.

—Kohn 1993, p. 10

As Alfie Kohn points out, every educator has a theory of learning. But a profound difference often exists between what people profess and what people actually believe, and this difference also applies to learning and teaching. The difference can be expressed in terms of "mental models," which are theories in use, and "espoused theories."

Mental models are deeply ingrained assumptions, generalizations, or even pictures or images that influence how we understand the world and how we take action. We often are not consciously aware of our mental models or the effects they have on our behavior (Senge 1990, p. 8).

The difference between espoused theories and mental models is important because

> Although people do not [always] behave congruently with their espoused theories [what they say], they do behave congruently with their theories-in-use [their mental models] (Argyris, in Senge 1990, p. 175).

Mental models shape day-to-day decisions and interactions. They constitute real beliefs about how children learn and fundamental assumptions about what teaching and schools should look like. In terms of our theory, mental models are aspects of dynamical or perceptual knowledge—the way we perceive the world and make sense of it. These fundamental beliefs are powerful because they organize experiences, information, and strategies.

We have traveled all over the country and have asked the following questions of many people:

What is learning?
What is teaching?
Where is school?

Answers invariably reflected some of the finest thinking of our time. We heard: "Learning is change in thinking and behavior due to new understanding"; "Teaching is guiding learners to do their own, best learning"; and "School is anywhere where this can happen, and it doesn't have to be a classroom."

Then we asked people: "If you really believe this, to what extent does your own school and your own teaching reflect it?" This turned out to be a provocative exercise. At its best, it led to sincere questioning about the difference between what we say we believe and what we actually believe. At its worst, the exercise became an invitation to do a great deal of blaming.

Most teachers, other educators, and the public have a mental model of learning and teaching formed and, we would maintain, physiologically entrenched by their early experiences in school. Five or six education courses in a postbaccalaureate program or college lecturing tend not to genuinely challenge teacher's mental models and do little to disturb these deeply held assumptions about schools, teacher roles, and learning. In short, we all tend to reduce what is new—and that includes innovative strategies and thinking—to fit (or accommodate) our current mental models.

Based on our studies, we believe that one reason why education continues to go through so many phases with "strategies that work," only to ultimately end up with business as usual, is that mental models of teaching and learning are not changing. Changing on the surface means acquiring new vocabulary and new formal explanations without challenging the basic beliefs that drive our moment-to-moment actions. We end up like the principal who was overheard excitedly telling a friend, "Oh, we did brain-based learning last year; this year we are doing constructivism."

To Change Practice, Change Minds

If mental models drive the decisions that we all make, the implication is that to successfully improve education, we have to change the mental models that educators have of learning and teaching. We therefore wanted our theory to form the basis of a new mental model in the people with whom we worked. We set out to demonstrate that our theory can act as a practical guide for a living, dynamic new way of approaching learning and teaching for schools, teachers, and students.

We believed, and wanted to test the belief, that our theory, properly understood, would naturally drive changes in instruction and influence decisions that the school, staff, and faculty made. By looking at learning and the learner in a new way, we expected teachers to more or less naturally create, modify, expand, and adapt their own teaching to reflect new understandings. In effect, if educators changed their minds about how education worked, changes in practice would inevitably follow.

Teacher Change and Transformation

When we first attempted to use the theory as the basis for restructuring, we discovered just how challenging it is to translate words on a page to a living, present-day school context and practice. Although educators loved the ideas expressed in *Making Connections*, implementing the theory turned out to be another matter entirely. All of us had to learn that instant solutions did not automatically surface from the theory and that working with the theory in mind meant, first of all, taking time to share and change powerful assumptions about learning and teaching. We were looking at assumptions that guide our moment-to-moment decisions about what we actually do when we teach.

Our understanding came with time. Our learning embraced elements of action research and hermeneutics. This kind of research is qualitative, quantitative, participative, and dynamic. We observed, connected to our knowledge, collected data, asked questions, searched for answers, read profusely, modified and expanded our assumptions, and started the process all over again. This was the same process, we should add, that we sought to induce in the people with whom we worked.

On the one hand, we found enormous enthusiasm and excitement. People had a sense of possibility and were exhilarated by the phenomenal range of projects, potential for creativity, and variety that brain-based learning supports. On the other hand, we faced (and still face) the constant threat of exhaustion and frustration that accompanies any change process. We found human beings whose routines and relaxed interactions with family and friends have been severely strained.

Real change is also extremely difficult because it challenges traditional and personal beliefs and asks us to revisit and reinterpret our own experiences and our own sense of self. Here's what one teacher participating in brain-based restructuring said about it:

> I don't think it can be overemphasized how scary all this change is. I've always been willing and quite good at rearranging the deck chairs; I've never been asked to transfer from a steamship to a starship before. I can sagely intellectualize about why and even how. Maybe the key is to remember it's not a leap but a journey where I can control the pace.

Our process together was an exercise in honesty and frustration as we began to uncover the forces that held current assumptions in place. The tension between teachers' need for techniques and strategies for the next day and our own emphasis on changing beliefs about learning and teaching required not only patience but the capacity to admit and accept that such a fundamental change does not happen overnight.

Our Main Surprise: Different Ways of Perceiving the World

As we worked with and observed teachers, both in our schools and around the United States, we began to see and confirm differences in what we call "instructional approaches." Though the details had not been clear to us, the central thrust of the differences was expected. After all, it was clear that those who used a stand-and-deliver model had to differ in significant ways from those who elicited student interests and then embedded content as appropriate. We ultimately distinguished between what we call Instructional Approaches 1, 2, and 3. Figure 1.2 (see p. 25) is a summary of the approaches, and we describe them in depth in Chapter 10.

As we pursued the matter, we also found something more. It is clear that the different instructional approaches reflect different mental models of teaching and learning. Mental models, however, go much deeper and further than we expected. Mental models about teaching are themselves grounded in even more fundamental ways in which people look at things and interpret their world. The differences were something that we had intuitively felt but had not adequately anticipated or understood. Richard Elmore recounts an experience in restructuring:

> I recently gave a talk about school restructuring to a gathering of high school principals and superintendents from school districts that identified themselves as reform oriented. The common theme of their reforms was changing the high school schedule to lengthen the standard 45- or 50-minute class to something longer, perhaps as much as 90 minutes. . . . When I asked them why they chose to concentrate so much energy and attention on changing the schedule, they first looked at me as if I had descended from another planet. . . . To them it was obvious that changing the schedule would lead to a different kind of teaching, but it wasn't necessarily obvious what kind of teaching that might be. My favorite commentary on this problem is the teacher who was quoted as saying, after his school changed from 45- to 90-minute periods, "Oh, good, now I can show the whole movie." It is not obvious, in other words, that changes in teaching practice follow from changes in structure (Elmore 1995, pp. 23-26).

FIGURE 1.2
SUMMARY OF THE THREE INSTRUCTIONAL APPROACHES

Instructional Approach 1 can generally be described as a "stand-and-deliver" model. This approach relies on top-down thinking and the control of information and facts to be disseminated by teachers.

Instructional Approach 2 is considerably more complex and sophisticated than Instructional Approach 1. It is still primarily a command-and-control mode of instruction, with many of the same beliefs and practices as Instructional Approach 1, but there are some critical differences. Teaching tends to be organized around concepts with an eye to creating meaning rather than just for memorizing. To this end, it uses complex materials and can incorporate powerful and engaging experiences.

Instructional Approach 3 is what we had envisioned as brain based. It differs radically from Instructional Approaches 1 and 2 because it is much more learner centered, with genuine student interest as its core. This kind of teaching is more fluid and open. It includes elements of self-organization as students focus individually or gather collectively around critical ideas, meaningful questions, and purposeful projects. Instructional Approach 3 teaching is also highly organic and dynamic, with educational experiences that approach the complexity of real life.

We finally described these more fundamental ways of looking at things as "perceptual orientations." The perceptual orientations frame the ways in which educators can think and perceive. The orientations set limits on what teachers can conceive of. Thus, those at Perceptual Orientation 1 cannot think out of the Instructional Approach 1 box. Those at Perceptual Orientation 2 can think about and potentially do both Instructional Approaches 1 and 2. But only those who are at Perceptual Orientation 3 can think in sufficiently fluid and integrated ways to embrace all three instructional approaches. One aspect of the perceptual orientation is a core difference between those who rely on the external power given them by the system and those who have a sense of self-efficacy and are self-reliant. The former find a stand-and-deliver model of teaching quite natural. The latter are much more capable of accepting and working with the individual choices expressed by students.

We describe the differences generally in terms of a distinction between Perceptual Orientation 1 and Perceptual Orientation 3. We suggest that there is a transitional phase, what we call Perceptual Orientation 2. And we argue that most work on restructuring education is currently directed at a shift from Perceptual Orientation 1 to 2, and that this thrust is essential.

Our Theme

A new way of thinking is required by the paradigm shift—but that way of thinking cannot be taught. As we explored the differences in perceptual orientations, we came to believe that system change requires educator change, and that educator change is a matter of personal transformation. The source of the resistance of schools to change lies in a system that is itself maintained by a set of absolutely compelling deep beliefs about learning, teaching, and the nature of reality itself.

In a sense, the traditional system was well served by the old paradigm. There was a good match between system and beliefs. That reciprocal relationship is now breaking down. A turbulent system requires a different set of beliefs—a different perceptual orientation. We need a new match.

All educational issues need to be reconceived in terms of the new sciences and a basic understanding of perceptual orientations. For example, people are legitimately concerned with raising educational standards. However, our conclusion is that the people who are capable of teaching to a new and more complex set of standards are those who see complexity as natural. Perceptual Orientation 3 must be supported in educators, therefore, if standards are to be raised significantly. However, the system itself is going to have to be reconfigured and must function in different ways if the fluid and dynamic instruction associated with Perceptual Orientation 3 is to be possible.

That, therefore, became the focus of our work, and of this book.

This Book

Ultimately, this book describes a journey involving two specific schools and an unlimited and unnamed number of others that engaged in a process of restructuring based on changing mental models. It also includes corporations and businesses that were involved in exploring our process. It draws on more than 100 hours of recorded video and audio documentation showing the changes that took place in thinking and practice. In addition, we sent our own research questionnaire to numerous schools and individual educators.

Our objective is to contribute to a broader understanding of the change process—to help redraw a map of what it takes for educators and, in particular, teachers to change how they think and what they do as a result. This map will show what happens to men and women when they let go of the limitations of their old beliefs and expand them to include new lenses.

We divide the book into three distinct sections; each can be read separately as a "book" by itself.

Section 1. Theory: The Foundation

Section 1 deals with the changes in our collective philosophy as the new sciences, systems thinking, and comparable developments in other fields come to replace a Newtonian frame of reference. The new view is that reality is much more fluid, less predictable, and far more interconnected than we had understood it to be. We see that traditional education was built on a machinelike model where educators "owned" the information and distributed it much as an industry would develop a product and control production. Coming to terms with the fact that we no longer own the information, and that information is everywhere available in the world of instant access, is critical to genuinely rethinking the nature of the education system and our roles as educators. What that rethinking then needs is a view of the brain and of learning that is compatible with the new sciences and with the whole person. The section therefore concludes with a "new paradigm" view of the brain and mind, and with a summary of a theory of learning that can guide new approaches to teaching and education. It is the theory that we previously spelled out in *Making Connections* (Caine and Caine 1991, 1994).

Section 2. Practice and Implementation

This section describes how we worked with educators to help them implement brain-based learning. We begin with our overall scheme for working with schools and describe in depth the small-group process that we used. This process had the most profound effect on changing the sense of community in the schools with which we worked, and we describe the consequences for community.

We also describe the more practical interventions and changes we collectively explored with teachers and with as many of the school community as we could involve. We describe and illustrate several processes and strategies that we introduced, including suggestions for orchestrating complex experience and for active processing, and we examine some of the results. We show how we helped educators to take chances, experiment, do the things they and we believed in, and change. In the course of three years, the entire process also unleashed teacher creativity; and although everyone explored a coherent model of learning and practice, we found that each teacher and school pursued different paths in translating the theory into day-to-day activities and strategies.

Section 3. What We Learned

The book concludes with our description of the three instructional approaches that we identified, each with its own identifiable parameters. This description can be extremely helpful in creating a clearer picture of our goals for instructional change. We include a discussion of the perceptual orientations, focusing particularly on Perceptual Orientation 3. (Note: Both the instructional approaches and perceptual orientations are outlined in greater depth in an upcoming book to be published by ASCD: *Unleashing the Power of Perceptual Change: The Potential of Brain-Based Teaching.*)

2

System's End

Equilibrium is the stage closest to death for a living system, but we haven't known that. We have thought that when we are at equilibrium, everything's fine, and that it is change that causes our disintegration.

—Wheatley 1995, p. 3

Why Is It So Hard to Change Education?

Anyone involved in the most basic restructuring is struck by just how hard it is to implement even minor changes if those changes come up against the way the system has always run. Seymour B. Sarason (1990) wrote a provocative book entitled *The Predictable Failure of Educational Reform*, in which he recalls:

> For almost half a century I have witnessed and have been a participant in efforts generally to improve our educational system. . . . I came to see what should have been obvious: The characteristics, traditions, and organizational dynamics of school systems were more or less lethal obstacles to achieving even modest, narrow goals. How does one deal with the abstraction we call a system embedded in and reflective of a society that created and nurtured that system? (p. 12).

We have observed similar difficulties, even when there seem to be good intentions all round. In one of the schools we worked with, Park View Middle School, in Yucaipa, California, it took three years to change to flexible scheduling; and this change remains controversial in the school, dividing friends and colleagues. Some teachers were committed to it because they felt that it gave their students time to delve more deeply into subject matter, and other teachers were angry because a two-hour block was too difficult to "prepare for." The school board needed proof that time spent on teaching equaled some documentable amount that could be calculated. The only way that initial changes in scheduling could be handled was through a system where teachers had to "bank" the minutes and hours of the day and week.

Additional questions include many issues of assessment and instruction: Why are new and more complex modes of assessment so difficult to implement? Why are quantifiable measures, such as grades, built on hairsplitting percentages still so pervasive? Can knowledge really be that precisely measured? Why do we still act as though a student's appreciation of art or a particular literary work or enthusiasm for physics can be analyzed and evaluated in this way? Why is school content still so separate from the complex real world in which students live? Why do we still focus so hard on prespecified tasks and outcomes that relate neither to student purposes nor the real world?

We are certainly not the only ones raising these questions. Rather, we join a host of educators, some of whom have dedicated their lives to changing education with meager results. Arthur Combs (1991), one of education's most illustrious statesmen, replies to the question of why we haven't changed:

> It isn't because we haven't tried. We've tried a hundred things. Here are a few: the Palmer method, phonics, teaching machines, psychological testing, audio-visual . . . techniques, open schools, open classrooms, team teaching, teacher aids, social promotion, the New Math, the New Sciences, languages in the early grades, tracking, homogeneous grouping, inquiry learning, behavior modification, rewards and punishment, systems analysis, grades, competition and . . . behavioral objectives, competency based instruction, "back to basics," computer technology, and voucher

systems. Each of these, in its time, was enthusiastically advanced as a solution to education's major ills. As it became evident that it, too, was as disappointing as its predecessors it was soon laid aside. Changing public education is like punching a pillow or, as someone has suggested, "Like moving a cemetery; after you've done all the work, you still have a cemetery" (p. 1).

Most educators who have been in the system a few years share a cynicism about reform. Along with Art Combs, they see movements introduced with great fanfare, only to blow over as others take their place. The movements become "fads" that ultimately do not change anything.

Why don't these change efforts have more impact? How can it be that programs deeply grounded in both research and experience, and strategies that clearly work in some contexts, do not appear to have much overall success? Even worse, why do some programs that have impeccable research backing up their claims of successful learning actually end up with the popular belief that they make things worse? After all, this is the charge that has been leveled recently at the apparent failure of "whole language" (an emphasis on using children's literature and student interests in language arts instruction, with phonics being incorporated and embedded, rather than depending on basal readers and phonics drills) in California. And yet, the whole language approach, as developed and practiced by people such as the Goodmans (Goodman 1986, Goodman and Goodman 1979) and Harste (1989) and their students (e.g., Flores, Cousin, and Diaz 1991), is totally consistent with the best of modern learning theory and practice and is highly effective in improving the reading and language skills of children.

Finally, what is it that drains so many teachers, and that renders it so difficult for teachers and students alike to express their creativity, demonstrate their competence, and function at much, much higher levels?

The Educational System Was Designed to Be Stable and Resist Change

We suggest that schools have resisted change for two main reasons. First, the education system is part of a larger system that is grounded in a way of thinking—a paradigm—and that way of thinking is deeply entrenched. Second, the paradigm has led to the design of social systems as social machines, the essence of which is to remain stable and unchanging over long periods of time, even when they are perturbed. Our first need is to bring this underlying thinking of the system into the light. That is a difficult, challenging, and potentially unpopular thing to do.

We Are in the Grasp of Compelling Ideas

There are always compelling, central organizing ideas that permeate society as a whole and, therefore, education. Dawkins, a British biologist, coined the term *meme* to describe a cultural belief or "unit of cultural information" that literally has a life of its own. A meme starts as an idea but ultimately has the power to organize and structure society in a specific way:

> A meme is "any permanent pattern of matter or information produced by an act of human intentionality." . . . Although we might initially adopt memes because they are useful, it is often the case that after a certain point they begin to affect our actions and thoughts in ways that are at best ambiguous and at worst definitely not in our interest (Csikszentmihalyi 1993, p. 123).

Memes are the social counterpoints to genes in the physical organism. Memes and paradigms overlap but are not the same thing. A meme (or cluster of memes) can become a paradigm. When that happens, a meme, or compelling idea, has become a frame of reference. Another way of defining a paradigm, therefore, is a compelling frame of reference that has a life of its own.

Mechanism Plays a Part

Mechanism tends to portray things in terms of separate elements connected by lawful relationships into a working system that produces well-defined, controllable outcomes.

—Goerner 1994, p. 5

The dominant view of reality—the major paradigm—for several hundred years has been labeled as Newtonian. One aspect of this view is that almost everything can be conceived of as machinelike. The world itself, in this view, is explained as a gigantic bit of clockwork. That view of reality has carried with it a set of basic thinking tools with which we try to analyze and fix every situation. Indeed, even the idea that a problem can be solved by "fixing it" is a mechanistic notion. The notion of "fixing" human beings even permeates a great deal of instruction.

In this way of thinking, any problems and any system can be divided into separate parts, which can then be dealt with in isolation. Thus, a car can be taken apart, and each piece can be worked on, whether it is wheels, carburetor, or gear box. Pieces can be repaired and replaced, and the vehicle will continue to function.

Psychology and the social sciences have also been imbued with these types of beliefs. They gave us behaviorism and the applications of rewards and punishments so compatible with a mechanistic belief system in controlling behavior one bit at a time. All of us in education recognize how well we accommodate such scientific understanding in the form of smiley stickers, grades, training, detention, promotion, awards, incentive schemes, penalties, and so on. They are the "tools" or "implements" with which the parts can be fixed and the school and students can be made to do what is necessary for them to become a "part of," or take their "place in," society.

Bureaucracies: Social Machines

One of the most powerful and successful expressions of the machine metaphor has been the development of and reliance on bureaucratic modes of organization. While hierarchical organization has been with us for millennia, and some forms of bureaucracy were developed by both the Romans and the Chinese, bureaucracies have now become a pervasive way of structuring human interactions. Bureaucratic modes of organization are the perfect answer to organizing a society on the model of a machine. In fact, a bureaucracy can be defined as a social machine.

In *Restructuring Our Schools,* W. Patrick Dolan (1994) recalls the origin of the Roman military model, which parallels a pyramid: "Power and authority for the direction of the enterprise are centered at the top of the pyramid. The military command orientation has powerful ramifications on decision making and information flow" (p. 12). What Dolan calls the "middle tier" then has at least some say in the interpretation of authority and hence some degree of power. At the bottom, however, are the grunt workers who "live, work and die. . . . Their job is to do what they're told and not to ask questions" (p. 13). Dolan summarizes:

> Thus, it is very important where you find yourself in the pyramid. In this top-down, command-demand structure you are reminded every day where you belong in the hierarchy. Your rank tells the world how much you need to know, and how much say you have about it (Dolan 1994, p. 15).

He goes on to document how this model was adopted by the Church of the Holy Roman Empire and later by the Industrial Revolution. Apparently, we had other models to choose from; but this pyramid model, which successfully held the Roman Empire together for hundreds of years, eliminated all other potential competing organizational models.

In a bureaucracy, everything is compartmentalized. People have roles that entitle them to make specific decisions, and they are given only the information that those at the top believe is appropriate for those decisions. Hierarchies are used to maintain an orderly division of labor and responsibility and are evident in almost any type of administrative organization, including schools, district offices, and state and federal organizations.

It is important to acknowledge that in many respects, this way of running our everyday affairs has served us well, particularly in the

Industrial Era, when factories served as the social models for schools. Both government and industry have capitalized on bureaucratic modes of organization. Science and technology have thrived by using mechanistic modes of thinking. And schools and universities have both adopted the framework and prepared the people needed to function in and operate these systems. We can point with genuine pride at the structures, institutions, and processes we created in response to the knowledge and understanding we were provided by the Newtonian/Mechanistic paradigm.

Schools as Social Machines

Looking closely, we recognize that as educators, we have perfected the mechanistic view of reality. We are actually experts in creating, maintaining, and controlling a well-ordered and organized social machine:

● *Machines—and schools—have parts.* One aspect of the machine metaphor is that all the parts, including teacher and child, tend to be seen as "objects" that we do things to—whether it is an empty container to be filled with facts or a malfunctioning part that needs to be improved.

Another aspect of the metaphor is that the part can be fully understood and worked on without examining other elements of the context. A teacher may be called "good" or "bad," for example, without any attention being given to salary, size of classes, or what else is going on in the school or district.

● *The parts have specific functions and purposes.* In a machine, parts have clear and distinct functions. This notion has been translated into educational structures with specific responsibilities and job descriptions. A teacher teaches, a parent parents, an administrator manages, and a child learns. Each function is treated as separate and only connected in a specific and limited way. Such a view is linked to seeing teaching as a job that has more to do with assembly-line production, rather than with creating experiences linking learning to genuine shifts in understanding.

• *In a machine, causes and effects can be clearly identified, separated, measured, and related to each other.* Embedded in this approach to replacing or fixing parts is a straightforward belief about the nature of cause and effect. Causes and effects can be clearly identified, separated, measured, and related to each other in direct and proportionate ways. This belief is partly what is meant by the notion of linearity. This way of thinking, which carries with it such a strong sense that outcomes can be predicted and controlled, has penetrated all of education and our other institutions. The system therefore requires accountability based on linear cause-effect relationships and offers rewards for things done right.

Thus, we say that "poor results are caused by poor teaching . . . or poor textbooks . . . or an inadequate curriculum," and so on. If students are not learning enough, we say that they need even more "on-task behavior," the assumption being that more such behavior translates into better results. We then go about improving or repairing or fixing these defects. Thus, in teaching, we contend that the greater the input through hard work, practice, and rehearsal, the greater the result in the form of test scores and grades. We keep focusing on fixing or altering the structure when we really need to understand what keeps the structure in place.

What Is It About the Machine Metaphor That Is So Compelling?

That the dominant view of reality has been colored and shaped by mechanism and a set of related ideas is well accepted. Post-modernism is largely an attempt to repudiate that view. The question that we find intriguing is, Why has mechanism proven so compelling?

We begin with the notion that Newton himself was not a mechanist in the way that "mechanism" is used today. He believed in God and explored astrology. However, what his combined interests suggest to many scholars is that he was passionately attached to the idea of a well-ordered universe. In this he was not alone. We concur with the belief that a desire for order, and explanations of apparent disorder, have been at the heart of human existence for millennia, as much for the safety and comfort that come with the explanations as for any other reason. We will argue later that human brains are designed to make sense of experience. And making sense means that each one of us yearns for a grasp of "the patterns that connect." Mechanism is extremely compelling because it combines an explanation of reality with immense power to take charge of that reality. That combination, we suggest, has been intoxicating.

The larger problem, we further believe, is not simply with the idea of mechanism itself but with one of its corollaries. If a well-ordered universe is like a well-oiled machine, then disorder, uncertainty, sudden change, unpredictability, and turbulence are signs of a machine that is malfunctioning. They suggest that something is wrong. In short, Western society, in particular, has bought deeply into the notion that stability, predictability, and planned change are the real signs of health, and fears their opposites. For many people, stability, power, and mechanism represent security and safety.

Resistance to Change Is Embedded Everywhere

The mechanistic paradigm has led us to perceive and act in such a way as to enhance the forces that keep us from changing. Indeed, the paradox—and the frustration—is that most of the effort that has been put into changing education has actually reinforced the basic dynamics that make change exceedingly difficult. We have been doing it to ourselves! How does this happen?

Our research has led us to these conclusions:

1. Continuous grade-based evaluation acts as feedback to control the system. Almost every teacher in every school will acknowledge that one of their consuming focuses is to "teach to what will be on the test." This means that the course content is tied to prespecified outcomes, and any ventures off course are being corrected all the time, using grades and evaluations. Specifically, multiple-choice and other paper/pencil tests are set to give feedback on memorized facts and skills. They provide little opportunity for assessing individual variation and creativity in thinking.

Although most teachers use grades and evaluation as we describe, the consequence is that the very process of teaching for prespecified information leads to a form of compliance or agreement to learn only that which is required. Grading and testing, therefore, all too often actually limit creative thinking and questioning that goes beyond the basic facts required to "get a good grade." In these instances, students are being corrected so that they give back exactly the responses and reinforce assumptions that have been established as correct by an outside, authoritative source. Genuine variance in thinking and questioning is not encouraged by such testing. And other potentially generative conditions that are essential for student growth as thinkers and decision makers are constantly neutralized. More "authentic" assessments, which encompass student self-assessment, performance assessment, and portfolio assessment, encourage student growth and creativity. Many schools, districts, and states are developing such assessments; but, unfortunately, the process is slow and not without its detractors. For example, one such authentic assessment, the California Learning Assessment System (CLAS) was initiated in 1993 and eliminated in 1995. The CLAS test was sophisticated and brain based. It needed changes and better community understanding, not elimination.

Grace Arnold, the current principal of the Open Charter School in Los Angeles, laments the demise of CLAS:

> The CLAS [California Learning Assessment System] test was really the right kind of test for how this school teaches. It was a beyond-the-basic-skills kind of test. We teach for higher skills, critical thinking, independent thinking, and collaboration among children. Now that the CLAS test has been canceled, something that could have had a huge effect in educational reform has been taken away.

2. Schools as subsystems are constrained by the larger system. Other events in California illustrate how large systems influence what happens in schools:

> A sweeping proposal by [California] state schools chief Delaine Eastin to improve education by freeing local districts from state regulation has run into serious hurdles and is evolving into a far less ambitions strategy that is unlikely to produce the wholesale changes needed to reform California Schools.

> Facing financing obstacles, opposition from the powerful teachers union and legal questions that cast doubt on her power to waive state regulations, Eastin has been forced to back off on some of the more innovative aspects of her "Challenge" plan (Colvin, *L.A. Times,* December 8, 1995, pp. A1–A40).

Every school is a part of the larger education and social system that influences it. For example, when confronted by the call for change, high school teachers tell us that until the demands for university standards shift, they are bound to provide lectures, encourage note taking, and use modes of assessment that enhance potential performance on standardized tests. The constraining power of the larger system is illustrated by the sources of funding (with contributions from the state, local communities, and others); legislative and local controls over such items as school architecture, times of operation, teacher credentials, textbooks, and curriculum; political and religious issues as exemplified by the fierce battles for positions on school boards; and community participation in school functions. For instance, here is an excerpt from an *L.A. Times* article that demonstrates both the engagement of the community and how emotional the objection to change can be:

> California's schools aren't starving. They're choking to death on educational fads and bureaucratic mandates. This will not change until local communities, parents and the press get on the schools' case and make sure that the money spent now is spent better (Boychuk, *L.A. Times,* December 22, 1995, p. B9).

The emphasis on grades, as a further example, stems from the larger community. For many years, the focus of education has been on college admission of high school students, even though most students do not complete a four-year college degree. The primary source of information about the quality of students has been their grades and their scores on college admission tests. Employers have also regarded grades as important indicators of employability (though the reliance on grades in the workplace is declining). And grades are the primary or rule-of-thumb indicator of student competence used by parents and politicians.

With rare exceptions, grades and test scores dominate almost every educational consideration. They are almost exclusively the ways in which we judge whether children, teachers, and schools are succeeding. Much of the debate at every political level is informed by and infused with debate over test scores and standards. Colleges, in particular (with the exception of those with a large number of the most exceptional candidates to choose from), demand translatable, easy-to-assess symbols of one type or another that match universal admissions criteria.

The result is that educators in schools are constrained by the criteria used by all those outside the schools.

3. Current conditions lead to downshifting, which leads to the imposition of control. We have defined *downshifting* as a psychophysiological response to threat associated with helplessness or fatigue (Caine and Caine 1994a). Downshifting inevitably results in less sophisticated use of the brain and a reversion to behaviors and patterns that have been previously "programmed." Thus, the conditions that cause downshifting are compatible with memorization and repetition. That is, downshifting can foster memorization but interferes with higher-order and critical thinking and with creativity. In schools we have worked with, we have identified some of the more subtle conditions that we believe collectively contribute to downshifting. These conditions increase a sense of helplessness in the learner and discourage genuine self-efficacy:

    o *Prespecified "correct" outcomes have been established by an external agent.* Under this condition, students must learn the answers the teacher has determined to be correct, and teachers must perform in ways that others deem to be correct. That significantly closes the options available to both students and teachers.

○ *Personal meaning is limited.* What is to be learned or taught does not have to connect with what students already know or desire to know. Student purposes or innovative or chosen ways of dealing with problems and situations are all too often treated as irrelevant.

○ *Rewards and punishments are externally controlled and relatively immediate.* The result is that the consequences of action, including salaries, testing, and grades, are not under personal control.

○ *Restrictive time lines are given.* Though deadlines are important in their place, a constant barrage of time limitations determined by others drives people to do what has to be done to meet the deadline, rather than to reflect on options.

○ *Work to be done is relatively unfamiliar, with little support available.* Isolation exacerbates uncertainty without the reassurance of necessary feedback. This situation applies equally to teachers and to students working alone. Students and teachers are judged on the basis of performance criteria determined by others, are held to rigid deadlines stipulated by others, and often see little or no meaning in work that is tied to rewards and punishments controlled by others.

Underlining all of these conditions is a belief structure that denies the learner's own purposes and meanings, even though they are a critical part of the learning process.

When these conditions exist, learners' ability to solve problems is impeded. As they encounter feelings of helplessness, they tend to revert to early programmed behaviors indicative of conformity to the status quo. Additional reactions include becoming territorial, using and yielding to hierarchical command-and-control behaviors, and having little tolerance for the thinking appropriate for complex issues like diversity and individuality. We argue in depth in *Making Connections* (Caine and Caine 1994a) that the design of the educational system induces downshifting in administrators, teachers, and students. The combined effect is to reduce the capacity of participants at all levels to think and act "out of the box."

The Essence of the System:
Foundational Information as a Controllable Commodity

The life blood of any system is information. Without seeking to define "information" in any detail, there are at least two types that matter in an education system. One is the curriculum content—the "stuff" that is disseminated. The other is information about people—the grades and assessments and reports. To function, bureaucracies need almost total control over both the nature of the information and the direction and way in which it flows. Schools survive and thrive for as long as they are central players in the flow and control of information.

When asked, "What is the desired outcome of education?" people almost automatically say something like "well-informed students." In many respects, that response is appropriate. When parents send their children to school because they want them to be educated, they want their children to have access to the information and to the skills that will ensure the children's survival and success as adults. Educators and education have as their primary function the delivery of essential information. The core commodity of education is the information that is to provide a foundation for success in life.

In a sense, this information is detached from the minds of people and has an independent existence. Facts and skills are conceived of as owned by the system and warehoused in schools, where they are packaged and then delivered to students. This distribution-and-delivery system is controlled in many mutually reinforcing ways that are familiar to all of us. Here are some of those information-delivery systems:

• Policy decisions on curriculum requirements are made at state and district levels and, in some cases, at federal levels. The curriculum is separated by subject; and there tends to be a set of core subjects, at the heart of which are "the basics," such as reading and math, with others as secondary.

• Each subject is assumed to have a logical developmental sequence, with one segment sequenced in each year of a student's education.

- An intricately designed system of administration is used to make certain that the appropriate information is being dispersed in classrooms. Children are organized into groups by reference to age, grades, and academic year. In elementary schools, one group of children—often far too large—tends to be the responsibility of one teacher. In later years, teachers are allocated groups of children for small chunks or blocks of time, the purpose being to deliver prescribed curriculum content.

- The actual day-to-day distribution of information is ultimately a task for the teacher. The teacher has a significant degree of freedom in how to "teach" the material, usually with the use of texts, film, and videos. However, teachers are isolated within classrooms and subject-specific departments, with little time or opportunity to connect knowledge to other subjects or to the real world—or to students.

- Teachers are supervised by administrators. The structure and information are linked through a timetable so that places (classrooms), teachers, and subject matter are connected and managed.

- The modes of assessment that we described previously are used to ensure that information flows in the right ways and that people, both students and adults, are performing in the right ways.

Although this description is an oversimplification, we are convinced that it is essentially accurate. An enormous amount of time and effort is invested in selecting and controlling the flow of information. Moreover, each aspect of the system sustains other aspects. The result is like a conveyor-belt, packaging-and-delivery system, where products that conform to design specifications (e.g., *A-grade* and *B-grade* fruit) are identified and selected, and where much that does not conform is discarded or rerouted as an inferior product.

It is no wonder that attempts at change are inordinately difficult. How can we really expect significant amounts of innovative teaching or administration when innovation, by definition, means that the heart of the system itself—the identification and direction of flow of information—will be disrupted? When change is attempted, the energy demands will be high. There may be some innovation and some good results, particularly when a teacher or school is given a moderate degree of autonomy. However, we would expect schools that went beyond the norm to revert to the pattern of the basic system when highly innovative people leave. That reversion is demonstrated time and time again. We would also expect the personal cost, where people do seek to buck the system, to be extreme.

Education Is Losing Control of Its Commodity: Information Is Available Everywhere

The very same skills of separation, analysis, and control that gave us the power to shape our environment are producing ecological and social crises in our outer world and psychological and spiritual crises in our inner world. Both these crises grow out of our success in separating ourselves from the larger fabric of life.
—Kofman and Senge 1993, p. 10

The current organization of schools as stable systems created to control and disseminate information is being undermined on multiple fronts. The reason is that many aspects of the larger system that sustains education are crumbling. Changes in technology, developments in the sciences and other disciplines, and the growing cultural crises previously noted by Kofman and Senge all call into question traditional ways of thinking about schooling and the bureaucratic structure that supports it.

Such changes do not mean that there is nothing of value in the traditional ideas, only that we have to merge those ideas into a bigger picture.

Information Is Running Free

A key contribution . . . to the hyperlearning revolution will be what Bruce R. Schatz, a scientist at Bellcore, the regional phone companies' research center, calls "telesophy"—the potential ability to make all knowledge available to anyone, anywhere, anytime."It's actually going to be possible to have all the world's information at your fingertips," says Schatz. Those with the greatest ability to pay will still get greater access to the most valuable knowledge. But the cost of access will be so greatly reduced that vastly more knowledge will be available to everyone.

—Perelman 1992, p. 37

The amount of information being created and made available almost exceeds the imagination. Moreover, the information is overwhelming traditional channels. In time, these channels will be unable to cope with the flood; and unlike most floods, the information flow will not dissipate. In fact, it can be seen that the channels of information flow in the larger system are being redefined and reshaped by technology as digital signals replace mechanical action, as people become capable of working together though separated by thousands of miles, and as time constraints crumble in the face of high-speed computers. The core elements of the education system are consequently being changed. There is no way that education can remain in charge of information. Pertinent information is beginning to be available anywhere and everywhere.

Curriculum Is Changing

Developments are taking place at the edge of every domain of knowledge to the point where many reports in authoritative journals are out of date before they are published, products are obsolete before they hit the market, and many current events change their configuration on a minute-by-minute basis.

As a result, traditional sources of information for students are fundamentally inappropriate. Irrespective of whether textbooks are effective, few textbooks can be the primary source of important and current information. Similarly, even teachers who are constantly updating their own professional expertise can only keep pace with a small fragment of what is becoming available.

The Competition for Disseminating Information Is Becoming Fierce

Information technology can be used to deliver both facts and skills in powerful, engaging ways. Such information can be stored in prodigious amounts in compact ways, and much of what teachers currently "deliver" can be done more simply and cost effectively using information technology. This situation is analogous to the use of expert systems to compete with doctors in providing medical diagnosis, the use of automated teller machines (ATMs) to replace bank tellers, and even the use of computers to run massive ocean liners.

In addition, information is becoming openly available to more and more people in multiple ways. That means that the sources of information and the opportunities to learn are now becoming so vast that they threaten to engulf classrooms and schools. Tomorrow's children are inheriting a world that will be profoundly different. They will live in a world of unlimited information. The Internet, World Wide Web, virtual reality, unlimited international access to television viewing, encyclopedic information of all types, and instant access to the world's greatest minds mark only a few of the possibilities. As we write, for instance, an intensive effort is under way to connect every classroom in the United States to the Internet.

According to John Abbott of Britain's "Education 2000," and the "21st Century Learning Initiative," it is now estimated that roughly 20 percent of families are Technologically Advantaged Families (TAFs) (personal communication). This number is expected to increase significantly over the next 10 years. Home schooling also has increased significantly over the past 20 years and is expected to continue increasing as more and more teaching tools become available in the form of software that parents can provide for their children. If the product of schools continues to be seen as the dissemination of facts and skills, then there will be cheaper, more efficient, more personal, and more effective ways to do the job schools are now set up to do.

Traditional Authorities Are Having Their Credibility Questioned

Teachers can be second-guessed when genuinely contradictory information is available to students from multiple sources, ranging from the Discovery Channel on television to the Internet. Many teachers and professors complain about students who come to class and voice the opinions of talk show hosts and others as unquestioned authorities.

Many messages from the media and in the arts directly challenge some taken-for-granted value systems. And many adults who advocate strong views are sometimes seen as not practicing what they preach. Insofar as the control of information depends on the prestige of adults and their unquestioned authority, the dam has truly burst.

Information About the System Itself Is Flowing Freely

Educators used to have a significant degree of autonomy from the larger community. Hiring and firing, curriculum decisions, instructional methods, and academic standards used to be set within the system. That wall has also been breached. Media investigations, litigation, school board politics, and larger ideological campaigns all mean that system personnel can be exposed to public scrutiny in a way that is fundamentally different from the past. The information used to run the system no longer flows through relatively closed channels. Here is an introduction to ways in which information might unexpectedly become available in a class:

A parent recently told us that her daughter's teacher had assigned papers to be researched. Each student was to select a U.S. state to research. Reports were to describe topographic features, weather patterns, any industrial and commercial specializations, and so on. Her daughter, who was quite computer literate, searched through her encyclopedia software and promptly typed out not only her own report but reports for all her friends. She provided her friends with reports that they discussed with each other, reported on in class, and turned in as completed assignments. The teacher was angry when she discovered what the daughter had done and considered it cheating. The mother took exception to this accusation saying that the assignment was too simple.

Our concern is to highlight the way in which students will begin to access more information and more possibilities than teachers expect, and the real turmoil that teachers will experience in the current system.

Beyond Mechanism

As Sarason noted at the beginning of this chapter, the education system has been sustained as a part of a larger system. It has been difficult to change because its structure is based on ideas that pervade a much larger way of thinking.

But now the core idea—the Newtonian paradigm—is reaching a limit of applicability. We live in a world where massive amounts of information flow freely, in multiple guises, and at a time when adults are also confused. The foundational structures of the larger world in which education resides are themselves changing. Education has no choice but to follow suit. When information flows in a way that can no longer be contained, old forms and structures and processes are overwhelmed and must adapt:

> What Prigogine and others found is that a system can be at equilibrium and when confronted with change, it will fall apart, but it will fall apart so that it can reorganize itself (Wheatley 1995, p. 3).

This larger breakdown is evident in such activities as calls for vouchers, charter schools, satellite and computer-based delivery systems, schools run by businesses, changes in funding, and more active school board participation in curricular and instructional issues. We find ourselves in a fluid, turbulent, and changing world, and yet we still need to educate children.

An Example

Many scenarios exist for what education will look like as information begins to flow differently. The following is a scenario being developed by Creative Learning Systems of California (16510 Via Esprillo, San Diego, CA 92127-1708; telephone: 1-800-458-2880) (see Figure 2.1 on p. 51). In their words:

> A Creative Learning Plaza is a large open environment for up to 150 people, working together for several hours at a stretch. In this

environment, everyone is a learner and both young people and adults can be facilitators. . . . [In] the interior landscape, . . . the furniture is reconfigurable, the reference materials are delivered on demand through networked interactive multimedia, and the place is constantly buzzing with activity.

The plaza provides for videotaping on location, has the capacity to simulate physical and computer-generated models of real-world projects, and promotes the use of concept-mapping software. Works of art can be downloaded, software is available to assist in literary text analysis, and provision is made for intimate small-group discussion.

The plaza is guided by a team of about five teacher facilitators who move around and maintain a big picture of what is happening with the group as a whole.

Such a plaza is being funded by Arthur Andersen as part of their "school of the future" for grades 9–12; it was launched in Alameda County, California, in the summer of 1996. The Creative Learning Plaza will call for what we mean by brain-based teaching. It also matches our view of one way that schools of tomorrow may be organized. We also believe that teachers will not be able to function in this type of environment without a radically different view of learning and teaching.

Everything Changes

In a sufficiently complex system, when one element changes in essential ways, so do the others. The issues interact and merge, even though people caught in the middle may not grasp that fact easily. The questions that we ask and the ways of asking will now be different. Grades, methods of instruction, curriculum, discipline, physical plant, the role of parents and the community, economics and politics, system structure and resistance to change, values and beliefs, and mental models of how children and adults learn are all interconnected.

In *Mindshifts* (Caine, Caine, and Crowell 1994), we wrote that

We will finally turn education around, in our classrooms and in our communities, when we adequately grasp the nature of . . . connectedness. Then we will also see how to deal with our problems simultaneously (pp. 4-5).

FIGURE 2.1

Creative Learning *Plaza*™

*The Ultimate Environment for
Collaborative Learning*

Patent Applied For

Creative Learning Systems, Inc.

Image courtesy of Creative Learning Systems, Inc. (1-800-458-2880)

What we need to do is grasp the nature of this fluid and dynamic interconnectedness; and we need a new set of tools for thinking about the situation. To change successfully, and to deal successfully with change, we need to begin by reframing the issues and the description of the situation itself. Then we will be able to move forward.

* * *

Physicists have caught a glimpse of the infrastructure of the *real* world. Yet oddly enough, they have been able to do this only through the use of advanced technology. And all of our technology—the panoply of tools and devices at our disposal—has been developed starting from the assumption that the world can be taken apart and analyzed. Our map-making, bounding, and classifying are what have given us power over nature. But now, because of the sophisticated technology that has allowed us to experimentally probe the subatomic domain, we found that reality has no boundaries (Darling 1996, p. 137) (emphasis in original).

3

Reconceiving the Problem

We are not at the end of science, we are at the end of the potential of linear science, but at the beginning of a new science.

—Ilya Prigogine, Nobel Laureate

We stand at a turning point in human civilization, the magnitude of which we are only barely aware but whose importance cannot be doubted. The changes in thinking will affect every segment of the culture. And the key factor is an understanding of how order emerges and change is driven. The bigger picture, of which chaos is a part, is the physical understanding of how order evolves naturally, why change is inevitable, and what factors underlie transformations.

—Goerner 1995, p. 17

When we began working with schools, we worked with the belief that everything was interconnected. We knew that we were dealing with a huge system called *education,* which included teachers, students, administrators, parents, society, and politicians. We began to see that we needed to invoke systems theory to grasp the essential connection of things. A system is "a collection of parts which interact with each other to function as a whole" (Kauffman 1980, pp. 1–2). Many theorists and practitioners have emphasized this point. W. Edwards

Deming, John Goodlad, Ted Sizer, and Michael Fullan, among others, all point us in this direction.

Almost from the beginning, we found that orthodox views of how systems work were simply inadequate to explain what we were experiencing. We therefore had to take a detour through some of the ideas of the new sciences to better understand our process and the power of the context to resist change. More specifically, we needed new tools for thinking about the nature of the relationships within and beyond a system.

New Paradigm: New Science

The changes that we are looking for in education are part of a response to a much larger force for change. What all of us, educators and citizens alike, are experiencing is a shift in our most fundamental assumptions. In part, this shift is being led by discoveries in relativity theory, quantum mechanics, biology, and chemistry. It is affecting everything, from the way science is being interpreted and how we assess business and economic trends, to how we view brain research for clues to better understand teaching and learning. The shift is being supported by the explosion in technology, which allows us to see more dynamism inherent in interconnectedness and complexity. In effect, technology is beginning to spawn questions we never thought of asking before. And the resultant answers parallel and touch major shifts in many other fields and domains.

We encounter or bump up against the new science most obviously when we become aware of the way some terms have entered our everyday world. Words and phrases such as "mechanistic thinking," "feedback," "networks," "nonlinearity," "chaos," and "complexity" have taken on new meanings as we explore the limitations of "classical dynamics" with respect to the dynamic, fluid nature of reality. Systems are now dealt with in an entirely new way, with features such as emergence, self-organization, and wholism. And although most of the vocabulary was spawned in science, this new way of thinking has great implications for the social sciences and for just about every field, including education and teaching.

In the universe we now see as much more fluid and turbulent, we believe it is more appropriate to talk about discernible patterns than quantifiable certainties. The new systems thinking and quantum theory help us see our human experiences in a new way. Instead of a machine, the universe and everything in it is more readily described as a sort of primordial soup out of which things emerge and take form, and into which they ultimately return. While there can be some stability over time in many systems, that stability is now explained and understood in different terms.

The "new science" view of the universe is profoundly different from the machine metaphor that has guided our thinking thus far, but its view still provides us with an orderly view of reality. That is, many phenomena that had seemed random, chaotic, or inexplicable are now known to be expressions of deeper patterns that had been invisible.

Therefore, we do not throw out everything we learned about quantification; we simply extend our picture of reality, which has suddenly become much larger. Nor does the new paradigm mean that the new sciences are in some way fully formed and fully understood, or that different theorists and practitioners even fully understand and agree with each other. Rather, we are finding immensely powerful and all-embracing new ways to perceive and describe trends and patterns over time. With that come new ways of acting and interacting with our world. This exploration is currently taking place in every field of human endeavor, including education (Garmston and Wellman 1995; Cleveland, Neuroth, and Marshall 1995). In education, our exploration can ultimately lead us to ponder how we could ever have subscribed to the notion of classrooms as a stable system, which is indicative of the military or factory model. Here, our goal is simply to begin to unpack some of our current understandings in a way that can assist educators.

Let us begin to explore these ideas through a story. It is not the story of any one place or time, but a composite. However, we expect the elements to be familiar to our readers.

The Story of Education in Calichusetts

Imagine, for a moment, that you have spent several years watching education at work in a fairly large and prosperous state. We will call it Calichusetts:

> For a long time, the education system had been conducting business as usual, although several individuals had expressed some concern that things could be better.

> A few years ago, concerns about the quality of schooling seemed to mushroom into a blaze of activity. A parent's group made a presentation to the state legislature because, they claimed, schools were not teaching the basics. The media started sending teams into schools that seemed to be underperforming. Teachers complained about class size. In fact, there was so much unrest that the legislature passed one bill freeing some schools from normal constraints and giving them opportunities to become charter schools. At the same time, a move for more effective management along business lines spurred activity toward site-based reform. And a host of new instructional methods were introduced, extensively supported by the department of education.

> Still, concern persisted. There were some cases of improved performance on standardized tests. In fact, a few schools raised their reading scores significantly as they implemented whole language teaching, a move that received a great deal of support in much of Calichusetts. However, as you read your daily paper, you come across an article saying that literacy standards have actually declined statewide as whole language has been implemented.

> One particular innovation that had bothered but interested you was the participation of business in education. Indeed, a few years back, one city had handed all control of education over to a business—Advanced Academic Enterprises (AAE)—that promised both better results and lower costs. What intrigues you is finding out that the business (AAE) has not produced the promised results and that control of the city's schools has been taken back by the system.

At this point, you are intrigued. There are so many configurations out there—vocal home schoolers who have banded together in groups that function a bit like ordinary schools; businesses that are setting up schools for the children of employees; virtual schools on computer networks; more and more site-based management and theme-based schools; and a vast traditional school system that seems to be fraying around the edges as massive amounts of time, money, and effort are invested in new strategies. And yet . . . standards and performance don't really seem to have changed that much. What is it really all about?

Clearly, some aspects of education in Calichusetts have changed. There are so many new players, and new relationships between such players as business and political interest groups. In fact, the changes are so dramatic that the system clearly is not a rigid machine. It reminds you more of Silly Putty. It can take on a dozen different shapes and be molded by whoever works on it, and yet the consistency remains just the same. Actually, what the system is doing is changing its shape and its configuration so that it can adapt to varying elements of its environment. However, it is not really changing its nature. What is happening?

Dynamic and Dynamical Systems

The difference between a mechanistic and an ecological vision is striking. In an ecological view, people are intrinsically motivated, self-organization will occur spontaneously if the environment is conducive, emphasis on control is bad for structurally sound growth, the future is not an extrapolation of the present.
—Goerner 1995, p. 30

The answer begins with what seems like word play. It is with the difference between systems that are dynamic and those that are dynamical.

Dynamic systems, according to Mark Michaels (1994), have a lot of movement, but the input and the output are totally predictable. An assembly line is an example. And so is the engine of a motor vehicle.

They are also relatively closed in that they do not interact much with their environment, nor are they sensitive to it. Machines, from this point of view, are dynamic systems.

Dynamical systems are different in a peculiar way. They are much more open to the environment, exchanging matter, energy, and information. An example is the weather. It does interact with the environment, with all the interplay between temperature and evaporation and land mass and energy—in fact, it's difficult to tell where weather begins and ends. At the same time, even with advances in Doppler radar and other technologies, people find it difficult to make specific predictions about what will happen as a result of all the activity.

From this perspective, schools and social systems seem to be *dynamical* systems. People flow in and out through employment, enrollment, graduation, and so on. Money flows between the system and the larger environment, whether we are talking about state budgets, federal grants, or fund raising by the local PTA. Parents ask questions, meet with teachers, and campaign to get on school boards that then direct teachers on matters of curriculum. Kids watch TV and bring what they see and learn to school with them. In short, there is an enormous flow of energy and information and matter between schools and the larger context. Yet none of this movement guarantees that results will improve. In fact, it sometimes seems as hard to "control" education as it is to control the weather!

The difference between dynamic and dynamical systems is important because both resistance to change and the nature of change are explained in very different ways.

System States:
Dynamical Systems Can Be Stable or Unstable

Dynamical systems have different system states. Understanding these states is crucial to understanding what is happening with education. One essential factor is whether the system is stable or perturbed. It is easier to live in an orderly way when things are stable; we are much more put out when everything is perturbed. More technically, there is a strongly ordered, stable state, in which the flow of activity continues, but nothing much changes. And there is the much more disturbed state, in which all sorts of different things can happen. That second state is one of *disequilibrium*. It tends to develop when the interaction between the system and its environment becomes more active and unpredictable. It is like the stock market that becomes much more volatile when more money flows in or more disturbing political news is broadcast.

What has been happening with education is that for many years, it has been stable, dwelling quite comfortably in an ordered state. However, over the past several years, there has been more and more interaction with the environment—more intensive media coverage, more concern from political and religious groups, more demands from business, more special needs to accommodate, and more impact from technology. All of these have perturbed the system. Thus, it is moving out of stability and into disequilibrium.

The Story of Calichusetts Continued ... Something Is NOT Happening

Something about Calichusetts has been puzzling you. Even though you might expect some disasters, with all this change, you should surely find extensive evidence of much better results. There ought to be some configurations working so well that they could be copied.

How was it possible, you had asked, for all that change to take place without any significant differences really occurring? What you see is that the system is actually quite dynamical—there is lots of activity, much of it very intense. Yet the underlying pattern of what is done in schooling has not shifted much, including grades, periods, time expectations, and curriculum. That all remains stable. Within all the change and turmoil, there is profound stability. In systems thinking, stability means that the essential underlying dynamics do not change. In social systems, these dynamics translate into powerful beliefs, assumptions, and values that hold the system in place.

You decide to stop being an armchair watcher. Instead, you are now interested enough to go and visit some of these traditional and new parts of the educational system. As you visit them, you are delighted to find that there are, indeed, some examples of spectacular success: young children doing sophisticated thinking, older children engaged in high-quality projects, creative teachers, and some results that are breaking the ceiling on standardized tests. And yet, these schools are in the minority. Most are not even known. And when they are discovered and attempts are made to replicate them, the attempts do not work.

What you find, in fact, is that something quite fundamental has NOT changed and is not changing within the larger system. How could that be possible? And what could it be?

Because you are not a professional, and you do not really know what to look for, you begin to ask people involved in education a simple question. You ask teachers and principals and board members and parents and politicians and journalists. What you ask is: "What are the schools actually trying to do?"

Most people look at you as though you are an idiot. However, they are polite enough not to tell you. They say things like "We're trying to teach kids"; "The kids have got to have the right skills"; and "We're trying to cover the curriculum."

For a while, what they say makes sense. But as you think about their answers, you recall some ideas that you recently read about. It seems to you that underlying the answers given by all the people that you interview is a more basic idea. You have heard the idea described as "treating information like a commodity." You recall that someone actually set it out in three basic principles:

1. *Only experts create knowledge.*
2. *Teachers deliver knowledge in the form of information.*
3. *Children are graded on how much of the information they have stored.*

There may be other ways of stating these beliefs, of course. What staggers you, however, is that almost everybody in this constantly changing yet stable system actually has the same set of beliefs.

The effects of these beliefs are everywhere. They infuse every decision, every relationship and chance meeting between parent and teacher, every story in the media, every deliberation over budgets—even research studies on teacher effectiveness. It's like a field effect, that "invisible web of relationships," where the basic set of beliefs are present everywhere and in everything. And it is these beliefs that are not changing!

To answer what is happening, and what is not happening, we have to explore more of this territory of "system-speak."

Adaptation and Coevolution

Some dynamical systems, such as the weather, respond to and interact with whatever forces are "out there." As a result of El Niño, California may experience significant changes in rainfall, for instance. Other, higher-order dynamical systems can do more than simply interact with their environment. They can actually adapt and change themselves so that they evolve as the environment evolves. This mutual and reciprocal adaptation is called *coevolution*. In Capra's (1988) words:

> Our natural environment consists of ecosystems inhabited by countless organisms which have coevolved over billions of years, continuously using and recycling the same molecules of soil, water, and air (pp. 390–391).

If we stand back and take a long view, coevolution is happening with education right now. From the perspective of the big picture, large-scale changes in education—such as charter schools, business participation, and distance education—are all facets of a system changing its shape and configuration as society and culture themselves change. For example, as more information becomes available on computer networks, we would expect education to change so that computer networks play a bigger role. And when there is real ease of access to the information on a computer, the role of teacher as deliverer of information will be forced to change.

Although education as a whole seems to be evolving, there is no guarantee that the system that emerges will best meet our needs. The system adapts to the environment in which it actually finds itself, and not simply to the environment that we want. For example, while technology is rapidly penetrating education, so is entertainment and a "sound-bite" mentality. The new configurations of the system, therefore, may not favor excellence and demanding intellectual performance.

Our challenge is to understand the features and forces that drive adaptation. That understanding will give us the opportunity to influence the emergence of new systems of education and not just be bystanders as the entire system modifies itself around us. As Wheatley asks:

> What are the sources of order? How do we create organizational coherence, where activities correspond to purpose? How do we create structures that move with change, that are flexible and adaptive, even boundary-less, that enable rather than constrain? How do we resolve personal needs for freedom and autonomy with organizational needs for prediction and control? (Wheatley 1992, p. 8).

Complex Adaptive Systems Self-Organize

The systems that can change themselves and interact with their context as they change do not yet have a name that everyone can accept. Sometimes they are called "self-renewing systems" or "living systems." The label that we like is "complex adaptive systems." And the property that is most important for our purposes is *self-organization*. Thus, Capra (1996) says, "self-organization has emerged as perhaps *the* central concept in the systems view of life" (p. 83) (emphasis in original).

Self-organization is the ability of living systems to organize into patterns and structures without any externally imposed plan or direction. Systems self-organize without strategic plans, without leaders being visionary for others, and without having to think it through ahead of time. A self-organized system emerges (Wheatley 1995, p. 4).

We can see self-organization operating in Calichusetts. There, you notice something about the way that the system keeps changing shape. No one person or group is in control. Although many people have input and influence, the shape that the system takes from moment to moment is the cumulative result of all the different inputs and interactions. The system actually seems to be reconfiguring itself. This is self-organization, and it is a fundamental property of complex adaptive systems.

One example of self-organization is the Internet and the World Wide Web. There are many players, and each responds to its own situation and to innovations as the user comes on line. In fact, the system actually cannot be controlled. And yet it is a sort of "dynamic entity" (Goerner 1994). It is a sprawling, messy, interactive, almost alive, self-organizing system of which no one has control.

Self-organization is one of the most potent messages of the new science. It is fundamentally different from a traditional view of organization, which depends on top-down control, the specification of rules of behavior and communication, the use of constant supervision, oversight, and predictable outcomes. Such a view represents an optimistic view of human nature. It is the power of self-organization itself that we have to tap. Our task is to grasp what happens that fosters self-organization, and then to introduce those conditions into classrooms, schools, and education generally in a way that helps us serve our purposes.

Simple Processes That Guide Self-Organization and Shape Massive Systems

We need a simpler way. And there is one. As we will see, however, the fact that this way is simple does not mean that it is easy.

Self-organization occurs when several basic conditions are met (see Freeman, in Abraham and Gilgen 1995):

• The system needs to be open and exchanging energy and information with its environment.

• There should a large number of distinct elements (e.g., in education, we could call these "elements" teachers, students, and parents).

• The system should be excited or energized. An example of such excitation is the affiliations and partnerships that came into being, and the activity that was stimulated, in response to the actions of the New American Schools Development Corporation several years ago. (In the early 1990s, a national competition sponsored in part by industry was set in motion for the purpose of developing "world-class" education in ways that could be replicated throughout the United States. Literally hundreds of partnerships between schools, businesses, universities, and others sought to participate.)

All three conditions are beginning to be met within the larger system of education.

In addition, there are at least two more related and important features of a complex adaptive system that are critical to self-organization:

• There are some core relationships between the parts. Often they can be formulated in terms of principles or "rules" that actually spell out basic relationships. We are not talking about the traditional rules or regu- lations that exist in schools. We are referring to intrinsic relationships that run deep. In human systems, these include and revolve around fundamental values and beliefs.

• Each semiautonomous part of the system then adjusts its own behavior so that its behavior and sense of identity are consistent with those relationships or rules of relationship. This is called "self-reference." In practice, individuals or participants are continually checking out their relationships to others by referring to personal values, beliefs, and principles (not necessarily articulated), many of which are shared. This entire process is automatic and proceeds through personal reflection and feedback on how others are functioning.

An example of self-reference organized around a basic value like, "What's in it for me?" is likely to be one in which opportunism is rampant and compassion is absent. Such an example seems to be what many societies are becoming today. These societies can be compared with other societies having systems that follow another rule, "Do unto others as you would have them do unto you." The two principles combined would lead to a much more compassionate system. We have to understand that all of us subscribe to some version of rules as individuals and as a system and that these often unarticulated rules have profound consequences, reaching into all facets of human life.

Background

Let us step back a moment and see one way in which the interaction of rules of relationship and self-reference came to be understood. We begin in the early 1990s, when complexity theory was being popularized with one experiment. It was a computer program called BOIDS (Waldrop 1992).

Craig Reynolds of the Symbolics Corporation in Los Angeles had developed a computer program to simulate birds in flight. He set up a "large collection of autonomous birdlike agents—boids—into an on-screen environment full of walls and obstacles" (Waldrop 1992, p. 241). He also gave them some simple rules to function by. One was that a boid was to always move toward the perceived center of mass of boids; the next was to match velocities with boids in its neighborhood; the third was to stay a minimum distance away from every other object, including other boids. Then he set the program in motion. What he found was that the objects began to act exactly like a flock of birds in their movement and configuration. They moved in one direction, veered around, expanded as a group, and contracted again. He had used some simple procedures to create complex, dynamic order. He NEVER said "Create a flock," and yet flocking behavior "emerged" as the system self-organized around some basic rules.

Another self-adapting computer program—an artificial stock market created by economist W. Brian Arthur—extended these principles. He set up some "agents" in a computer with rules that were like the simple "buy" and "sell" rules that operate in trade and markets, except that there were random rules that competed. "They [Arthur and his colleagues] started their agents off from total stupidity—random rules— and let them [the agents] learn how to bid" (Waldrop 1992, p. 274). What they found after letting the program run was that patterns began to develop. The patterns had not been programmed in. But they looked very much like the typical behavior of the stock market! There were bull markets and bear markets, "bubbles and crashes" (Waldrop 1992, p. 274). The researchers felt that they had found an emergent property in the system.

These examples show something of how self-organization actually works. In the words of Stephanie Pace Marshall (1995):

> Complex behavior, like flocking, need not have complex rules. Simple rules will yield profoundly complex results (p. 12).

Brian Arthur put the same thought differently when he said, "the parts are smart" (Arthur 1994). Self-organization as a systems concept, then, describes the overall response of the system that occurs as a result of the way in which each part monitors and adjusts according to its sense of the core relationships. That is, self-organization is the result of the ways in which the parts "learn"! But the learning is driven by some basic principles and relationships.

Does self-organization explain what is and what is not happening in education in Calichusetts? Are all the players and participants basically guiding their reactions and behaviors in the light of some traditional relationships that operate at a deep level in their psyches? Could it be that such relationships are expressed in terms such as the following?

Only experts create knowledge.
Teachers deliver knowledge in the form of information.
Children are graded on how much of the information they have stored.

Could these traditional relationships be why the underlying pattern—the way in which the basic education is administered and implemented—is not changing? Everything that is being done may be the result of an unchanging set of basic beliefs. Following this set of beliefs would mean that the system is internally designed to function in a particular way, irrespective of how much additional activity there is and irrespective of how meaningless or ineffective it might be.

If what we have described is correct, then we have one solution to our problem. The immense promise within this view is that by changing the core relationships—the deep beliefs that express the nature of the connectedness between the people and elements of the system—and by adequate self-reflection and self-reference, the system can reorganize itself in ways that actually assist education. What would happen if the core relationships, beliefs, and values were as follows?

Dynamical knowledge requires individual meaning making based on multiple sources of information.

The role of educators is to facilitate the making of dynamical knowledge.

Dynamical knowledge is revealed through real-world performance.

The question to ask ourselves is, "How would education, including research, teaching, school buildings, administration, and funding change if we all adopted the notion of learning as the acquisition of meaningful knowledge instead of the delivery of information developed by experts?"

An Example

In a personal communication, Joann Neuroth of On Purpose Associates in Michigan showed us an example of such an approach. She introduced us to Lakeview School in Battle Creek, Michigan, which has been seeking to apply several ideas from complexity theory to restructuring. One idea is the continuous improvement tools of Total Quality Management. The other has been an attempt to explore the implications of "learner-centered" learning principles.

What the teachers did was to select one specific purpose, namely, the creation of "thoughtful learners," and combined that with the vision of learner centeredness. Here we see a clear focus of relationship. Next, they took the relationship seriously, both individually and in cross-functional groups and teams. That is, they engaged in extensive self-reference with respect to the core idea. The consequence was, and continues to be, a massive rethinking and change of the system, with changes emerging as natural consequences of the ongoing reflection and learning. Part of their process is illustrated in Figure 3.1 (see p. 68).

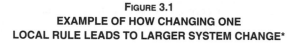

FIGURE 3.1
EXAMPLE OF HOW CHANGING ONE
LOCAL RULE LEADS TO LARGER SYSTEM CHANGE*

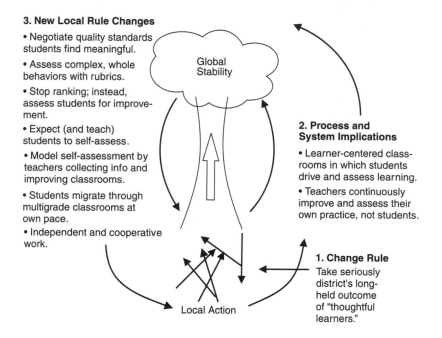

3. New Local Rule Changes

• Negotiate quality standards students find meaningful.

• Assess complex, whole behaviors with rubrics.

• Stop ranking; instead, assess students for improvement.

• Expect (and teach) students to self-assess.

• Model self-assessment by teachers collecting info and improving classrooms.

• Students migrate through multigrade classrooms at own pace.

• Independent and cooperative work.

Global Stability

2. Process and System Implications

• Learner-centered classrooms in which students drive and assess learning.

• Teachers continuously improve and assess their own practice, not students.

1. Change Rule
Take seriously district's long-held outcome of "thoughtful learners."

Local Action

*Source: Lakeview Schools, Battle Creek, Michigan.

What Else Influences Self-Organization and Adaptation?

The inside-out approach of taking a few core ideas and principles of relationship really seriously is a counterintuitive but exhilarating possibility—so strange, in fact, that it strikes you that such an approach can't be all that simple. A torrent of questions comes to mind: How can so much come from so little? What changes? What does not change? What needs to change? Does all of this mean that there will not be any significant change until beliefs change? Does change need to take place inside and outside the system? And what *are* the inside and outside, anyway?

There are so many questions, in fact, that you feel compelled to seek answers from those who have been keeping pace with all these ideas. Those people are not difficult to find. What is unsettling as you meet them, however, is that there are so many versions of how it all works. What is compelling is the growing consensus. You decide, now, that you need to select one point of view to maintain coherence and find enough that will guide you. You settle, serendipitously, on a couple of educational searchers who first began exploring brain research and are now trying to make sense of an entire new paradigm. We will call them Marguerite and Patrick. You meet with them and attempt to marshal your questions, knowing that the questions are all intermingled and that for the time being, all you seek is a big picture.

Dialogue Between You, "Marguerite," and "Patrick"

You: *Isn't it just a matter of understanding what causes what, and fixing it? After all, in a car, press the accelerator and the car goes faster; remove your foot and (provided that you are on level ground) the car will slow down. Surely results are proportional to activity?*

Patrick: That is possibly the greatest conceptual shift that we all have to make. It simply is not true, in the case of most phenomena, that input and output or cause and effect are proportional. Nor is it possible to always tell what causes what. What you are describing with your accelerator is a linear relationship—an idea that has enormous cultural weight. One example is a legal system that tries to make the punishment fit the crime. Another is a scientific system that looks for understanding by trying to identify and then measure the individual impact of independent variables. In both cases, much of the context and other things are ignored.

The awkward problem with a belief in the linear notion of cause and effect is that such a belief does not describe most of what happens in the universe. It does not apply to most aspects of health, business, or the weather; nor does it apply to most of what happens in education. We adhere to it because we have never really had the scientific tools to investigate other possibilities. And those tools are now becoming available. The result is that we are coming face to face with the prevalence of nonlinearity. Sally Goerner tells us that

> A nonlinear system is any system in which input is not proportional to output. . . . For example, 140 Fahrenheit is not twice as pleasant as 70; 8 aspirin do not reduce a headache 8 times as much as one aspirin. . . . Nonlinearity is as simple as that. It is everything whose graph is not a straight line—and this is just about everything (Goerner 1994, p. 16).

Marguerite: To take Sally Goerner's example further, taking 64 aspirin does not mean that I will not get a headache for two weeks. Much of what we do in restructuring is the equivalent of pushing harder on the accelerator or giving more aspirin. More time. More effort. Add more strategies. Try more things. And yet the result is often negligible and frequently counterproductive. Things may, in fact, get worse instead of better. On the other hand, sometimes a slight input can have enormous effects. An example is what happens in a spontaneous encounter between a student and a caring adult when a few words can change a life! More does not necessarily mean better. And sometimes, less is more.

You: *But the implications of that are mind boggling! More "on-task" behavior does not guarantee understanding. More teacher work on lesson plans may interfere with learning. More funding for special programs may lead to no improvement whatsoever for special needs or other children. Prescribing higher standards may have no impact on student understanding. Less teacher input may be exactly what students need. Fewer rules and regulations may lead to more order and more courtesy.*

Marguerite: We feel the same way. That is why it is so difficult to answer when people ask us what to do and why we hesitate at this point to enter the national standards debate. Excellence is vital, but the underlying paradigm doesn't make sense any more, which means that we can't address the questions in the old way.

You: *Surely that cannot be totally correct. There are lots of straight-forward examples where linearity has worked and where some things lead directly to other things. These include examples where hard work led to better results or where clear management policies could be implemented. If what you are saying is right, why have problems not shown up before?*

Patrick: Good point, though I would quibble with your final statement. Lots of these problems have shown up before, but they were ignored, partly because of a mechanistic mind-set. After all, we have seen superb accomplishments from people who did not finish school or who did not like it. We have also seen some of our best students drop out or get low grades simply because they are different. The bigger issue, though, is that nonlinearity becomes more of an issue as a system becomes more unstable—as it moves away from equilibrium. As you know, people are talking about the fact that even the pace of change is increasing everywhere. What that means is that the entire system, of which education is a part, is becoming more and more unstable. When that happens, nonlinearity shows up more. The instability is then made even greater because the effects are fed back into the system and amplified; and so change begets more change, and there is more and more instability.

Marguerite: We should add here that nonlinearity is actually essential for self-organization to work, so nonlinearity is a *plus* and not a problem.

You: *Now wait a moment. You are saying that the system is experiencing instability, and that that's a good thing. Yet you are also saying that the education system is resisting change and is stuck. Perhaps you would care to clarify?*

Patrick: Oh dear. I'm afraid you're right. What we see, first of all, is that all of society is becoming more unstable. This instability is partly what we mean by nonlinearity. From the point of view of education, instability shows up in all the agitation and activity, the political action and the media interest, the rewriting of standards and curriculum, the legislative action, and so on.

You: *So tell me again, where are we "stuck"?*

Marguerite: I hope that you are ready for this. Being "stuck" is what you found in Calichusetts. At the same time all this activity is going on, people don't seem to change some core beliefs about the nature of learning and teaching and schools. You remarked on how so many different people with different goals seemed to have the same set of basic beliefs. Those beliefs are some of the compelling ideas that Dawkins called *memes*. The ideas seem to be set in stone, and people don't even question them. The memes seem to be *stuck* in the minds of the people who make decisions about education. Since these basic beliefs guide people in what they do, we end up with the same sorts of underlying patterns and behaviors. No essential change is made.

Patrick: Most people in the community seem to have a common set of expectations about schooling, based on the first three assumptions mentioned previously. Well, nowadays, the expectations have not been met; but neither have they changed. And so more and more people are actively intruding into the day-to-day activities of the schools. And more and more people are telling teachers what to do and are saying that they have better ways to teach and are trying to find new modes of teaching kids. The movement for vouchers and charter schools is an example. So the structure is being destabilized. But the delivery model of education, where information is treated as a commodity, is not changing. The system is adapting in that it is making some responses to its perceived environment, but it is resisting evolution.

Marguerite: That is ironic. You see, many school-based educators have been trying to change people's minds, if you like, for quite a long time. And powerful new approaches based on new "rules" have been tried. But the broader system—the universities and parents and businesses, all of whom love *A*'s and "objective measurements" and the like, would not change. So education struggled. Now the broader system is saying that what education has is not good enough—but those in the broader system have difficulty changing the way they think or the bureaucratic procedures they have developed. This is what happened in California recently. A wonderful new mode of assessment was introduced by the department of education. It had the potential to take schools beyond traditional approaches to evaluation. But it was poorly handled and frightened some members of the public who proceeded to have it rejected. They succeeded. In this example, a set of prevailing beliefs in the larger system basically prevented the smaller subsystem from changing to something more complex and, paradoxically, more simple.

Patrick: There is another irony there, we think. People in the larger community are pushing to introduce technology, which works differently from schools. And at the same time, they want schools to do the same things and go on working in the same old way.

You: *There seem to be other factors at work that you are not addressing.*

Marguerite: Now you're touching on one of the most difficult aspects of all this. Yes, there is more. Much more.

You: *Is this hopeless or what? You seem to be a fairly optimistic couple. What's good about all of this?*

Marguerite: Actually, we are cautiously optimistic. We see much to appreciate in what is happening—yet we hear a clear warning signal. We see reasons for both hope and concern.

Reasons for Hope; Reasons for Concern

Living on the Edge of Possibility

Young children, like young kittens, are in a constant state of excitement (unless they are sleeping). They are into and around and through and play with everything. Life for them is a constant exploration (and, for parents, a sustained lesson in patience). We do not like babies to be unhappy, but in essence we do not question this life lived on the edge of continuous discovery. We just need to make sure that the life is also safe. This combined condition is crucial for their early learning.

Just as there is an optimal state for the young learning mind, so it transpires, there is also a state for all complex adaptive systems, where adaptation and change are optimal, without jeopardizing the integrity of the system. This state hovers between disequilibrium on the one hand and disintegration on the other. In the language of complexity theory, this state is called "far from equilibrium" (Prigogine and Stengers 1984) or "the edge of chaos" (Waldrop 1992) or "bounded instability" (Stacey 1992). Prigogine suggests, in fact, that "disequilibrium is the necessary condition for a system's growth" (Prigogine, in Wheatley 1992, p. 88). Our preferred term is "living on the edge of possibility." It is a state of constant exploration and opportunity. The critical feature is that the system itself needs to sustain or move into this excitement for self-organization to be possible. But when it does, self-organization is actually inevitable.

What does the system look like? One key feature is viewing oneself as a continuous learner instead of the possessor of answers. Individuals try out new ideas and processes. People join with others in different groups and for different purposes. People bounce ideas off each other, with one thing leading to another in a way that was never anticipated. They play with endless variations and possibilities. In business, new products and materials are developed and tested; and new uses are found for old materials. There is a sort of buzz of activity, experimentation, innovation, reaction, and creativity. In fact, this activity looks just like young children at play. Implicit within possibility and variety is uncertainty. In the words of Peter Senge: "A reverence for uncertainty is one of the unrecognized implications of systems thinking" (Senge, in Briggs and Peat 1989, p. 200).

Because of this variety of options—and the possibility of generating more—the system can adapt to changing internal and external needs.

Here is what a teacher said about exciting activities in a learning system (captured at a recorded group meeting):

> They [the students] are taking what they are learning home. For probably the first time, they are talking to parents about it and they are extending it even further. Some of the projects that are taking place in my classroom—one little boy is trying to make a

flying gecko. . . . Anyway, he said that he was going to go home tonight because he knew they had an old . . . model airplane engine in the garage and he was going to get his dad to work on this airplane engine with him and they were going to make a flying gecko. So they're taking what they are learning home. They're excited about it and they're transferring that by talking about school to their parents. And in this area where we are in Rio Linda, that's so valuable. And I think that makes the parents have a link to the school.

When we think of systems in this way, we actually find ourselves moving out of the metaphor of the machine, and even of technology, into the realm of biology:

Biological systems are adaptable, resilient and capable of generating perpetual novelty. That's not a bad list of attributes for the company of the future. To achieve these qualities, however, biological systems make sacrifices—in efficiency, controllability, predictability, and immediacy. That's not a bad list of attributes for the company of the past (Taylor 1994, p. 68).

We lose tightness and control and predictability. We gain flexibility and extraordinary resilience.

The influx of new strategies, coupled with the major changes taking place in the larger society, indicates that education is now on the edge of possibility, or moving toward it. That is precisely where education needs to be to make the dramatic changes that are necessary.

The New Paradigm Is Bridging the Divide Between Individualism and Community

We know that we need community. As individuals, we "long to belong." More practically, groups can accomplish some things that simply cannot be accomplished alone. Yet as theorists talk about self-reference and the reflection of the "individual parts," they often seem to be speaking of something exclusively individualistic—that working together is irrelevant. Not so.

What we find is that if appropriate processes are used (an example is the one we describe in Chapter 7), powerful and authentic community begins to emerge. In part, a renewed sense of community emerges simply because everyone participates. In part, as people reflect in depth on their own beliefs, they become aware of how they might be blocking out other ideas—and people. Thus, participants gain a growing openness to each other. In part, by collectively engaging in self-reference, people find it easier to identify common purposes and meanings and to value many relationships. This process is how group identity develops.

We see one more benefit. For as long as the process persists, and provided no limitations are set on how deep the self-reference is permitted to go, we find that even the core rules of relationship themselves can be changed by consent. As Kelly says, "Natural systems not only change, they change how they change. They organize around self-changing rules" (Kelly, in Taylor 1994, p. 68). Thus, even more integrated and sophisticated groupings and communities can emerge and evolve, groups that are then equipped to handle the more complex situations in which we find ourselves. These solutions are finding expression in management—union relations, government, health organizations—and in schools.

Warning Flags

The problem with the impending changes in education is that at least one absolutely fundamental idea is not changing. Most people still seem to think that learning means memorization. And even when they pay lip service to meaningful learning, they really want to control the ways in which students form meanings. That is impossible. The practical consequence is that the larger system may rearrange itself, but much of what it ends up doing will not be significantly different from what is done today. Thus, education could become increasingly irrelevant in preparing students for possible futures. It also means that students will be less able to make intelligent decisions.

Self-organization can occur around all sorts of different beliefs and common principles. There is simply no guarantee that the way systems will organize will always be positive. Some communities, of which gangs or the Mafia are examples, also organize around common purposes and beliefs.

What We Need

If there is one central precept that needs to change, one basic idea that needs to become a meme—a compelling idea—it is that people understand how the human brain makes sense of things, and that influential people decide to take meaningful learning seriously. As that happens, people will begin to examine how their own thoughts and behaviors affect meaningful learning—both for them and for their children. Until that happens, notwithstanding all the time, money, and effort poured into educational reform, the system itself will adapt to be compatible with whatever complex beliefs it spawns, devoid of conscious reason or intelligence. That type of adaptation is precisely the opposite of what is needed for the 21st century.

There is another critical point. Those who become comfortable with change and process, and with the ideas embedded in the new science, will frequently be at odds with those who rigorously hold on to the fundamentals of mechanism. The two groups will speak profoundly different languages and have different assumptions and meanings. Bridging these perceptual chasms will be one of the most crucial tasks for all of us in the coming years.

4

From Machine to the Possible Human

Simply stated, the problem we have been saddled with for the past three-quarters of a century is: exactly how does man maximize his being? If we answer—as we must—that man maximizes his being by creating rich, deep, and original human meanings, this leaves the further question: how exactly do we talk scientifically about maximizing human meaning?

—Becker 1968, p. 169

The ways in which we treat the human mind and brain mirror the tension between the old and the new paradigm. Traditional approaches in the neurosciences, and approaches that educators have adopted in interpreting the neurosciences, have led us to persist in viewing the learner in fragmented and limited ways. This view has been quite consistent with a mechanistic view of the world.

The new paradigm, however, is now playing itself out in the neurosciences as well and is providing us with a radically new view of how the mind/brain functions. Recent years have produced a flood of information about the brain, with varying degrees of use to educators. Some information has come from neuroscientists. Damasio (1994), Edelman (1992), Freeman (1995b), and Kelso (1995) are examples. Other contributions have come from the work of professionals in related or connected fields—psychologists such as Ornstein (1991) and biologists such as Sylwester (1995). Yet others, such as Russell (1995) and Cleveland et al. (1995), cross disciplines freely, as we did, to make sense of it all. And the whole subject is making its way into the general media, as illustrated by the cover story in *Newsweek*: "Your Child's Brain: How Kids Are Wired for Music, Math, and Emotions" (Begley 1996).

The practical consequence is that we can begin to understand the capacities of learners in fundamentally new ways. This new understanding is at the heart of the new views of learning and teaching. A fundamental shift in perception is critical for living successfully in the information-rich world into which we are moving. More specifically, the time has come to think in terms of what is possible for people to be and become, rather than in terms of how they can be assisted to function at survival levels.

The path toward this new way of thinking, however, is muddy. Some developments take the form of new understandings about the brain alone. Others begin to trace more complex connections between mind and brain. In this book, we are suggesting the need to see that body, brain, and mind form a dynamic unity, the nature and possibilities of which far exceed, and are qualitatively different from, those of the constituent parts. To that end, we have a need to examine profound issues that go beyond brain research. How we interpret and use the research will have a much greater impact than the research itself. Such inquiry presents new challenges:

> The deep difficulty here lies in the fact that the complex whole may exhibit properties that are not readily explained by understanding the parts. The complex whole, in a completely nonmystical sense, can often exhibit collective properties, "emergent" features that are lawful in their own right (Kauffman 1995, pp. vii–viii).

One fundamental difference between the old and the new paradigm is that the new paradigm is grounded in a sense of wholeness rather than in fragmentation. Moreover, as Kauffman notes, the whole has certain properties and characteristics that simply are not evident in the parts treated separately. What this means for education is that to the extent that we concentrate on the parts, say, of a human being, we are incapable of helping that person realize his or her full potential. Our strategies are inevitably too narrow, and our results are necessarily too limited.

How the Paradigm of Man-as-Machine Plays Itself Out

The Newtonian paradigm treats the brain largely as predictable, fixable, and controllable (if we could just find the right formula or medication). To the extent that Newtonian science has been able to separate us into parts, the function of the parts can be described with an eye to control. With this view, our feelings, including love, empathy, awe, and spiritual longings, are seen as artifacts of how the physical machine interacts. And our institutions have reflected this belief.

Mechanism

Mechanism is part of a set of larger philosophical ideas. One such idea is materialism, which is the view that all of reality is grounded in matter and that mind and consciousness are properties of matter. For our purposes, the thrust of materialism is that the human mind is a property and product of the brain. Mind is what the brain does. We are nothing more than the functioning of our brain. The implication, then, is that the way to deal with the mind is to understand the brain better, and human problems can be solved by "fixing" the way that the brain works. A related idea is reductionism, which means a complex phenomenon is not explained on its own terms but only in terms of the constituent parts.

Most Orthodox Brain Research Is Mechanistic and Reductionist

It seems to us that much of the new research about the brain adopts the traditional attitude that the mind is simply a product of brain functioning. Take a moment to note the following:

This flood of neurobiological data lets us understand more clearly than ever how the brain's centers for emotion move us to rage or to tears, and how more ancient parts of the brain, which stir us to make war as well as love, are channeled for better or worse. This unprecedented clarity on the workings of emotions and their failings brings into focus some fresh remedies for our collective emotional crisis (Goleman 1995, p. xi).

On the surface, indications are that science has advanced our understanding of ourselves. Upon closer look, however, science is also subscribing to the notion that "we" are not in charge. It is our "brain's centers for emotion [that] move us to rage or to tears." Furthermore, who we are as emotional beings is determined by evolution and the mechanical functioning of our brain. This kind of conclusion begs all sorts of questions: Who or what is responsible for the emotions I feel? If my emotions are merely the result of neurons firing, who can "fix" my emotions? Why shouldn't I take chemicals to make me happier? Where do "I" fit in? What about self-reflection and insight? The above author writes a helpful book on "emotional intelligence," but the lack of questioning of the basic premise and lack of a discussion and search for a more human and complex foundation for emotions should disturb us.

We Acquire a Profound Sense of Helplessness and Dependence on Experts and Drugs That Can "Fix" Us

The "fix-me" or "fix-it" philosophy plays itself out best in pharmaceutical intervention, particularly in fixing unpleasant and frightening emotional states. The fix-it approach supports us in ignoring our own power to change conditions or behavior.

Mechanistic thinking focuses on the physical parts that can be identified and their functions, which can be categorized and classified. When coupled with reductionism, this way of thinking has been constraining. At its most absurd, this combination can lead to thinking that instead of memorizing, using multiple experiences, practice, and rehearsal, I need some acetylcholine; instead of self-control, I need more or less dopamine (to deal with my hedonistic nature); I need some endorphins for pain relief, histamine for arousal, melatonin to keep me from having to give up habits that influence my ability to sleep, serotonin to relax me, and vasopressin before I go in to fight for my raise or to mediate my feelings of jealousy (adapted from Freeman 1995b, p. 119).

We are not arguing against the use of medication. We are suggesting, however, that an inappropriate set of beliefs may lead to an inappropriate use of medication. With children, this kind of thinking can lead to even more insidious consequences, culminating in a lifetime of dependence and sense of helplessness. The following story illustrates our concern about using the fix-it approach to deal with "problem" children.

Jeremy's Story

I (Renate) was sitting in the conference room of a middle school, making some notes. The room is large and used for multiple purposes. Quite frequently, errant students are set in the room to reflect on behavior issues, and I talk with them. I have been continually surprised at how frank students are and how willing to discuss the pros and cons of their offenses.

On this particular day, Jeremy is sitting across from me. We begin to talk, and he tells me that he is here because he yelled out in math and bothered the other students. I ask him why he did this. He explains that the lesson was too simple for him—that he was bored and thinks that adults think they can just dish out any boring old thing and kids will just do it. I am intrigued by the intelligence of his argument and the choice and variety of the language he uses. I am enjoying this child.

At some point, an adult walks in and says, "I hear you didn't take your medication again, Jeremy. You know how you behave when you don't take your medication." I am appalled. I don't live with Jeremy and do not want to judge his parents or doctor too harshly. But I also know Jeremy's teacher, and everything Jeremy described was accurate. What is going on here?

Jeremy's behavior appears by all counts to be rational. Yet he is, or his behavior is, a problem for others. There is no time in the school day for dialogue or dealing with his interpretations of what is happening. It is clear that he does not like his teacher (he does not respect the teacher). But why have all the adults chosen to use medication as the answer to Jeremy's behavior problem?

Purpose, Meaning, and Relationship Are Lost

One of us can remember reading a book on the cognition of music:

Bit by bit, the book described what was happening in the brain and nervous system as we listen to music. Neuronal responses to music were identified and categorized. Human beings became nothing more than a machine that was sensitive to certain impulses. The book was written in the best scientific fashion of our time, yet it applied all the strictures of a science founded in Newton's thinking. Before I finished the book, I was overcome by a sadness bordering on panic and depression. There was no music in all of the definitions and identifications. The music and my joy in the spontaneous response had been reduced to some sort of mechanistic process, and my inner experience was nothing more than an artifact.

If I am, in fact, a product of Darwinian selection and my DNA determines my abilities and ultimate quality of life, and if I am the victim of my brain functioning, then what is my purpose here other than to live out my life in a way that pleases me, those I care about, or some authoritative other who punishes or rewards me? Is it any wonder that our schools and our society are filled with a "me-first" generation?

Mechanistic perspectives leave little room for processes like "emergence," which cannot be traced along an identifiable and quantifiable cause-effect line. Purpose and meaning are not seen as intrinsically real. Hence, a mechanistic view insists that mind is an artifact or accident of nature. Freedom, therefore, is an illusion.

We Place an Impenetrable Limit on What Human Beings and Human Society Can Do and Become

The fix-it approach has resulted in a belief in an external control, which has robbed us of an understanding of and trust in our own strengths. This approach supports a vision of equilibrium, nongrowth, and control, which depend on agents that ignore our own capacities. It is a way of keeping things the same. Life is not seen as complex, emergent, and organizing at ever higher levels of complexity. Instead of looking for a child or adult to self-actualize, access creativity, live in dynamical balance, and grow in spirit, we view the very experiences that open such possibilities as too painful. Here again, pharmaceuticals are all too often given to keep an individual in a dysfunctional situation, from a miserable job to a destructive marriage, by taking relaxants regularly and thereby avoiding the growth inherent in taking a personal step toward positive change.

For example, recent research suggests that those who watch the evening news are more depressed than those who don't. Let us suppose we go to the doctor because we are generally depressed. Our doctor has not heard of the connection between the evening news and depression, or has heard about it and is generally pessimistic about the ability of humans to change their behavior. He therefore prescribes an antidepressant. The consequence is that we can now watch murder and mayhem without feeling depressed, the news media doesn't have to change anything, and the stock of the pharmaceutical company rises in value.

Are our students merely future consumers whose primary purpose is to work, earn money, and buy or use products? Here is a possible scenario:

From the moment we are born, we use products and therefore enhance the economy. The food industry looks for ever more efficient food (often devoid of "life") production, and restaurants give ever greater portions as they encourage children and adults alike to "consume" more food. When such eating results in gaining too much weight because we lack self-control, and ultimately leads to illness, we become consumers once again as patients for doctors and hospitals. Even our death results in one final act as a consumer in the form of a decent burial. Or is there something more noble that human beings can aspire to?

There Is More

The time has come for educators to rethink why we educate. Are students simply individuals who must ingest some form of the basics to survive, consume, and produce, or is education about helping children, who are capable of self-reflection and self-organization, and of enjoying a life where they explore their abundant potential? Is it educational to enjoy listening to and playing music, or is it only education if we are taught about the mechanics of music? Those questions will not be answered only by research that focuses on the brain as a separate anatomical device. We must decide what the brain is a part of, and what it is for.

Anyone who has ever observed a child figure out how to play a game, become bored with it, and then observe the boredom disappear as something in the child's thinking or imagination spurs the child on to add a new twist to the game has seen what machines—and the brain alone—cannot do.

Human beings are purposive. Human beings are adaptive. Human beings are dynamical. Human beings learn.

When human beings learn, they self-organize. And as Bill Doll (1993) suggests:

> The details of how such self-organization occurs are still a mystery—as are the details of gravity, electricity, and quantum mechanics. But it seems evident that the process depends on reflective action, interaction, and transaction—key points in the curriculum theorizing of Jean Piaget, Jerome Bruner, and John Dewey (p. 72).

When asked to explain why we do something or engage in a certain behavior, we may initially explain what we do by applying simple notions of cause and effect. Only when we search deeper, however, do we find more deeply held beliefs and assumptions that also exert a powerful influence on our actions. Changing fundamental beliefs is at the heart of meaningful learning. When human beings engage in that deeper type of learning, they are capable of purposefully changing themselves. In Piagetian terms, assimilation and accommodation are not limited to acquiring new information, but are actually transformative. We change as people. This process of change is at the heart of Maslow's (1968) theory of self-actualization.

Human beings are not machines. Human beings are complex adaptive systems living on the edge of the continuous ability to self-actualize. We are creative, and in that creativity, we can reinvent our own lives by moving from the focus on problems to solutions. We are remarkable creatures.

It is time to appreciate what we can be and to educate to those possibilities:

> Among the tasks of neuroscience are those of understanding the neurodynamics and the neurochemistry of . . . feelings in education, which should be explored in the context of a social process of interaction among peers and leaders, not as an assembly line for conditioning behavior and using diet and drugs to raise IQs, ameliorate attention deficits, and reduce the hyperactivity in exceptional individuals (Freeman 1995b, p. 147).

First Steps Beyond the Old Paradigm

It is clear that even when we look at the brain as an entity in its own right, mechanism is inadequate to describe brain functioning.

The Brain Is a Complex Adaptive System

Complexity theory has now entered the neurosciences. It is now much more accurate to say that the brain is a complex adaptive system, a primary characteristic of which is self-organization (Kelso 1995). As Klaus Mainzer suggests:

> The process of network self-organization is fundamental to the structure of the brain. . . . Self-organization as a learning procedure demonstrates that organisms are not fully determined by the genes containing a blueprint which describes the organism in detail (Mainzer 1994, p. 139).

The recognition of self-organization is extremely important because it forces us to discard the view that our brain can be controlled by simple, direct, cause-and-effect mechanisms and procedures. The regions of the brain are both separate and connected to a larger whole. They also interact in ways that are nonlinear and indirect. The functions of the brain are wholistic, interdependent, and complex. The brain continually shifts and changes because of what is happening in the "outer" and "inner" world. If we recall that a system is a collection of parts that interact with each other to function as a whole, then this description fits the brain as it adapts dynamically and monitors physical functions as readily as it facilitates the organization of thoughts and behaviors.

Seeing the brain as a complex adaptive system helps us somewhat. For example, we can identify many physiological or anatomical parts within the brain, but the minute we attempt to attribute a function, such as memory, learning, behavior, or feelings, to any one portion or part of the brain, we are inevitably ignoring multiple connections that are involved and engaged simultaneously. Elements of memory can be detected and "localized" as a primary function here and there, as can emotions, but in the brain, everything is connected. And a new theory on volume transmission (Agnati, Bjelke, and Fute 1992) paints an even more complicated picture by hypothesizing that not only does communication occur between neurons and axons but information passes through the extracellular space as well.

Body and Brain Are One

A second major step toward a better appreciation of how a brain works is to grasp the fact that the body and the brain are not separate. For instance, the unity of body and brain is supported by the emerging understanding of peptides. These chemicals are molecular messengers that so link the nervous system, the endocrine system, and the immune system that "the three systems must be seen as forming a single psychosomatic network" (Capra 1996, p. 282).

Thus, systems that had once been thought of as discrete and separate are now seen to be deeply interactive. Indeed, as Damasio (1994) says:

> The brain and the body are indissociably integrated by mutually targeted biochemical and neural circuits. . . . The organism constituted by the brain-body partnership interacts with the environment as an ensemble, the interaction being of neither the body nor the brain alone (pp. 87–88).

The body is in the brain, and the brain is in the body. For most purposes, treating them as separate no longer makes sense.

Problem: Mind Still Seen as Nothing More Than Brain

Notwithstanding this interconnectedness of body and brain, and even though we can now describe the larger system as complex and dynamical rather than as static and machine-like, the same reductionistic approach is often applied. Ken Wilber (1995) calls it "subtle reductionism" when descriptors for brain functioning are based in systems and complexity theory that still ultimately sees the brain as a machine, only more complex.

In this view, we are still simply cells and sinew and metabolic processes and brain activity that result in consciousness. In effect, who we are turns out to be an "artifact" of nature and our physical existence, the point still being that "we" are not in charge. "We" are the result of this causal relationship. This kind of thinking continues to ignore our own intuitive conclusions about ourselves and life.

Some of the leading edge theories of brain functioning clearly carry with them these reductionist overtones. One example is Gerald Edelman's (1992) theory of neural Darwinism. A nonlinear model coming out of biology rather than technology is described in the words of Robert Sylwester (1995):

The electrochemical dynamics of our brain's development and operation resemble a rich, layered ecology of a jungle environment. A jungle has no external developer, no predetermined goals. Indeed, it's a messy place characterized more by organic excess than by goal-directed economy and efficiency. No one organism or group runs the jungle. All plants and animals participate in the press, each carrying out a variety of ecological functions (p. 18).

On the one hand, note the wonderfully rich view of the interactive dynamism of the brain and its environment. On the other, note the irrelevance of purpose, meaning, and goals, features of mind that are essentially derivative from biology.

A similar view in many respects is held by Kelso (1995), who also subscribes to the belief that processes such as perceiving, intending, learning, and remembering are little more than artifacts of brain functioning. Again, we find a materialist and reductionist philosophy buried in the application of the new science. Mind and consciousness are still treated as byproducts of brain functioning:

More to the point, quantum models are new wine in an old bottle . . . . The elemental building blocks (reflexes, quanta, and microtubules) change with the centuries, but the underlying concepts of transmission and reception pass whole from one generation to the next. The qualities of consciousness, sentience, experience, comprehension, intent, and awareness are not conceived in terms of independent spirit, soul, or Bergson's elan as in Cartesian dualism, but they are assigned as aspects of brains, neurons, and particles (Freeman 1995b, p. 38).

Appreciating the Brain/Body/Mind Connection

Humankind likes to think in terms of extreme opposites.
—Dewey, in Doll 1995, p. 1

If characteristics emerge at higher system levels that are qualitatively different from those at lower levels, then the sciences appropriate to different system levels will be qualitatively different. The science of cells is qualitatively different from the science of organism, which in turn differs from the science of ecological systems.

—Harman 1988, p. 91

We do not plan to venture into the debate about the origins of mind. Even if mind is simply an evolutionary development, the essential point is that mind is more than just the activity of the brain and the body. Insofar as it is an emergent property, it works at a different system level and cannot, therefore, simply be explained in terms of the physiology alone. This is analogous to the fact that the properties of an organism cannot be explained exclusively by the characteristics of molecules. But just as molecules and the larger organism interact, often in inextricable ways, so do body, brain, and mind:

> It is the biological evolution of social brains that has been sadly neglected . . . a neglect deriving from the engineering viewpoint of "the brain" as an adaptive filter, information processor, and symbol manipulator having keyboards, microphones, and scanners for input channels. Children deserve better (Freeman 1995b, p. 147).

Our next challenge, in order to more fully understand ourselves, is to further transcend the either/or way of thinking. We have seen that the body and brain so interpenetrate each other that at some level they need to be treated as a single system. We have also seen that the mind can be affected by what is done to or with the brain and the body. We now find that, in addition, the mind can also influence the body and the brain. That is, all three—body, brain, and mind—totally interpenetrate and influence each other.

Fortunately, there is a growing body of evidence that points the way, much of it led by neuroscientists:

• In an interview with Bill Moyers, Candice Pert, a leading researcher into the nature of peptides (described earlier), stated that intelligence is in every cell of the body. In her view, the mind is found throughout the brain and the body and is not confined to the space above the neck (Moyers 1993, p. 183).

• Every time we make a decision to change our behavior on the basis of personal volition and meaning, we also change the composition of the chemistry in our brains (Miller 1995).

• Because body, brain, and mind are so inextricably interconnected in many ways, the brain is actually shaped by its experience (Diamond 1988). Moreover, experience in one domain (such as music) can impact the capacity of a child in other domains (such as spatial ability and intelligence) (Boettcher, Hahn, and Shaw 1994; Rauscher, Shaw, Levine, Ky, and Wright 1995).

• In children, debilitating experiences can actually "hard-wire" the brain and induce dysfunctional thinking for life. For example, constant stress and threat also rewire emotion circuits (LeDoux 1994). We have already introduced the notion of downshifting—the response to a threat accompanied by a sense of helplessness or fatigue. Downshifting can be hard-wired into the mind/brain so that the brain remains on high alert. Because a child is so vulnerable to any input, and because downshifting can be so debilitating, safety, security, and relationship are indispensable ingredients in education. Thus, we need to maintain a balance—environment needs to be rich in stimulation, and yet be imbued with orderliness and care.

Ultimately, therefore, "*events in the mind can become causes in their own right*" (Csikszentmihalyi 1993, p. 46).

Reclaiming Our Humanity: Becoming Ourselves

To understand human behavior, . . . it is necessary to understand the behaver's perceptual world, how things seem from his point of view. This calls for a different understanding of what the "facts" are that we need in order to deal with human behavior: it is not the external facts that are important in understanding behavior, but the meaning of other facts to the behaver.
—Combs, Blume, Newman, and Wass 1974, p. 16

Recall that a system is a collection of parts that interact with each other to function as a whole, and that the whole is greater than the sum of its parts. The potential and the possibility that are available to us are always set by the properties of the system with which we are dealing. To realize the potential of what it means to be human, we need to better appreciate the nature of the human system. Specifically, we need to appreciate that body, brain, AND mind constitute one dynamic unity. This unity is what operates at the level where educators work. We have to come to terms with this complexity—we must deal with what someone once called the "squirming, active whole being of a child."

Purpose and Intentionality

The wholistic view sees human beings as active, dynamic, self-organizing systems with a mind or a self capable of self-reflection, continuous growth, and change. This view therefore ascribes some intentionality or organized focus that is inseparable from the whole person as that person searches for meaning and determines purposes. Intentionality is critical because it makes the mind the executive function or intelligent organizer and receiver of brain activity. Freeman (1995b) gives us three aspects of intentionality:

> To stretch forth and modify the self in conformance with the world.
> To seek wholeness in growth.
> To maintain the unity of self (pp. 18–19).

This intentionality is profoundly different from the mechanistic view. We are obliged to understand the nature of the mind as purposive; self-reflective; creative; and having freedom to create meaning, and through meaning and purposive action, enhance itself. Thus, there is a "whole" known as "self" or "I," which has the ability to observe, participate in, and take charge of its own growth.

The Self and Change

The self is a dynamic unity that is the total collection of an individual's psychological and physiological makeup, together with past experiences. Some people (e.g., Gazzaniga 1985, 1992) argue that the self is actually a construct—the product of the interaction of many different modules and aspects that are often in conflict with each other. And there is evidence for the view that many people are "houses divided against themselves," most potent, perhaps being the existence of multiple personalities in one "person."

Incontrovertible evidence, however, shows that people can grow and that the self can become more integrated. Thus, Sperry (the "father" of split brain research) contends that the "I" is an emergent property that is greater than the sum of the parts of the brain or mind (see Hooper and Teresi 1986). The view that the self has properties that are more than the sum of the individual parts is a direct consequence of the new understandings of systems. In the words of Wheatley and Kellner-Rogers (1996):

> Life's natural tendency is to organize. Life organizes into greater levels of complexity to support more diversity and greater sustain-ability.
>
> Life organizes around a self. Organizing is always an act of creating an identity.
>
> Life self-organizes. . . . Organization wants to happen (p. 3).

The implication is that for people to function at higher levels, which means that we can access properties of wholeness, we need to intentionally work toward more complexity and integration.

We become more complex through self-actualization. The further growth of the self, the capacity to become more complex, is at the heart of all transformative learning.

Like any complex adaptive system, the self seeks to maintain its identity: It seeks to adapt without changing its internal organization. But the self also continually seeks to enhance itself and to become more complex. And these two forces, to maintain the status quo and to change and go with the possible, represent a continuous tension. When convinced of the need to change, usually when old behaviors no longer work, or when provided with challenging opportunities that minimize a sense of helplessness, the self will change. But usually, like a school or school system, we, too, will try to adapt without actually changing.

Genuine growth requires change, and change often hurts because we temporarily lose our sense of self. Letting go of an old belief means letting go of how we define ourselves. This entire enterprise is often a frightening process and why Carl Rogers and Rogerian therapy place such emphasis on the need for empathy, congruence, and positive regard. These conditions must surround people if we want genuine change to take place. In our own work with restructuring, these conditions are what our process groups provide (see Chapter 6) and what is at the heart of low threat/high challenge. The good news is that we can all change, but we will not risk redefining ourselves if the appropriate conditions are not present.

Self-Reference

A key insight of Maslow is that in some circumstances, the transformative path becomes natural, compelling, and fulfilling. The self begins to seek further emergence as a matter of course. Thus, although disequilibrium exists, often substantial disequilibrium, it tends not to be accompanied by a sense of panic. The threat has been transmuted into challenge.

A particular type of self-reference is needed for self-actualization to take place in this way. What has been called instrumental self-reference is limited to examining plans of actions and strategies. A deeper type of self-reference, one that involves the self observing itself—almost in its entirety and in a detached way—is crucial for some types of growth and transformation. The self grows through constant observation of its own parts in interaction with itself and its environment.

Our argument is that the thrust of higher education should be transformative in the sense in which we have described it here. Every subject in the curriculum is a frame of reference for examining and perceiving the world, and thus, for coming to better know ourselves.

Children Need the Freedom and Opportunity to Explore Ultimate Questions and Larger Purposes

One major battle of ideas in this century has been between fundamental approaches to the meaning of life. One approach is scientism, which places a particular view of the scientific process at the heart of all human endeavor and denies spiritual reality in its entirety. The other is an approach to religion, in which a particular set of teachings is perceived as the absolute truth—no questions whatsoever can be entertained. Both are extreme approaches that diminish education. This diminution occurs primarily because it denies people and the system the right and the opportunity to genuinely explore fundamental questions and seek alternative answers.

We should repeat that it is not our intention here to actually engage in the debate about these fundamental issues or questions. We are not addressing the issue, for instance, of whether or not humans exist as the result of some intentional or planned effort. Some—Murray Gell-Man (1994), a Nobel prize winner in physics being one—argue that where humanity finds itself today ultimately derives from basic physical forces supplemented by a vast series of accidents. Others, such as Stuart Kauffman (1995), one of the leading edge thinkers in complexity theory, suggest that we are at home in the universe, that intelligent life is expected. He contends that

> The theory of life's origins is rooted in an unrepentant holism,
> born not of mysticism, but of mathematical necessity (p. 69).

Still others contend, as does Deepak Chopra, a physician and best-selling author, that consciousness is primary and the material world and humanity's participation in it is an expression of the play of consciousness. And the question of the nature of consciousness and its interaction with mind, brain, and reality is now reaching out to the mainstream and is generating a great deal of interest, and some heat, in academic circles (see e.g., Csikszentmihalyi 1993; Dennett 1991; Eccles 1989, 1994; Penrose 1989, 1994; and the new *Journal of Consciousness Studies*, which began in 1994):

A half century ago, educated people in North America and Europe tended to be convinced of the reality described by scientific materialism. But these materialistic premises are now being challenged, and many of the best-educated people today appear to be persuaded by some sort of transcendentalist beliefs. Thus, we have the paradox that science has increasing power to predict, control, and manipulate the physical world, but decreasing credibility as a complete world view suitable for the guiding of human affairs (Harman 1992, pp. 16–17).

People who do become more complex frequently do so as a consequence of a deeply personal search for greater meaning. What matters to us is opening these issues for consideration and exploration by society at large, including students and educators within the context of education. To advocate teaching for meaning and then to deny students the opportunity to explore and ask the most profound questions about how what they are learning relates to a meaningful life is absurd. It is precisely through the pursuit of the answers to such profound questions that the learning that leads to self-actualization is made possible. Moreover, it is at the heart of the biggest questions that learners find the capacity to grasp the big ideas that help make sense of life.

At this point, we find ourselves moving into the realms of the ontological, the transcendental, and the nature of being (see, e.g., Oliver and Gershman 1989). We ask what Chopra means when he is reported to have said that you are not your mind, you are not your body, you are the one who has a mind and body.

In our opinion, the gateways will be really opened for individuals to "become what they can be" when the deep and profound questions are invited into education. This search, in particular, should be part of the mission of universities and institutions of higher learning, many of which have abandoned such explorations in favor of the more practical aspects of the professions. Clearly, we are now at the meeting ground of science; spirituality; and in many countries, the law and the constitution. These are questions with which educators and society have to deal, and which require extensive examination in intellectually rich and safe forums.

The Possible Human

Rather than discuss the knowledge that people should have, or the skills that they need to acquire, we would like to frame the purposes of education in terms of what sort of person one needs to be to develop sustainable communities and thrive within the new paradigm. If change really is taking place in the way that we have discussed, and if, as Kauffman (1995) and others contend, the development of higher orders of complexity is natural, then what we are working toward is the development of more complex and integrated people.

Many individuals have pointed the way toward the characteristics and attributes of such people. Examples include Jean Houston's (1982) notions of the possible human, Senge's (1990) set of five disciplines, and Kohlberg's (1981) stages of moral reasoning.

Here is our list of attributes that a more complex and integrated person might possess:

• *An inner appreciation of interconnectedness.* In a world where everything is relationship, more is needed than to intellectually understand the concept of relationship. Rather, people need to have a "felt meaning" for the whole (i.e., an inner sense of connectedness that culminates in insight [see Chapter 5 for a full explanation]), so that they naturally perceive interconnectedness rather than separation.

• *A strong identity and sense of being.* In a fluid and turbulent world, it is very easy to become confused and disoriented. People will need a coherent set of purposes, values, and beliefs. Moreover, those values should include an appreciation of life, opportunity, and respect for individual and cultural differences.

• *A sufficiently large vision and imagination to see how specifics relate to each other.* There is always more than we can know, and the extent of our ignorance is increasing. People will frequently, naturally, and inevitably come face to face with the unfamiliar, the unexpected, and the unknown. People will therefore need an internal frame of reference that enables them to make instantaneous connections, to relate the unknown to the known, to see patterns in the chaos, and to perceive commonalities. We call this capacity broader cognitive horizons.

• *The capacity to flow and deal with paradox and uncertainty.* We will all be living on the edge of possibility. It is a place of paradox, uncertainty, ambiguity, flux, emergence, and change. We need to have ways of thinking and interpreting that help us see pattern in paradox. Our modes of thinking will have to include and go beyond formal operations and formal logic. One type of thinking that is at home with paradox is creativity. Another is dialectical thinking, where "there is truth in all things but not one thing has all the truth," or where, in the words of Edward De Bono (1970), there is "yes," "no," and "po" (which induces other possibilities). At the same time, we will need to appreciate the constant mystery and to understand that at some levels, no fixed answers are possible. In essence, there will be a need for an understanding of process and the capacity to let go of many types of control.

• *A capacity to build community and live in relationship with others.* In a world where interconnectedness is fundamental and pervasive, we will need a new understanding of relationship, diversity, and community. Each person is deeply influenced by every other person. Thus, community becomes more than a caring group of people working and living together. Self-knowledge will be essential, as will authenticity and the ability to resolve conflict. All these skills will become more critical as we understand that our sense of self is partly defined by our sense of, and the nature of, our communities. Consequently, we will have to be able to function both as individuals and as parts of greater social wholes.

Surviving Together

Survival has always been a primary concern of individuals and nations. What has changed in recent times is the type of threat we face:

Like horrified passengers on an airplane who are told that the
pilots have mysteriously vanished from the cockpit as the plane
is cruising miles above the ground, we know that we must find a
way to master the control, or the trip will end in disaster. But will
we conquer ignorance and fear before the fuel runs out?
(Csikszentmihalyi 1993, p. 149).

There is now no way that individuals, communities, or nations can
isolate themselves from each other or the larger problem of survival.
Even if the United States manages to curb air pollution, it is growing
exponentially in China, and the air and atmosphere know no national
borders. Although some diseases may be curbed, others long thought
to be under control are making a comeback, and some bacteria are
emerging that show themselves to be resistant to the most powerful
antibiotics. Inflation, employment, and economic security can no longer
be regulated by any one nation. We are all participants in, and
influenced by, the global economy.

Paradoxically, the bad news is also the good news. We all share in
a global, interdependent world. We exist here because of everything
else that exists here, from ants to trees to mountains. We live within an
ecological system that makes sense:

The farther and more deeply we penetrate into matter, by means
of increasingly powerful methods, the more we are confounded
by the interdependence of its parts. Each element of the cosmos
is positively woven from all the others. . . . It is impossible to cut
into the network, to isolate a portion without it becoming frayed
and unraveled at all its edges. All around us, as far as the eye can
see, the universe holds together, and only one way of considering
it is really possible, that is, to take it as a whole, in one piece
(Teilhard de Chardin, in Miller 1992, p. 44).

The new paradigm carries with it renewed understanding. Order
is embedded in what we experience as chaos and turmoil. Everything
is separate and connected. There are parts and wholes. And with a
growing awareness of the interrelationship of everything with everything, we can all rediscover what it means to belong.

Our Vision and Process

Listen to any political debate, examine any dominant issue in our times, and you will find a call for education to solve problems. Although we were not clear about our goal when we embarked on our journey with schools, we sensed then and know now that it was to grasp the process of how education could function to produce the sorts of people who can lead us toward sustainable community in the next century.

We knew that it was not a matter of knowledge acquisition or of training in new skills (though both are important). Clearly, we sought to understand teaching and education as transformational processes that help people become what they need to become.

We do not claim to have solved the problem. We do claim to have found a path. It consists of our theory—our frame of reference for thinking about learning, together with the process that we set in motion and describe in the following chapters. Our experience is that educators who walk the path diligently undergo a major personal and perceptual transformation. We ultimately describe this as a shift in perceptual orientations—from what we call Perceptual Orientation 1 or 2 to Perceptual Orientation 3. And these are the people who have the qualities that make it possible to educate children in a way that is appropriate for survival and success in the next century.

5

How the Brain/Mind Learns

Biology is a staple at most American high schools. Yet when it comes to the biology of the students themselves—how their brains develop and retain knowledge—school officials would rather not pay attention to the lessons. Can 1st graders handle French? What time should school start? Should music be cut? Biologists have some important evidence to offer. But not only are they ignored, their findings are often turned upside down.

Force of habit rules the hallways and classrooms. Neither brain science nor education research has been able to free the majority of America's schools from the 19th century roots. If more administrators were tuned into brain research, scientists argue, not only would schedules change, but subjects such as foreign language and geometry would be offered to much younger children. Music and gym would be daily requirements. Lectures, worksheets, and rote memorization would be replaced by hands-on materials, drama, and project work. And teachers would pay greater attention to children's emotional connections to subjects.

—Begley 1996, p. 58

When we wrote *Making Connections* (Caine and Caine 1991, 1994a), we were making the same argument as that in the *Newsweek* article. Brain research can guide us in being much more effective educators. In the preceding chapters, we tackled two additional issues. The first had to do with why the system is still grounded in 19th century thinking. The second was to explore the issue in terms of the brain and mind working together—we need to think in terms of human possibility, and people are more than biology alone.

In this chapter, we seek to reframe the general ideas about mind/brain functioning in a way that makes the concepts available to educators. Originally, we synthesized research in the form of 12 principles that we called "brain" principles. Five years later, and after much discussion and examination, we stand by them, but have renamed them "brain/mind learning" principles. In general, they are sound. They move away from looking at the learner as a blank slate, and they do not limit learning to information processing.

The brain/mind learning principles also avoid our natural tendency to segment the learner into separate cognitive, emotional, or physical functions, independent of a self-organizing whole that constantly interacts on multiple levels with its environment. Continued learning, however, leads to change; thus, we have changed the principles and theory in some respects, as we describe shortly.

We complete the chapter by examining the types of knowledge and types of meaning that help us understand what education should be aiming for: surface knowledge, technical or scholastic knowledge, and dynamical knowledge. In the next chapter, we supplement the theory of learning with a theory of instruction that paves the way for educators to implement brain research.

How We Derived the Principles

To illustrate how the principles were derived, we begin our discussion with Principle 11: Complex learning is enhanced by challenge and inhibited by threat.

We focus on Principle 11 because it is the basis for the notion of downshifting, one of the core phenomena that we need to understand and with which we must deal if we are to improve education.

Figure 5.1 shows how we synthesized Principle 11 from research literature in each of several disciplines. The figure demonstrates the process we used to derive all the principles. Like all the principles, Principle 11 was the result of a cross-disciplinary search. We began with downshifting, which Leslie Hart (1978) had identified as a response of the brain to threat.

FIGURE 5.1
SOURCES FOR DOWNSHIFTING: THE BASIS FOR PRINCIPLE 11

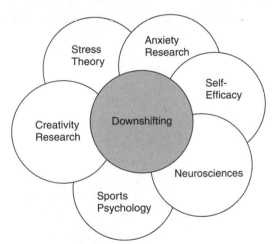

We now define downshifting as a psychophysiological response to perceived threat accompanied by a sense of helplessness or fatigue or both. Over time, it is associated with a lack of self-efficacy. We further define threat as any stimulus that triggers fear. Downshifting is an important concept to understand because when people downshift, they revert to more primitive instinctual responses or to early programmed behaviors. Downshifting has other effects:

> We are less able to access all that we know or see what is really there. Our ability to consider subtle environmental and internal cues is reduced. . . . We also seem to be less able to engage in complex intellectual tasks, those requiring creativity and the ability to engage in open-ended thinking and questioning (Caine and Caine 1994a, p. 70).

Thus, downshifting inhibits many of the basic capacities that education seeks to develop (for a thorough discussion of Principle 11 and downshifting, see *Making Connections*, Chapter 6 [Caine and Caine 1991, 1994a]).

The Brain/Mind Learning Principles

We went through a similar—and highly nonlinear and reflective—process as we developed the other principles. Here is a brief summary (see *Making Connections* [Caine and Caine 1994a] for a more detailed description). Readers familiar with our earlier work will see that the principles have been revised slightly:

• *Principle 1: The brain is a complex adaptive system.* Perhaps the most potent feature of the brain is its capacity to function on many levels and in many ways simultaneously. That is one reason why we have subsumed two former principles ("The brain is a parallel processor" and "Learning engages the entire physiology") to create a new Principle 1. Thoughts, emotions, imagination, predispositions, and physiology operate concurrently and interactively as the entire system interacts and exchanges information with its environment. Moreover, there are emergent properties of the brain as a whole system that cannot be recognized or understood when the parts alone are explored.

• *Principle 2: The brain is a social brain.* "For the first year or two of life outside the womb, our brains are in the most pliable, impressionable, and receptive state they will ever be in" (Darling 1996, p. 18). We begin to be shaped as our immensely receptive brain/minds interact with our early environment and interpersonal relationships. Vygotsky (1978) was partially responsible for bringing the social construction of knowledge to our awareness. For instance, therapy works through this dynamical interaction with others (Louis Cozolino, personal communication, March 1996). It is now clear that throughout our lives, our brain/minds change in response to their engagement with others—so much so that individuals must always be seen to be integral parts of larger social systems. Indeed, part of our identity depends on establishing community and finding ways to belong. Learning, therefore, is profoundly influenced by the nature of the social relationships within which people find themselves.

• *Principle 3: The search for meaning is innate.* In general, the search for meaning refers to making sense of our experiences. This search is survival oriented and basic to the human brain/mind. Although the ways in which we make sense of our experience change over time, the central drive to do so is lifelong. At its core, our search for meaning is driven by our purposes and values. Something of the extent of human purposes was expressed by Maslow (1968). Included are such basic questions as "Who am I?" and "Why am I here?" Thus, the search for meaning ranges from the need to eat and find safety, through the development of relationships and a sense of identity, to an exploration of our potential and the quest for transcendence.

• *Principle 4: The search for meaning occurs through "patterning."* In patterning, we include schematic maps and categories, both acquired and innate. The brain/mind needs and automatically registers the familiar while simultaneously searching for and responding to novel stimuli. In a way, therefore, the brain/mind is both scientist and artist, attempting to discern and understand patterns as they occur and giving expression to unique and creative patterns of its own. The brain/mind resists having meaninglessness imposed on it. By meaninglessness, we mean isolated pieces of information unrelated to what makes sense to a particular learner. Effective education must give learners an opportunity to formulate their own patterns of understanding.

• *Principle 5: Emotions are critical to patterning.* What we learn is influenced and organized by emotions and mind-sets involving expectancy, personal biases and prejudices, self-esteem, and the need for social interaction. Emotions and thoughts literally shape each other and cannot be separated. Emotions color meaning. Metaphors are an example, as Lakoff and Johnson (1980) so aptly describe. Moreover, the emotional impact of any lesson or life experience may continue to reverberate long after the specific event that triggers it. Hence, an appropriate emotional climate is indispensable to sound education.

• *Principle 6: Every brain simultaneously perceives and creates parts and wholes.* Although there is some truth to the "left-brain–right-brain" distinction, that is not the whole story. In a healthy person, both hemispheres interact in every activity, from art and computing to sales and accounting. The "two-brain" doctrine is most useful for reminding us that the brain reduces information into parts and perceives wholistically at the same time. Good training and education recognize this, for instance, by introducing natural "global" projects and ideas from the beginning.

• *Principle 7: Learning involves both focused attention and peripheral perception.* The brain absorbs information of which it is directly aware, but it also directly absorbs information that lies beyond the immediate focus of attention. In fact, it responds to the larger sensory context in which teaching and communication occur. "Peripheral signals" are extremely potent. Even the unconscious signals that reveal our own inner attitudes and beliefs have a powerful effect on students. Educators, therefore, can and should pay extensive attention to all facets of the educational environment.

• *Principle 8: Learning always involves conscious and unconscious processes.* One aspect of consciousness is awareness. Much of our learning is unconscious—experience and sensory input are processed below the level of awareness. Thus, much understanding may *not* occur during a class, but rather hours, weeks, or months later. Educators must organize what they do to facilitate that subsequent unconscious processing of experience by students. In practice, teachers should properly design the context; incorporate reflection and metacognitive activities; and provide ways to help learners creatively elaborate on the ideas, skills, and experiences. Teaching largely becomes a matter of helping learners make visible what is invisible.

• *Principle 9: We have at least two ways of organizing memory.* Although many models of memory exist, one that provides an excellent platform for educators is the distinction made by O'Keefe and Nadel (1978) between taxon and locale memories. They suggest that we have a set of systems for recalling relatively unrelated information (taxon systems, from "taxonomies"). These systems are motivated by reward and punishment.

O'Keefe and Nadel also suggest that we have a spatial/autobiographical memory that does not need rehearsal and allows for "instant" recall of experiences. This is the system that registers the details of your meal last night. It is always engaged, inexhaustible, and motivated by novelty. Thus, we are biologically supplied with the capacity to register complete experiences. Meaningful learning occurs through a combination of both approaches to memory. Thus, meaningful and meaningless information are organized and stored differently.

• *Principle 10: Learning is developmental.* Development occurs in several ways. In part, the brain is "plastic," which means that much of its hard wiring is shaped by people's experiences. In part, there are predetermined sequences of development in childhood, including windows of opportunity for laying down the basic hardware necessary for later learning. Such opportunities are why new languages, as well as the arts, ought to be introduced to children very early in life. And finally, in many respects, there is no limit to growth and to the capacities of humans to learn more. Neurons continue to be capable of making, and strengthening, new connections throughout life.

• *Principle 11: Complex learning is enhanced by challenge and inhibited by threat.* The brain/mind learns optimally—it makes maximum connections—when appropriately challenged in an environment that encourages taking risks. However, the brain/mind "downshifts" under perceived threat. It then becomes less flexible and reverts to primitive attitudes and procedures. That is why we must create and maintain an atmosphere of relaxed alertness, involving low threat and high challenge. Low threat, however, is *not* synonymous with simply "feeling good." The essential element of perceived threat is a feeling of helplessness or fatigue. Occasional stress and anxiety are inevitable and are to be expected in genuine learning. The reason is that genuine learning involves changes that lead to a reorganization of the self. Such learning can be intrinsically stressful, irrespective of the skill of, and support offered by, a teacher.

• **_Principle 12: Every brain is uniquely organized._** We all have the same set of systems, and yet we are all different. Some of this difference is a consequence of our genetic endowment. Some of it is a consequence of differing experiences and differing environments. The differences express themselves in terms of learning styles, differing talents and intelligences, and so on. An important corollary is to appreciate that learners are different and need choice, while ensuring that they are exposed to a multiplicity of inputs. Multiple intelligences and vast ranges in diversity are, therefore, characteristic of what it means to be human.

Learning Outcomes and the Making of Meaning

The principles make quite clear that there are different types of learning. For example, one distinction that most of us now take for granted is the difference between memorization and understanding, such as, "the students who are 'good in science' understand, while all the rest memorize" (Anderson and Smith 1985, p. 6).

Precisely the same message is spelled out by the brain principles. Principle 9 says that we have different ways of organizing memory, and that part of our brain is geared to rote learning, while other parts of our brain do other things. Principle 3 says that we are innately motivated to search for meaning, and Principle 4 suggests that the search for meaning occurs through patterning.

Recognition that the brain both perceives and generates patterns is at the heart of constructivism:

> Learning is an active process in which meaning is developed on the basis of experience (Duffy and Jonassen 1992, p. 21).

> Humans do not passively encounter knowledge in the world; rather they actively generate meanings in accordance with what they choose to pay attention to. Knowledge is thus generated by individuals in ways that are coherent, meaningful, and purposeful for the person who is creating the meaning and in the social contexts in which the person functions (Benson and Hunter 1992, p. 92).

Our bottom line is that the search for excellence and higher standards across the board has been and is being frustrated partly because we have not had a clear notion of the differences in learning outcomes. It is also being frustrated because of the fragmentation of body, mind, and brain and the artificial separation of people from each other. The moment we separate these, we gain a false sense of what it means to learn. The result is that we may think we are teaching for meaning and complex understanding when in fact we are functioning at a much more superficial level. The moment we start to connect and integrate different aspects of brain functioning and relate the functioning of individuals to each other, we acquire a more practical and complex sense of what "understanding" really means.

Figure 5.2 (see p. 110) shows how we conceive of the different types of knowledge and meaning with which education needs to deal.

Types of Knowledge Traditionally Favored in Education

The less concern educators have with the whole student, the shallower the learning and knowledge. Here is how we conceive of traditional learning outcomes:

• **Surface Knowledge.** Surface knowledge is the product of rote learning. This type of knowledge involves programming the taxon memory systems (those mentioned in Principle 9) and is likely to occur when students and educators are downshifted. It does not matter whether the learner understands the content, only that the content is memorized. Thus, content includes facts and skills that are memorized irrespective of how the learner feels about them or what the learner thinks about them.

Surface knowledge has genuine practical importance. It includes training in basic social responses (such as toilet training). It includes routines and procedures that must simply be implemented accurately, such as a secretary who boots up, or starts, the office computer system in the morning. It includes the tricks and techniques for memorizing faces, names, dates, and other information. The essential limitation of surface knowledge is that meaning and understanding are frequently

FIGURE 5.2
BRAIN-BASED LEARNING MODEL

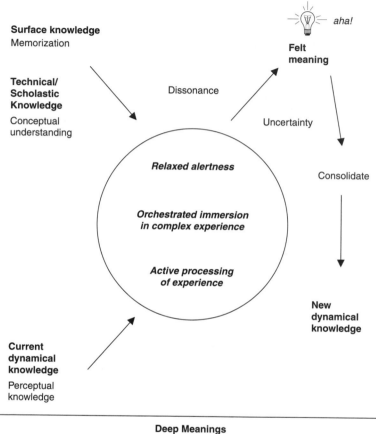

Deep Meanings
Underlying purposes, values,
assumptions, and beliefs

irrelevant. Consequently, the knowledge is simply instrumental. The ability to transfer and apply such knowledge to other more dynamic contexts is extremely limited.

• ***Technical or Scholastic Knowledge.*** In *The Unschooled Mind,* Howard Gardner (1991) alternately refers to scholastic or conventional understanding. Scholastic knowledge consists of the ideas, principles, and procedures that are traditionally regarded as the core content of any subject or discipline. This type of knowledge requires, therefore, an element of intellectual understanding. It is extremely important, irrespective of whether it is acquired in school or elsewhere; but it is limited because technical or scholastic knowledge, by itself, excludes what Gardner calls "generative" or "deep" or "genuine" understanding. That is, scholastic knowledge lacks a quality that makes it available for solving real problems or for dealing with complex situations. In our terms, technical or scholastic knowledge lacks felt meaning and a grasp of practical application.

Gardner gives the example of someone who may have studied physics for several years and passed exams that indicate the acquisition of technical knowledge, and yet when asked to actually describe the forces operating on a coin that is tossed in the air, gives the answer of a five-year-old. The schooling in physics leads to an ability to describe and explain a concept or process so that there is a sort of formal intellectual understanding. This technical knowledge by itself, however, provides little or no grasp of how the world actually works or how to apply such knowledge to novel situations.

Going Beyond Traditional Outcomes: Adding Meaning

Both surface and technical/scholastic knowledge are meaning deprived. As we engage more of the whole person, that person's learning is immeasurably enriched. Meaningful learning includes both *deep* and *felt* meanings:

• **Deep Meanings.** We need to begin with purposes and values. Principle 3 says that humans are innately motivated to search for meaning. We drew from *Making Connections* and other sources to develop the notion of deep meaning:

> Deep meaning refers to whatever drives us and governs our sense of purpose. It includes all the instincts embedded in our reptilian brains, from survival and territoriality to nesting and flocking. It includes our needs for social relationships and an emotionally rich life. And it includes our intellectual and spiritual needs. Maslow

(1968) expressed something of the range of deep meanings with
his hierarchy of needs (Caine and Caine 1994a, p. 105).

These are the fundamental purposes and values that make life itself
worthwhile. They can be innate or instilled. They are at the heart of
what a person sets out to do; and they are, ultimately, the forces that
drive the selection and interpretation of life experience. Thus, "deep
meanings provide a sense of direction that govern what people look
for and what they are willing to do, whether in sports, computing,
music, finance, or writing poetry" (Caine and Caine 1994a, p. 106).

Deep meanings are extremely important from the perspective of
learners and educators:

  ◦ Deep meanings are the source of most intrinsic motivation.
They are the source of our reasons to keep going even when we do
not understand. Thus, deep meaning is an initial source of energy that
spurs inquiry.

  ◦ Deep meanings shape what we are willing to look at and
how we interpret our experiences. Purposes and values have an
organizational component that necessarily and inevitably participates
in the actual framing of our knowledge.

Because all human beings innately organize their thinking and
perception around what they regard to be important (a form of
self-organization), educators must deal openly and effectively with
what children believe to be important—if we wish the children to
acquire real understanding. When we disregard student purposes and
values, we are tossing out the essential glue that acts as the key to the
depth of understanding we wish students to acquire. We then obstruct
meaningful learning.

Just as students' values and purposes are important, so too are the
concerns of parents and communities. The concerns that parents
expressed about education from all points on the political and religious
spectrum are quite legitimate. Values and purposes are intrinsic to
effective education. We therefore welcome the debate on these issues.
What troubles us is that so many participants in the debate are unaware
that values are at the heart of all expertise, mastery, and genuine
understanding.

• *Felt Meaning.* Genuine understanding always has an emotional component. Genuine understanding is much more than intellectual understanding. It includes what Gendlin (1962) calls a "felt sense" or "felt meaning" (Caine and Caine 1991, Chapter 8). Felt meaning is an almost visceral sense of relationship, an unarticulated sense of connectedness that ultimately culminates in insight. An insight, an "aha!" is a gestalt. It is the coming together of thoughts and ideas and senses and impressions and emotions, something like a chemical reaction. Thus, one's larger insights are profoundly exciting. This reaction is energizing and analogous to the energy that is released in many chemical reactions. In short, genuine understanding links thought and feeling, mind and body.

A growing body of evidence supports the emotional component of real meaning. Indeed, emotions of some type are intrinsic to rationality itself. Scheffler (1991), who wrote *In Praise of the Cognitive Emotions,* points to the experience of surprise as an example. It is now known that the structures of the brain themselves link emotion, memory, and perception (Sylwester 1995, LeDoux 1994). Cognitive scientists use other avenues to arrive at a similar notion, namely "hot cognition" (Dole and Sinatra 1994). Recently, Goleman (1995) published what has become a bestseller on the notion of emotional intelligence. And one of Damasio's (1994) central theses is that

> reason may not be as pure as most of us think it is or wish it were. . . . Emotions and feelings may not be intruders in the bastion of reason at all: They may be enmeshed in its networks, for worse and for better. The strategies of human reason probably did not develop, in either evolution or any single individual, without the guiding force of the mechanisms of biological regulation, of which emotion and feeling are notable expressions. Moreover, even after reasoning strategies become established in the formative years, their effective deployment probably depends, to a considerable extent, on the continued ability to experience feelings (p. xii).

The point is that any in-depth understanding of any subject, skill, or domain requires some integration of thought and feeling. The practical implication for educators is that we must do more than help students feel good so that they can study. Part of our job is to help them actually relate to the specifics of the curriculum.

Dynamical or Perceptual Knowledge

When deep meanings are engaged, and when information is processed so that students both acquire intellectual understanding and generate felt meaning, the students end up with we call "dynamical" or "perceptual" knowledge (and what, in *Making Connections*, we call "natural" knowledge). Dynamical knowledge is Gardner's "genuine" or "deep" understanding. And dynamical knowledge is what Morris (1995) refers to in his work on corporate management: "Knowledge comes about only under specific conditions, only when information is integrated with theory and with experience" (p. 4).

Fernlund (1995) makes the same point in different terms: "Concepts can be seen as human inventions that reflect a person's unique combination of personal knowledge with formal knowledge" (p. 45).

Dynamical knowledge is what we end up with as a result of our constructing our own meanings. That is why such knowledge consists of the total of the categories, ideas, and thoughts that we naturally and innately use as we interpret and interact with the world around us, and why it is perceptual. This type of knowledge is indicated by "the capacity to represent a problem in a number of different ways and to approach its solution from varied vantage points; a single, rigid representation is unlikely to suffice" (Gardner 1991, p. 18).

Perceptual knowledge is the way we take our world for granted— the ways in which we perceive our world. Paradoxically, both the ordinary knowledge of children and the sophisticated knowledge of experts are perceptual in our sense, because in both we are talking about their categories of perception.

The practical implication for education is that dynamical knowledge is the type of knowledge that we wish students to have in any aspect of the curriculum. The degree of genuine mastery or competence that they have is the degree to which what they have studied has been incorporated into their perception of the world. Here is an example from a novel by Dick Francis (1995): "I'd had a mathematical friend once who said he thought in algebra; Moncrieff, director of photography, thought in moving light and shadows" (p. 16).

Ultimately, then, our mental models or theories in use are aspects of our perceptual knowledge, while our espoused theories are essentially a combination of surface and technical/scholastic knowledge.

* * *

To summarize, three interactive types of knowledge are possible:

• *Surface knowledge* consists of memorized skills and facts. Personal meaning is usually ignored and not necessary. Most traditional education leads to surface knowledge.

• *Technical or scholastic knowledge* consists of complex skills and conceptual knowledge that lead to formal understanding. Critical thinking, information processing, and understanding necessary concepts are facets of technical or scholastic knowledge. To the extent that it is separate from deep beliefs and purposes, it remains incomplete. This type of knowledge is the source of espoused theories.

• *Dynamical knowledge* is perceptual in the sense that it is what a person actually believes and perceives at the moment of action. This knowledge is much more personal and taken for granted than technical or scholastic knowledge. It derives its power from deep meanings and intrinsic motivation. It is meaningful because it is based on genuine insight. The insight manifests as "felt meaning" or "aha!" Mental models are aspects of dynamical knowledge.

6

Teaching for Meaning and the Expansion of Dynamical Knowledge

A Hint of the Future

By way of illustrating what brain-based learning might look like, we refer to a story in the *L.A. Times* entitled "High School Students Mount Global Bid to Design Space Shuttle Pit Stop" (Johnson 1995). The article says that

> Thousands of high school students, from Finland to Taiwan to New York, are working via the Internet on the Space Islands Project, a global educational effort to design an orbiting refueling station for the space shuttle made of retooled shuttle fuselages (p. B4).

How did this program come to be? A book had been written suggesting that the federal government could save money by using, rather than disposing of, the bright orange external tanks employed to launch the space shuttle. Meyer, the author, contacted Peter Romero, a teacher at Bosco Institute. Romero in turn spoke to students and contacted other teachers on the Internet, and the idea of a joint venture between students and schools took off. According to the story, more than 300 schools in 38 cities and hundreds more schools around the world are participating in the project:

- Students from Bosco Institute are working with students from Mission High School in Monterey Park to design living quarters for 300 residents. They hope to create a life-sized model using a classroom at Bosco.
- Teenagers in Korea and Taiwan are experimenting with hydroponics to work out how to grow food in space.
- In Finland, youths are attempting to design a universal language center for the crew.
- A team of students from New York is tackling the problem of waste products in space.
- U.S. students hope to influence Congress to adopt some of the design ideas by conducting a petition drive. They also want to name the first station after Christa McAuliffe, the teacher who died in the Challenger tragedy.

Particularly interesting are the intensity and informality of work and communication outside the classroom walls. An example is the students at Bosco Institute who meet regularly after school in sessions that can last for hours. Another example is discussions between teachers who connect via e-mail; Romero even had a chat session on America Online. The teachers are clearly aware of the project's power to integrate subjects such as math and politics. "We want this to be something to hang our hat on and capture a lot of students' attention," said Pat Sullivan, a math teacher in De Soto, Kansas.

The power of the project is enhanced by the viability of the ideas. For instance, the story reports that, according to NASA engineer Mark Holderman, some of the students' ideas are viable today and are being pursued by NASA.

In terms of brain-based learning, what is happening here?

Brain-Based Education

The brain principles provide some guidance in grasping the nature of different learning outcomes. We also believe that we should be able to extrapolate from them a frame of reference for thinking about practice. After all, how **do** we teach, or assist students to acquire, dynamical knowledge?

The essential idea is that people are biologically designed to make sense of life experience. The art of teaching for meaning is to activate and facilitate the self-directed, pattern-finding nature of the brain. And that goal can be accomplished effectively only when the whole body/mind/brain is engaged. Our task is to ascertain the central elements of that process and then to organize them in a way that informs instruction.

Learning as Process

If you look at any of the work on creativity and learning, or if you look at the lives of great scientists, or if you look at your own creative process, it's not a nice orderly step-by-step process that moves you toward a great idea. You get incredibly frustrated, you feel you'll never solve it, you walk away from it, and then Eureka!—an idea comes forth. You can't get truly transforming ideas anywhere in life unless you walk through that period of chaos.

—Wheatley 1995, p. 3

Ultimately, our view of learning is much more like the learning of an artist or a great scientist. The artist needs skills and tools, a sense of design, a creative imagination, and a sense of the process that comes when all of these aspects are "played with" over time. An artist begins with a "felt meaning" for the vase to be thrown or the painting to be painted.

Armed with a sense or idea of a beautiful vase or painting, critical skills, and essential tools, the artist begins to create a painting. This effort is inevitably accompanied by many changes, stops, starts, and erasures. This kind of learning has little to do with being graded on completing a task, checking off homework, or doing something because one is told to. Skills, tools, and seeing the emergence of something "felt" but unarticulated are all integrated. And even practice and rehearsal have meaning; that is, they have a purpose that will lead somewhere that has meaning for the artist.

This is the type of learning the United States is famous for in its top graduate schools. We apply this same process to all learning, from childhood to old age.

Facilitating the Learning Process: Brain-Based Teaching

Because we are all designed to make sense of experience, in *Making Connections,* we focused on the elements that go into the act of making sense of experience (Caine and Caine 1991). In our synthesis of that process, we identified what we regard as the three interactive elements essential for the expansion of dynamical knowledge:

The orchestrated immersion of the learner in complex experience.
The active processing of experience.
Relaxed alertness as an optimal state of mind.

Figure 6.1 (see p. 120) shows our theory of practice, which is beautifully illustrated in the Space Islands Project described previously.

Orchestrated Immersion of the Learner in Complex Experience

What the brain principles collectively describe is that to some extent all meaningful learning is experiential. They also point out the multi-faceted nature of experience. Our task is to ensure that anything that we wish to teach or to have children learn needs to be embedded in multiple, rich, interactive experiences where most of what is to be learned is left open ended, ready for discovery by and consolidation within the learner. Here are some features that turn an activity into an authentic experience:

• ***An event or situation that has some aspect of a narrative or story form.*** Note that the Space Islands Project was a large-scale project, with a series of smaller projects embedded within it. The smaller projects unfolded over time in a natural way. Such projects are also organized around issues that need to be dealt with or problems that need to be solved, as happens in the scenarios that fill life.

119

FIGURE 6.1
THE EXPANSION OF DYNAMICAL KNOWLEDGE

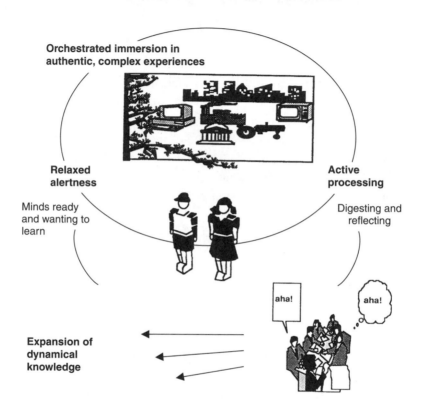

• *A physical context and peripheral environment that support the narrative.* The context within which the events occur may be real or may simulate the real world. Even a classroom with, say, genuine questions written on a chalkboard can become a supporting peripheral environment. After all, much of what transpires in business and in government occurs in offices or in simple contexts. What matters is that the contexts are appropriately tied into ongoing events.

• *Authentic social relationships.* Good communication skills and rapport help and, we argue later, are important in creating community. Crucial here, however, are social relations that embody authentic roles and functions—where issues are examined and problems solved in interactions, using relevant language, ideas, and concepts. Such activity happens automatically, for instance, when discussion centers around how to petition Congress or how to design a hydroponics experiment.

• *A variety of sensory input.* In most complex projects, we automatically find a wide range of sensory experience and input. In the Space Islands Project, for example, we may find both text and diagrams on computer screens. People move around as they meet in school and in homes after hours. Experiments conducted in a laboratory engage the body and the senses in ways that differ from experience in a meeting or classroom.

We use the word "orchestrated" because, although there is a great deal of randomness, the overall process is not haphazard. It cannot be tightly controlled, as we discuss later, yet can be influenced and guided. In the Space Islands Project, for instance, the selection and design of the project and subprojects bring some pattern to events. Communication after hours and on the Internet can both be influenced. Even the time parameters that are selected can be orchestrated to some extent. Thus, there can be significant educator influence, but the project is still so large and dynamical that much of what happens is self-organizing. This complex orchestration can be done much more effectively in the education system, but it will require the reshaping and reconfiguring of schools so that they exhibit much of the complexity found in life.

Active Processing of Experience

Although people find meaning in experience, they do not automatically extract all the potential meaning that is implicit or move beyond their current meanings without being challenged. Hence, our third element is the active processing of experience. In *Making Connections* (Caine and Caine 1994a), we defined "active processing":

> The consolidation and internalization of information, by the learner, in a way that is personally meaningful and conceptually coherent. It is the path to understanding, rather than simply to

> memory. . . . The pervasive objective is to focus on the process
> of our learning and extract and articulate what has been explored
> and what it means. In effect, the learner asks in as many ways as
> possible "What did I do?" "Why did I do it?" and "What did I learn?"
> (pp. 156–157).

Active processing includes thinking critically, using the Socratic method, asking probing questions, exploring alternative perspectives and points of view, solving problems, recognizing details, and searching for big ideas and broad implications. Thus, active processing leads to true understanding and mastery of content. It also dovetails beautifully with authentic assessment, which becomes more effective as an element of the instructional and learning process.

We hasten to add that active processing is not just a stage in a lesson, nor is it simply a time of reflection that occurs after some "experience" is over. It is a matter of constantly "working" and "kneading" the ongoing experience that students have. It needs to be embedded in, and a constant aspect of, all that is ongoing. Active processing involves frequent questioning and expansion of student thinking, as well as an articulation of facts, concepts, and details. That is why the three elements—immersion, relaxed alertness, and active processing—are present simultaneously on a continuing basis.

Active processing allows students to begin to take charge of learning and the development of personal meanings. It embraces reflection and metacognitive activities. It emphasizes self-reflection and deeper learning. Ultimately, then, active processing is self-referential. In really learning both material and exploring personal meanings, students get to deeply know themselves. This self-knowledge then becomes the key to functioning effectively in a complex world.

Relaxed Alertness as an Optimal State of Mind

The brain/mind principles, particularly Principle 11, indicate that the best learning takes place when students experience low threat and high challenge. This analysis has implications for the entire school context and sociocultural aspects of the learning environment. Our schools need a pervasive and specific state of mind, in learners and in the learning environment, that we call "relaxed alertness." All the methodologies that are used to orchestrate the learning context influence the state of relaxed alertness. It is particularly important for educators to understand the effect of rewards and punishments on student states of mind. Research shows most applications of reward and punishment in the behavioral mode inhibit creativity, interfere with intrinsic motivation, and reduce the likelihood of meaningful learning (Kohn 1993).

More specifically, we need to assist students to identify and use their intrinsic motivation, including their innate desire for knowledge and understanding. This task is difficult and complex but is at the core of genuine challenge. We must provide ways for students to satisfy their curiosity and their hunger for novelty, discovery, and challenge. Accordingly, Scardamalia and Bereiter (1992) demonstrate the importance of what they call "knowledge-based questions, [which] spring from a deep interest of the child or arise from an effort to make sense of the world" (p. 178).

A further subdivision is what Scardamalia and Bereiter (1992) call "wonderment questions, [which] reflect curiosity, puzzlement, skepticism, or a knowledge-based speculation, in contrast to a groping for basic orienting information" (p. 188).

Note that the Space Islands Project allows for a wide range of interests and sources of enthusiasm to emerge. Some students want to participate in projects related to space; for some, the memory of Christa McAuliffe strikes a chord. Others find that they can engage in political action as they petition Congress. Some students may find it exciting to work with and, to some extent, compete with NASA. Other students revel in the sheer joy of doing something that no one else has done and going somewhere that no one else has gone. And some students enjoy the good feeling that comes from working on teams and from connecting with others elsewhere on the planet. Thus, the project provides multiple opportunities for tapping into genuine interest, and for then relating curriculum to what matters to students.

Embedded within challenge, however, is always some degree of dissonance—some clash between what is "known" or "desired" and something equally real but incompatible. "To learn significant things, we must suspend some basic notions about our worlds and about ourselves" (Kofman and Senge 1993, p. 19). In describing a successful conceptual change strategy, for instance, Roth (1995) says:

> These students were reading to make sense of what the text had to say and to apply this knowledge to their real-world thinking and misconceptions about plants. They recognized the conflicts between what the text was saying and their own naive theories, and this conflict was resolved by abandoning or changing their misconceptions in favor of the more powerful, sensible disciplinary explanation (p. 21).

In our terms, students are poised on the edge of possibility. Dissonance, however, often provokes anxiety. Our task as educators is to prevent the experience of anxiety from triggering helplessness in our students. That is what we mean by reducing threat. We reduce threat by creating an environment in which students are safe to try, think, speculate, and make mistakes on their way to excellence.

The Space Islands Project can combine high challenge and reduce threat at the same time. Students have the opportunity to work together and to talk things out. There may be support from others in the real world. Time lines may be pressing but tend not to be artificial. All of these are factors that add meaning, reduce artificiality, support risk taking, and, therefore, reduce helplessness.

The teachers' beliefs in and about human potential and in the ability of all children to learn and achieve are critical. These aspects of the teachers' mental models have a profound impact on the learning climate and learner states of mind that teachers create. Teachers need to understand that students' feelings and attitudes will be involved and will profoundly influence student learning. We might ask ourselves, for instance, how likely the students in the Space Islands Project would be to take the time to work after hours if they felt that their teachers had no respect for their ideas or their ability to actually conduct experiments and solve real problems.

Because it is impossible to isolate the cognitive from the affective domain, the emotional climate in the school and classroom must be monitored on a consistent basis, using effective communication strategies and allowing for student and teacher reflection and metacognitive processes.

Finally, the learning environment needs to provide an underlying sense of coherence and orderliness. Schools need to ensure stability and familiarity—necessary for routine behaviors and procedures. In addition, a sense of community is important. Research confirms what most of us know:

> People need frequent personal contacts with others. They also need an interpersonal bond marked by stability, emotional concern, and continuity (DeAngelis 1995, p. 5).

Programs for gifted children take these implications for granted by combining a rich environment with complex and meaningful challenges. In our view, most of the creative methods used for teaching gifted students should be available to all students.

The Edge of Possibility

The process that we describe never ends. It matches the hermeneutic spiral in that the richer the experience, the deeper the processing; and the more that authentic purposes and meanings are engaged, the more profound and continuous is the learning. In fact, our experience confirms that the process acquires a dynamic of its own. It becomes intrinsically fulfilling and is accompanied by the constant urge to go deeper. It therefore becomes a process that thrives on possibility and that induces the pursuit of excellence, not as a dictated and mechanical outcome, but as a natural and joyful consequence of meaningful learning.

SECTION 2

Practice and Implementation

This section describes how we worked with educators to help them implement brain-based learning. We begin with our overall scheme for working with schools and describe in depth the small-group process that we used.

We also describe the more practical interventions and changes we collectively explored in two schools, both with teachers and with as many of the school community as we could involve. We describe several processes and strategies, including suggestions for orchestrating complex experience and for active processing; and we examine some of the results. We show how we helped educators to take chances, experiment, do the things they and we believed in, and change.

Our process had a profound effect on changing the sense of community in the schools with which we worked, and we describe the consequences for community.

7

Introducing Our Process

Western culture has taught us to "think apart" the world—to di-
vorce fact from feeling, spirit from matter, self from community. . . .
But these great opposites co-create reality. When we think them
apart we destroy the wholeness that they can bring to our lives.
—Source unknown

The Players and the Stage

Although our involvement with schools, school districts, and
teacher training over the past four years has been intensive, what we
emphasize here is our ongoing experience with two schools, both of
which were interested in a long-term program.

Dry Creek Elementary School

Dry Creek Elementary is a small K–6 school in Rio Linda, California,
a semirural area on the outskirts of Sacramento, about 450 miles from
where we live and work. Dry Creek enrolls 450 students and has 40
staff members; the staff members are categorized as classified (teachers)
and nonclassified (support staff). The school is a Title I school. Some

students come from middle-class families. Others are virtually homeless. There is also high student mobility, with a student turnover rate approaching 35 percent in the second year of our work together.

We began working with Dry Creek early in 1992. At that time, we jointly agreed on a five-year program. There was nothing magical about a five-year period, nor could they commit to more than one year at a time because of funding unpredictability. We simply agreed that, as much as possible, this would be an intensive, ongoing process.

The school had come to us and agreed to go "where no one has gone before." Our work together was funded by pooling the Title I money allocated to the school. Our goal with Dry Creek was to work with as many of the adults on staff, classified and nonclassified, as we possibly could. We were able to do that from the beginning.

Our initial team consisted of the two authors (Renate and Geoffrey Caine) and our colleague Sam Crowell, a former principal and an associate professor of education at California State University, San Bernardino.

Park View Middle School

The other school is Park View Middle School, in Yucaipa, California, about 45 miles from where we live and from Renate's university. Unlike Dry Creek, Park View is a new school. Park View educators applied for a California restructuring grant, and in their proposal, they selected Renate as their coach. The grant was awarded, and Renate began working with Park View in 1992.

Yucaipa is a rural, conservative, middle-class community. The school's physical surroundings are in stark contrast to those of Dry Creek. It is next to a park, surrounded by mountains and grand vistas. Yet the problems experienced at Park View are in many ways similar to those at Dry Creek. Parental interest ranges from high for some children, from both divorced and undivorced parents, to apathy or physical and emotional abuse for children caught in dysfunctional homes and broken or unhappy marriages. As with Dry Creek, many students with unique needs, from special education to English as a second language, are mainstreamed into the regular classrooms. Both of these schools are largely reflective of California schools: They have indefensibly large student-teacher ratios (35.5 to 1 at Park View), and the issues they confront are representative of the larger California population.

Differences

The two schools exhibited significant differences. From the start at Dry Creek, we worked with almost the entire staff, both certified teachers and support staff. In addition, the principal, Cindy Tucker, and the Assistant to the Principal, Kris Halverson, were superb, involved leaders. Kris had been a mentor teacher and had many opportunities to move to better and more prestigious positions. She declined all of them to participate in our restructuring process. Both Kris and Cindy modeled teaching, supported teacher effort, and more or less monitored the entire process from day to day.

Park View was profoundly different. Although we had started out with two whole-school inservice programs, the reaction to brain-based learning was far from positive. The original restructuring grant did not specify brain-based learning, and teachers had not read *Making Connections* (Caine and Caine 1991, 1994a). As a result, a group of only 14 teachers began regular workshops with Renate.

Although the original principal was supportive, he was not directly involved in the brain-based learning portion of restructuring. The vice principal, Melissa Proffitt, however, had participated in writing the grant and had been instrumental in contacting Renate and soliciting her participation. Melissa comments:

> Opening a new school is a unique experience. You are bringing staff together from a variety of backgrounds and experiences. I believe we got involved in restructuring for several reasons. First of all, being a new school, we had no "past practices" to overcome. We had a blank slate to create our traditions. Second, the window of opportunity was open from the state at the time. This funding was essential to try and break out of several of the old mental models. Third, we had the correct combination of administration,

association leadership, and teacher leaders to pull it off. I introduced the idea of working with Renate, and staff was interested
without threat because the principles appeared to validate some
of the practices they had stored in their repertoire. I don't think
at the time they (the teachers) realized the depth and challenge
of the commitment they made.

The reality is that unless we had the approval of the principal,
association president, vice president (Carol Lawrence), and me,
the entire effort would have failed. The four of us sat and discussed
the funding of such a grant and what it could do for our school
in a long meeting after school one evening. It was at that point
that the four of us got started. We enlisted the help of others and
based the grant on using Renate's research to improve instruction
(Melissa Proffitt, Principal of Park View Middle School).

After the first year, the principal retired, and Melissa became the
principal. At this time, the school also became a year-round school and
divided into four tracks: A, B, C, and D. Shortly after Melissa became
the principal, she married and a year later took an eight-week maternity
leave. A new vice principal took over the leadership of the school.
Consequently, although there was continued and critical support,
administrative participation in the process was less at Park View than
at Dry Creek. In addition, Park View is three times the size of Dry Creek.
Melissa's ability to work "hands-on" was much more difficult. Ultimately, however, this did not turn out to be a problem.

Most of the teachers involved in the brain-based restructuring
process at Park View were in Tracks A and D. In the second year,
enormous turmoil and many changes, including the change to four
tracks and a year-round schedule, occurred. For other reasons too
complex to detail here, the brain-based group felt singled out and bore
the brunt of much hostility. Renate's assessment was simply that the
pressure to restructure was too high, and the changes had caught
everyone off guard. In our terms, the school downshifted.

Fortunately, the teachers drew additional leadership from within
their own ranks. One person in particular, Carol Lawrence, was a focal
point and provided enormous support for brain-based restructuring and
for Renate. We are now in our fourth year, with almost the entire D-track

still participating. We have also added additional faculty from the other tracks, and Carol is guiding some of the nonteaching staff in a group process.

Because of differences in distance and funding, the overall design of our process has been different although we drew from the same basic philosophy and model. What follows is what we did and what happened as a result.

Our Process in Action

The problem in many classes is that we try to transmit information without realizing that the classroom is a community and what we learn has meaning in our community.
—Rugger 1992, p. 17

We argue in this book that the actions educators take and the decisions they make are driven by their mental models of how people learn. Our first objective, therefore, was to help participants really master the theory of brain-based learning, beginning with the brain principles. This mastery would lead to their acquiring a mental model of learning that actually corresponded to how human beings learn.

A second and simultaneous objective was to affect the system as a whole, but in a quite specific way. It was to create a climate in which everybody is naturally reflecting and learning all the time, and where learning by all is both safe and taken for granted. This climate is crucial for teachers and for inducing in students a sense of the naturalness of constant learning and inquiry. We knew from the outset that we needed to create an appropriate learning climate and learning community to support the changes in instruction, curriculum, and administration that a new mental model would facilitate. This climate is consistent with the rapidly growing general awareness of the link between learning and community, an awareness at the heart of the learning organization. As Driscoll (1994) points out,

> Community is the entity in which individuals derive meaning. It is not so much characterized by shared space as it is by shared

133

meanings. Community in this view is not a mere artifact of people living (or working or studying) in the same place, but is rather a rich source of "living tradition" (p. 3).

For both objectives to be met, a natural appreciation of wholeness at a deep level was needed as a foundation. Many ways to develop wholeness were available. In the words of Susan Campbell (1995), for instance, "this sense of the whole [is] exemplified by four essential principles: Community Ownership, Meaningful Work, Ecological Sustainability, and Respect for Differences." She suggests that these four principles promote "a shared experience of belonging" and allow individuals to contribute to something larger than themselves (p. 189). We agree with her that when this "we-feeling is present, people can accomplish amazing things," and that the feeling of synergy created is often profound.

This process guides the way in which each person interprets and responds to what is happening in the larger context. When we share common meanings and understand our own and other peoples' purposes, then we can support each other and our various projects. When all of us feel connected and included, an entirely different spirit pervades what we do.

Our approach was to model what we were looking for and to apply our theory, both to working with individuals and to the change process itself. We needed to introduce challenge and yet provide an adequate degree of safety *(relaxed alertness)*. We needed to supply the rich experience that is the essential raw material of all real change *(orchestrated immersion in complex experience)*. We needed to set in motion a depth of reflection and constant processing that would allow for the emergence of new and higher-order mental models *(active processing)*.

Perturbing the System—Dry Creek

From the outset, it was clear that we were going to rock the boat and disturb many (and perhaps all) of the sailors. More technically, we were going to heat up, or *perturb*, the system.

First, to affect the climate of a school as a whole, wherever possible we needed to include every adult who worked in the school—custodians, librarian, secretaries, cafeteria workers, and all staff or nonteachers engaged in the school in some way—in addition to teachers and administrators. Everyone contributes to a child's learning, and this contribution needs to be seen and believed. By introducing "nonteachers," however, we were going to significantly affect the relationships among the adults on campus.

Second, to deal with the whole system, we needed to break the relative isolation of teachers. In part, such work meant connecting them with each other in more ways—socially, intellectually, and as colleagues with common purposes and needs. In part, it also meant expanding the range of relationships beyond traditional groups and cliques. Much is to be gained when appropriate colleagues are seen as including others in addition to those teaching the same subjects or the same grade level.

Third, we were not primarily going to be informing or training teachers. Rather, we were setting out to literally change their minds. As we have already pointed out, changing a mental model is not just a matter of becoming acquainted with new research. Rather, teachers would experience some personal confusion, ambiguity, and disorientation; and because learning at this level is deeply emotional, their reactions could run the gamut from ecstasy to hostility.

Finally, although we had, and shared, a sense of what a new system might look like, ultimately we needed to facilitate the emergence of the system from the process itself. We did not set out to create a new structure. We intentionally set out to induce and support reorganization through self-organization. Although we were not then familiar with the theory of complex adaptive systems, we knew that a vision could not be imposed and that as people changed their view about what they were seeking to accomplish, the system would change. Consequently, we did not want premature closure as to what the end product would look like, just a sense that there would be one.

The Core of Our Approach

We felt strongly that we should use small "process groups" as the main vehicle of change. Small groups are a powerful tool for helping people bond and for building community.

We should also add that we thought a quality of community was important. In *Making Connections* (Caine and Caine 1994a), we described it in terms of *orderliness:*

> One aspect of the learning atmosphere seems to be indispensable in establishing relaxed alertness. It is orderliness, which, in our view, is different from order. Orderliness is reflected in a pervasive sense of acceptable behavior as practiced by everyone in a school. This sense is marked by an understanding of interconnectedness and hence genuine respect for the feelings of and concern for others. It minimizes an emphasis on power or control. In terms of Doll's (1993) metaphor, there is "more dancing and less marching." Orderliness creates a safe context within which students can be creative, excited, and spontaneous (pp. 150–151).

We knew that if we worked with the adults in the school in the right way, the "essence" of the community that emerged would spread to the students naturally. In terms of the new sciences, what we wanted was a *field effect*. Wheatley (1992) contends, "Without a coherent, omnipresent field, we cannot expect coherent organizational behavior" (p. 57). We had a sense of the nature of field effects from experience in other contexts and knew it to be important.

The Larger Program

Although we knew that the program would emerge as we progressed, we did have a conceptual framework within which the group process was embedded. Figure 7.1 (see p. 137) is a summary of the program. A half-day regrouping and review of all participants is recommended at least once after three months. Progress is monitored, and additional inservice education is provided as needed.

FIGURE 7.1
SYNOPSIS OF BRAIN-BASED PROGRAM AT TWO SCHOOLS*

Step	Activity
1	Make assessment visits and conduct meetings.
2	Ask that staff read *Making Connections: Teaching and the Human Brain* (Caine and Caine 1994a) to prepare for program.
3	• Two-day retreat for all staff on the change process and brain-based learning. • Form *Mindshifts* process groups to examine learning and change, enhance bonding, and create a self-sustaining structure that will facilitate change.
4	Groups meet for 1½ to 2 hours at a time, three times every four weeks, for at least three months.
5	Conduct a four-day workshop on brain-based instruction, focusing on orderliness, authentic assessment, innovative methods of instruction, and enhancing educator/staff creativity.
6	Work with principal, faculty, and staff toward institutionalizing a system of administration that will preserve educational developments.
7	Conduct a workshop on the Multilayered Curriculum and principles of connectedness. The workshop provides a philosophical and practical framework for an integrated curriculum that can accommodate all subjects and disciplines at an advanced level.
8	Develop a self-designed Apprentice Community as the ideal shape of the new school.

* Dry Creek Elementary School, Rio Linda, California, and Park View Middle School, Yucaipa, California.

We followed Steps 1–5 quite closely, but then found ourselves diverging as we began to have new insights and worked together in the longer term. We describe more of what we did in the next chapter.

Preliminaries at Dry Creek

As we mentioned earlier, Dry Creek had been exploring the need for change for at least a year, and a majority of the staff had agreed that something needed to be done. After a staff member heard Renate at a conference, and after a visit by Geoffrey to the school, a preliminary plan was developed. The following components were included in the plan:

• *The program would be an experimental partnership.* Although we were familiar with many specific processes, the particular combination that we suggested for Dry Creek was being attempted for the first time. In addition, although we were being hired as consultants, we knew that the process needed to be owned by the staff and that the "new" school would take a shape that emerged out of our combined explorations.

• *We were in this for the long haul.* Funding could never be relied on for more than one year, so we all knew that the program could be terminated at any time. Nevertheless, we wanted a verbal commitment that included us and the school, stating that the program would last for at least five years if possible. We wanted everyone to know that this was not a quick fix and that the program would entail ongoing, intensive work.

• *The program was voluntary.* People cannot be forced to change. We were attracted to Dry Creek because almost the entire staff really seemed to want to participate, and because they would do so without being paid additionally for their time.

Preliminaries at Park View

Park View was a new school with a faculty from different backgrounds. Many teachers had come simply because they taught at these grade levels (grades 6–7). They did not necessarily come to be a part of a restructuring school. Many elementary teachers had been involved in some type of restructuring already. Some who knew about Park View's restructuring efforts still didn't completely comprehend what would be involved in the process. The school started as a two-track school, traditional and D-track. Early comments that we heard emphasized that the traditional track was full of "traditional" teachers. The school was already split to some extent.

There were, therefore, some similarities between the two schools:

• ***The process was voluntary.*** To reiterate, this was a process, not an event. Those who did not want to participate did not, and they were not penalized for abstaining.

• ***The process was long term.*** The initial grant was for five years. Because funding at Dry Creek could not be guaranteed for more than one year, the Park View program had more financial security than the one at Dry Creek. There was no doubt in the minds of most of those who participated at Park View that the program would continue for at least the full life of the grant.

• ***The program was an experimental partnership.*** Although Renate had some Dry Creek experience by then, this context was new; and participants agreed to have joint learning and decision making, along with teacher involvement in a host of other programs. Renate was the coach, not the boss; and brain-based learning was only one aspect of the school restructuring.

The philosophy of the program matched that at Dry Creek, but overall design did differ significantly from Dry Creek in several respects. A major difference was that Renate would visit the school for two days each month. Because Dry Creek was 450 miles away, our visits were more infrequent, and classroom observations and feedback were rarer and briefer. On one day, she would facilitate a workshop. On the other day, she would visit classrooms, observe participant teachers, and meet with them privately. There was, therefore, a much earlier and a more direct participation in the process of instruction at Park View than at Dry Creek. However, the focal point was clearly going to be *Mindshifts* process groups, one consisting of all D-track teachers and another consisting of individual teachers from other tracks (about 14 teachers). Teachers were introduced to the theory and had the same readings. As with Dry Creek, the process group was going to drive restructuring.

Mindshifts Process Groups: The Core of What We Did

We wanted participants to develop a mental model and a sense of community by becoming more aware of the dynamics of their own learning and thinking. That is why we call our groups "process" groups. The main supplementary tool that we offered was our workbook *Mindshifts* (Caine et al. 1994), which we first tried out at Dry Creek and which spells out what we do in more detail. Here is the core of what we did:

• ***Outcomes.*** For the first few months of the groups' functioning, we had no designated outcomes. The goal was learning based on *Mindshifts*, not production. The groups were not intended to be used for developing materials or lesson plans, engaging in formal research, or debating about what should happen at the school.

• ***Membership.*** The ideal group size is 6 to 10 people who commit to meeting regularly. Membership in the initial groups should be across functions and divisions. Ideally, a group should consist of teachers and nonteachers, and the teachers should not be people who regularly work together. At a later time, group membership changes so that the groups can also be used to work on common projects.

• ***Meetings.*** Meetings are intended to last $1\frac{1}{2}$ to 2 hours and should be held weekly. Participants should meet in some part of the office that is not regularly used by them for work. As much as possible, we avoided comings and goings during the meetings. At Dry Creek, we found that the most that participants could manage was three meetings a month, lasting $1\frac{1}{2}$ hours.

• ***Procedures.*** Although there is substantial room for creativity and personal choice, we have found that groups succeed when they follow a basic set of procedures:

1. Beginning and ending on time. Punctuality contributes to orderliness and trust. Because so much about restructuring is uncertain, core protocols that everyone can rely on become important. Commitment to timely beginnings and endings is a little frustrating for some people but extremely valuable to most.

2. Starting with a simple and accepted procedure that gives everyone a moment to relax. When people come to the group, their minds are still full of the day's events and problems that they have to solve. We suggest that the group members find some way to relax their minds and bring their attention to bear on the group itself. There is no limit to the methods that can be used. A few moments of silence is one method. A short relaxation exercise is another.

3. Ordered sharing. This part of the process is perhaps most powerful in generating the spirit that we seek. It is particularly valuable because it helps to minimize the impact of roles and power. Everyone is perceived to be a genuine learner. Figure 7.2 (see p. 142) shows the steps in ordered sharing.

4. Learning about brain-based learning. The challenge for participants is to come to a deep understanding about how people learn best. This challenge, therefore, commands most of the effort and energy of the group in each meeting. The group should spend some time—at least an hour—working through the brain principles and the theory of brain-based learning. The key is to examine one's own learning. *Mindshifts* (Caine et al. 1994) provides a series of exercises that accompanies each brain principle. These exercises give the group the opportunity to "experience" the principle in operation, then to reflect on it and on the implications for their own learning and teaching.

An additional strategy to assist participants to learn about learning is, either individually or as a group, to select something new to learn—a subject or skill that is of genuine personal interest. Topics can range from music or a second language to golf, art, or a new business skill. The task is for group members to examine the ways in which they actually learn and to observe the ways in which the brain principles and the theory of brain-based learning are actually operating in their personal experience. This examination and observation occurs through reflection and through interaction in the group.

5. Closure. A procedure for ending the group meeting is as important as one for beginning. This is an opportunity to bring temporary closure. One method is for each person to share briefly, beginning with what was of most interest or importance to each in that meeting. Another is to play some theme music. The closure signals a

FIGURE 7.2
STEPS IN ORDERED SHARING

1. The group sits in a closed circle. A circle begins to eliminate hierarchy and engender a sense of equality.

2. Agree on some core material to read or explore. We recommend some "big idea" or pithy saying that applies across the board and is open to multiple interpretations and points of view. Material with many legitimate points of view offers something to which everyone can relate personally. At the same time, the range of possibilities fosters open-minded listening.

The following are some ideas that we use, partly because they begin to make sense of the notion of wholeness and connectedness:

- Everything is separated and connected.
- Whatever is, is always in process.
- The whole is greater than the sum of the parts.
- The whole is present in the part.
- Order is present everywhere.
- Everything comes in layers.
- There is always more than meets the eye.
- Inside and outside reflect each other.

Other process principles can be found in *Mindshifts*. Participants can also use their own pithy readings.

3. Participants are asked to take a moment to reflect on the reading or material. This is *not* a time to search for what the material "really" means, but an opportunity to think about what it currently means to each participant.

4. Each person expresses a personal opinion about the chosen subject, with a time limit of, perhaps, one or two minutes. The person on the left or right expresses an opinion next. The direction of sharing continues around the circle. Although this process may feel awkward and counterintuitive at first, people will begin to be comfortable with it. It eliminates competition for time and space and ensures that each person will have precisely the same opportunity to speak and listen. The procedure sets the stage for the in-depth communication that is ultimately the goal for the group.

5. No one makes any comment about what another says—no opposition or support. Every silent member, however, pays full attention to what is being said. The reason for the silence and for the absence of feedback is to provide legitimacy for whatever opinion a person expresses. The group gives people permission to hold and express their opinions. Later, people have plenty of opportunity for disagreement and debate in the main body of the process. The ordered sharing is needed to create a climate in which people can feel free to share what is on their minds without judging, without being judged, and without being interrupted. Such activity is needed to create the conditions for individuals to risk self-disclosure and engage in genuine self-reflection. We create a climate where participants begin to be willing to examine and test their

FIGURE 7.2—*continued*
STEPS IN ORDERED SHARING

opinions. Often this is also the only time they feel that someone is really listening to them.

6. The group leader for the meeting monitors timing and participation. Thus, someone has responsibility for calling "time" when the allocated time for any person has expired. The group leader also monitors the ordered sharing around the circle. If necessary, the leader can ask anyone who keeps on making comments to refrain from so doing; but maintaining the integrity of the process should really be the responsibility of all the participants.

7. Everyone reflects briefly and silently on what was said and on their own reactions to the content and the process.

8. If the group desires, the process can be repeated. An intensive experience in any one session, however, doesn't matter; repetition of the process every week does.

9. Proceed to the next phase of the group meeting, without discussion. Moving on is often extremely difficult for people, whose basic predilection is to jump into discussion and debate. This process, however, is precisely to generate a different sense of being together, in which debate and immediate advocacy and defense of a position are not the objective. We therefore ask participants to go on to the next step of the meeting without further exploring the topic.

clear ending and provides for a transition to whatever participants do next.

• *Group Leadership.* Although group facilitators may be selected for the first couple of meetings, the objective is for everyone to have many opportunities to both follow and lead. In our experience, leading a group is one of the best ways to create an understanding of how what we do affects others and to understand the responsibilities that we have to the larger community, irrespective of the role we play. We also agree with Ryan (in Gozdz 1995, p. 92) that leadership in learning communities is shared; it moves freely as needed among the group members.

Underlying Spirit and Philosophy of the Process

We appreciate that the process we describe sounds somewhat formal. We have been excited recently to find an emerging body of theory and practice that supports the underlying spirit and philosophy. The phrase that is now in vogue for what we are seeking to elicit is "the spirit of dialogue." It received its impetus from David Bohm (1989), a physicist. He felt that we are living in a highly fragmented environment and are being inundated by more information, itself fragmented—more than any one person can be expected to deal with. He therefore began searching for a way to help people get "below" the noise of opinion and fragmented fact. His answer is found in dialogue:

> "Dialogue" comes from the Greek word *dialogos*. *Logos* means "the word." And *dia* means "through." . . . The picture or image that this derivation suggests is of a stream of meaning flowing among and through and between us (Bohm 1989, p. 1).

Dialogue is *not* debate and argument (with winners and losers). It is *not* consensus building (where agreement is reached but underlying beliefs are unchanged). It is *not* sensitivity training (where "we" become sensitive to "them"). It is *not* discussion (which is an exploration and a breaking apart of ideas without going beyond intellectual analysis). All of these have a place and a role. Dialogue is

> A sustained collective inquiry into the processes, assumptions, and certainties that compose everyday experience (Isaacs 1993, p. 25).

Dialogue, therefore, is a process in which participants in a group gradually begin to shed masks, roles, and fixed ideas so that they can penetrate deeper meanings and come together in a genuine sense of communion. There is no competition for space or time, and everyone knows that he will have an adequate opportunity to speak and be heard. Participants are paying full attention to each other—and to their own reactions and intentions. As participants become familiar with the process, questioning can be introduced. The objective, however, is not to confront or to make a point. The questions can be for clarification or to assist a participant in her own deeper reflection.

The goal is to build and develop shared meaning and to use self-awareness as a resource. Or as Bohm (1989) indicates, the object is not to present and defend opinions but to look at opinions—to listen to others and ourselves to see what it all really means. It is out of this openness—this participatory consciousness—that deeper truths and insights can emerge. Ultimately, therefore, we use dialogue to become aware of and suspend the underlying assumptions that drive the ways in which we work. Using dialogue means that we bring our mental models into the open for self-examination. And that includes the mental models that we have of how people learn.

In practice, the precise ways for engendering the spirit of dialogue can vary. Here are two sets of suggestions. Gerard and Teurfs (1995b) advocate the following: Listen and speak without judgment, have respect for differences, suspend role and status, balance inquiry and advocacy, and focus on learning. Isaac's (1993) suggestions work at a slightly deeper level. He recommends that you "suspend assumptions and certainties, observe the observer, listen to your listening, slow down the inquiry, be aware of thought, and befriend polarization" (p. 3).

It may be apparent that a paradoxical flavor to dialogue exists. For instance, dialogue can often be understood to accomplish the following:

- Bypasses mechanically attempting to achieve results, yet produces results.
- Creates an atmosphere of safety for exploration, yet at times "dangerous" issues appear.
- Involves listening in a collective, yet requires intense listening to oneself.

Process Groups for a Diverse Society

The problems of educational renewal are compounded by the issues of multiculturalism and pluralism. Our experience indicates that community building, based on small process groups that embody the spirit of dialogue, is part of the answer. First, such groups have a genuine goal of seeking common meanings. Understanding other cultures and ethnic groups happens when we experience each other in dialogue as learners. Second, the processes that we emphasize have roots in many traditions (see Gerard and Teurfs 1995a). These traditions range from practices of Native Americans to the Society of Friends (the Quakers), from tribal councils in other cultures to practices of European intellectuals. Third, differences do not need to lead to conflict and confrontation. By virtue of the bonding and safety that can take place, the process groups have the capacity to neutralize much downshifting and so generate a better climate within which to deal with differences.

* * *

The real voyage of discovery lies not in seeking new landscapes but in having new eyes.
—Marcel Proust, quoted by Ryan in Gozdz 1995, p. 91

8

Implementing Relaxed Alertness

In the preceding chapter, we described the *Mindshifts* groups (see Caine et al. 1994), which were intended to be the vehicle for transformation. They were, in fact, supplemented by a parallel strand of activity that focused on specifics, including instruction and curriculum. We combined the two strands through regular visits to the school.

In the first two years, Dry Creek allocated all eight inservice days to our program. From the third year on, reduced funding forced a reduction to six days a year. In the first year, the program began with an initial two-day workshop in September. We administered our own "perceptual styles" instrument, introduced the group process, and reviewed the theory of brain-based learning. This workshop was followed by a four-day inservice training session in January. Thereafter, our inservice sessions varied. Sometimes we had a two-day program; sometimes we spent a day observing teachers in the classroom and then talked with them afterward; and sometimes we combined classroom visits with a one-day inservice session. All visits dealt both with the group process and some aspect of restructuring and curriculum.

At Park View, the sequence of events was different. After the first workshop, Renate worked with a core group of people regularly. She alternated her time between inservice programs with classroom visits and individual meetings with teachers. Because the school as a whole was not involved, the focus was more directly on the classroom and the relationships within the core group. The same general thrust and spirit, however, were maintained.

There was no magic combination of days and inservice programs, and the whole process was messy because so much was happening at multiple levels all the time. What we sought to do, therefore, was to maintain our presence and the spirit of the process and of brain-based learning through an ongoing joint assessment of needs. We also wanted to assist the teachers, individually and collectively, to begin the instructional and curricular changes that we felt were necessary.

As already mentioned, for the first two years of our program, we formulated and required no specific outcomes for teachers. The idea was that they would participate, experiment, and learn. We did, however, provide a significant number of ideas and strategies for them to test and to work with. As they began to acquire more insight into the essence of learning, we felt that they would take advantage of the strategies that we introduced and experiment with them. This process of experimenting and learning was intended to help them become more proficient in the classroom and to begin guiding them beyond the classroom and the orthodoxies of traditional lessons and curriculum.

Implementing the theory outlined in Chapter 5, we used our workshops to introduce some compatible information and experiences for each element—immersion in complex experience, relaxed alertness, and active processing. We worked with each of these elements to some extent in every visit because they are all related. This chapter focuses on relaxed alertness; the next, on immersion and active processing. Both chapters highlight our processes, include materials we used with teachers, and emphasize our own learning.

Because we felt that community and the intrinsic motivation of each individual were the most critical aspects of both restructuring and classroom activity, we began with the concept of relaxed alertness. We wanted to convey the notion that relaxed alertness needed to permeate every aspect of school life, from instruction to the school community and beyond.

Understanding Downshifting and Relaxed Alertness

We began our initial exploration of relaxed alertness with the adults in the schools by focusing specifically on *downshifting* as a living concept in their working lives. This initial exploration was followed by work on *orderliness* and *coherence*. Only after our first year together at Dry Creek, did we go into more depth by exploring ways to create low threat/high challenge in the classroom for purposes of instruction.

Assessing the Learning and School Climate

At Dry Creek, we explored downshifting and the school climate through observation and discussion. At our initial inservice program with Park View and in other contexts, we invited participants to gain a better sense of how downshifting manifests itself in schools by working with a survey (see Figure 8.1 on p. 150). Items on the survey represent conditions that can induce a sense of helplessness or dependence on the opinion and power of others. Many items, for instance, deal with the ways in which the system ignores personal meanings and purposes.

Having others do this exercise proved to be an eye-opener for us. This was a process document; it was never meant as a prescriptive evaluation. Completing the checklist required a great deal of honesty, something not every participant was willing to publicly risk. This unwillingness to take the risk was true even at Dry Creek, where most of the faculty participated in restructuring.

The exercise served best as a vehicle for open dialogue. Dialogue, however, was not always easy; and many staff members in our two schools were not initially prepared to deal with the more divisive issues openly. When we used the survey with other schools and districts, they tended to find it overwhelming. Looking at it from the point of "What do we do to fix it?" people saw too many individual elements that needed attention. Few schools had appropriate forums for genuine open dialogue in place, so the instrument sometimes *increased* downshifting, resulting in an increased sense of helplessness. Administering the checklist left us with a clear sense of the work ahead and with the realization that our work would require a different kind of effort. We were confirmed in our belief that the process groups were essential to our work.

FIGURE 8.1
SURVEY TO ASSESS YOUR LEARNING CLIMATE

We invite you to answer the following questions about your place of work.

This is a general survey, and it will be colored by your own state of mind at the moment. You may also answer differently at different times of the year. Nevertheless, it will provide you with a good general sense of the climate within which you work. We have not weighted any question.

Instructions: Circle **Yes** or **No** for each question. Specific answers may not be critical, but generally, the more yes answers you have, the more likelihood that downshifting occurs in your place of work. Note that in recording your responses, your control over the situation does not matter. In fact, the less control or input you feel that you have, the more likely you are to experience downshifting yourself.

Factors that cumulatively indicate the existence of downshifting

Yes **No**   Letter or number grades are the primary means of evaluation.

Yes **No**   Fragmented curriculum: Subjects separated from each other and from life.

Yes **No**   Your place of work is an age-grade organization.

Yes **No**   Achievement is based on age-grade criteria.

Yes **No**   Most outcomes are prespecified by teachers in the form of behavioral objectives.

Yes **No**   There is a lack of focus on alternative answers and solutions.

Yes **No**   Intelligence is narrowly defined (e.g., excessive emphasis on language and math).

Yes **No**   There is a general indifference to learning styles in teaching.

Yes **No**   There is a lack of group participation.

Yes **No**   Student groups are poorly developed.

Yes **No**   There is a general indifference to student interests and how they relate to subject matter.

Yes **No**   There is indifference to student experiences as rich sources of connection to the curriculum focus.

Yes **No**   Motivation is largely by rewards and punishments.

FIGURE 8.1—*continued*
SURVEY TO ASSESS YOUR LEARNING CLIMATE

Yes   No   Class time is dominated by the teacher (i.e., a "delivery model" of teaching prevails).

Yes   No   There are constant interruptions (e.g., bells and announcements).

Yes   No   Grades are the primary motivation for assignments.

Yes   No   Time schedules govern the length and duration of learning tasks.

Yes   No   There is lack of teacher planning time.

Yes   No   The curriculum is "prescribed," not faculty generated or developed by faculty/educator teams.

Symptoms of downshifting in the school as a whole

Yes   No   Staff factions

Yes   No   Extensive resistance to change

Yes   No   Extensive negativity

Yes   No   Limited concern for the system as a whole

Yes   No   Burnout

Yes   No   Few teacher teams or partnerships

Yes   No   Faculty accountability without power

Yes   No   Student apathy

Yes   No   Student absenteeism

Yes   No   Staff absenteeism

Factors that counter downshifting

Yes   No   Students participate in their own evaluation (including assessment of own strengths and weaknesses).

Yes   No   Students are given choices on tasks.

Yes   No   Tasks are related to student goals, concerns, and interests.

Yes   No   Tasks incorporate student experiences.

Yes   No   Tasks include open-ended assignments.

Yes   No   Student creativity is engaged and encouraged.

Yes   No   Teachers help students process "deep meanings" (i.e., the impact on their own values, drives, and purposes).

FIGURE 8.1—*continued*
SURVEY TO ASSESS YOUR LEARNING CLIMATE

Yes   **No**   Many time lines are flexible and linked to activities.

Yes   **No**   There is time for student-teacher conferencing.

Yes   **No**   There is time for teacher-teacher conferencing.

Yes   **No**   There is time for teacher-student-parent conferencing.

Yes   **No**   "Mistakes" are seen as a natural aspect of learning.

Yes   **No**   Students share and work with each other.

Yes   **No**   Students engage in reflection on content and on themselves (active processing).

From a Prescriptive to a Self-Developed Solution

We were beginning to see a genuine split between what we intended and what teachers and educators were looking for. They wanted strategies to implement; and we began to realize that we were asking them to make substantial "inner" changes. The reality of what we were trying to do was a shock. We reacted by "backpedaling." Our early reaction to teacher responses was to try to meet the teachers' needs by providing a summary set of behaviors. This summary would clearly tell people what we were looking for. We modified a model on "Relaxed Alertness" (see Figure 8.2 on p. 153) that we had used before.

Initially, this approach seemed like a good idea. A closer examination, however, showed that we were simply telling teachers what needed to be done. The prevailing mental model was extraordinarily deep. Just implementing the first recommendation, "Shares power with students by acknowledging their choices and perceptions," required a fundamental shift in values, beliefs, and thinking. We were falling into the restructuring trap that *words* and *directions* would suffice. Another problem was that teachers tended to want to implement every point, one at a time. It was the only way they could think of working with the ideas on the page. We were asking them actually to do *more*—we were asking them to change as people.

FIGURE 8.2
RELAXED ALERTNESS

Definition: Relaxed alertness is the state in which we experience low threat and high challenge at the same time. A runner at high speed is both relaxed and performing at her maximum. Threat and fatigue inhibit brain functioning, whereas challenge accompanied by safety and belief in one's abilities leads to peak performance.

Teacher behaviors

• Shares power with students by acknowledging their choices and perceptions.

• Sees child as a whole person, not just "a student."

• Empowers students by helping them to take responsibility for their own behavior.

• Uses music and art appropriately in the classroom.

• Orchestrates classroom as a healthy, living community of learners.

• Acknowledges different time requirements for different types of tasks.

School and classroom attributes

• Coherence among teachers, rules, and requirements.

• A learning community where everyone, both adults and children, learns.

• Orderliness as a natural result of children and adults' belonging and being recognized in a coherent environment.

• Supporting intellectual and artistic goals promoted in class.

• Children and adults supporting and respecting each other.

When we realized what had happened, we asked teachers simply to "play" with our ideas. We hoped they would reflect on them, discuss them, and slowly experiment with changing behaviors. We were not seeking to be prescriptive. We hoped that they would observe themselves and their community and begin to modify procedures and activities to include relaxed alertness and low threat/high challenge wherever possible. We began to understand the nature of the rift as we sought to help them literally "become" the types of people who manifested the behaviors naturally. We were asking them to reinvent their own teaching models; on the other hand, the teachers wanted to be shown what to do. All of us had to understand and manage this critical tension.

At this time also, we came to a deeper understanding of the importance of self-reference and a sense of process—both were needed for almost everything we hoped to have happen, yet were missing for most participants. The process groups in our two schools ultimately provided what was needed—but it took time. We began to see evidence of understanding as teachers began to make decisions on their own and change their classrooms.

First Changes

Some teachers rearranged their classrooms for student convenience. Others included tablecloths and plants to give the environment more warmth and naturalness. Others began to use music. At Dry Creek, the custodians and nonteaching staff did their part. We were grateful and excited to have them take charge of these changes. We had particularly emphasized the arts; and many teachers—and the school as a whole—began to put prints of notable paintings on the walls.

At the same time, we also found that what we had developed as instructional support documents were actually things they could use best after they had made their own changes. Our specific ideas and vision tended to stifle their own.

Understanding Coherence and Orderliness

Relaxed alertness has a system component—an almost invisible, underlying, collective way of interacting that we call *coherence*. Mountaineers have a sense of the *other*, even when that person is beyond visibility. This "sense" is evidence of coherence. This state is not achieved by magic but emerges out of other events and practices, including a common set of experiences or history; common beliefs, tools, and purposes; and even a common sense of rhythm. All these underlying elements, when flowing together, are what we mean by coherence.

Another way to conceive of coherence is in terms of *fields* (see Chapter 1). According to Sheldrake (1988), "Fields are nonmaterial regions of influence" (p. 97). Of course, many other types of fields exist, such as the electromagnetic field. A property of fields is "action at a distance," meaning, as Sheldrake notes, that "objects can affect each other even though they are not in material contact" (p. 97).

One reason we like dialogue as a process is because it embraces the notion of a field effect:

> Dialogue is a discipline that conducts . . . experiments that attempt
> to make conscious the underlying field in which different frames
> and different choices for action emerge (Isaacs 1993, p. 31).

Isaacs goes on to say that social "fields of meaning" are often unstable and incoherent. Though understanding how fields work is difficult, we conceive of coherence as a field effect that emerges out of appropriately deep and congruent processes. Coherence, then, is what replaces the use of rules and control commonly associated with frozen or static systems.

Orderliness Introduced

As we discussed in Chapter 3, self-organization is a consequence of some underlying procedures. The quality of the coherent field created is a consequence of these procedures. Self-reference is critical: Individuals take some rule or value seriously as they apply it to themselves and their community. By engaging in self-reference in this way, the participants actually create community.

We did not focus on the notion of coherence itself as much as we focused on the idea and practice of orderliness with the aim of having coherence naturally emerge. We intended to work with such issues as the value of a common set of assumptions about learning, the power of rhythm and routine, and other factors that we describe later. Ultimately, orderliness in brain-based learning is achieved when the entire community takes responsibility for their own actions and behaviors and when the entire community is always being considered.

There is an added bonus. Orderliness is important because it provides a conceptual and practical link that integrates aspects of what is happening in the school and society as a whole. On the one hand, orderliness provides a superb platform for instruction and curriculum. On the other hand, it supports the larger society by infusing society with children who have experienced "a world that works." The practice of orderliness in schools is part of what we mean when we say schools are apprentice communities, and is a central aspect of our view of the schools of the future.

At Park View, we concentrated on building a direct awareness of orderliness from the beginning. With the staff, we used processes that had taken some time for us to introduce into Dry Creek. We had learned a great deal by now. In our efforts to reduce the uncertainty at Dry Creek, we had not really used brain-based teaching. We were beginning to see that no matter what we gave to teachers in the way of instructional help, if we spelled out what to do clearly, then they would rehearse and replicate without ever having their basic beliefs about learning and teaching challenged. Also, they would not access their own creativity in implementing the new understandings. Almost everything was reduced to a prescriptive approach to learning. We began to be cautious about anything that looked prescriptive.

We also became aware of how much restructuring by the state department of education and others, well intentioned though it was, ultimately modeled prescriptive teaching. Frequently, complex and dynamic forms of instruction invented by researchers and academics, as well as other talented educators, were confined to a notebook binder of some type and taught by trained individuals. The binders and the teaching that accompanied the binders inevitably became prescriptive; and teachers were simply being taught what to do. Teachers then were deprived of exactly the process and the dynamism that gave life to the innovation in instruction in the first place. We began to seriously look at how we were modeling the theory.

We knew that what we were after had to begin with a felt meaning, which we usually introduce with a *global experience* of some type. Global experiences are authentic and challenge thinking and beliefs.

We decided to bring in a global experience before we went into "how to's" and details.

Orderliness: The Main Idea

Our central idea was that order is present everywhere, even in the midst of chaos. (This is a principle that has been around as an idea for much longer than chaos theory.) In the checklist on relaxed alertness (Figure 8.2), some questions were directed at the degree of orderliness in the school. Here are some examples of elements we would look for in a coherent and orderly environment:

- Teachers engage in personal and professional reflection.
- Teachers share burdens and tasks and work together.
- Mutual respect and caring is nurtured in classrooms and the school.
- Codes of behavior and conduct are consistent and respected.
- Parents are actively involved in the school.
- Nonteaching staff are openly respected and regularly acknowledged.
- New students are systematically welcomed into the school.
- New teachers are supported.
- The school board and community support the school.

In fact, "Order is present everywhere" is a global theme. We wanted the personnel to understand that global themes function as "big ideas" that can apply both to any curriculum area and to life in a school generally. A severe thunderstorm, for instance, may wreak havoc; but it is still a part of a weather system. The weather system actually frames the meaning of a thunderstorm. The storm makes sense in the context of weather. Whenever things change, either voluntarily or as the result of forces beyond our control, we have a much better chance of success if we maintain an underlying and pervasive sense of orderliness. Even a learning brain in the midst of confusion needs to feel safe and secure and to sense that there is order that may not yet have become evident. In individuals, this is what Ellen Langer (1989) refers to as creative uncertainty.

Instead of telling our teachers what orderliness was, we attempted to give them a feel for orderliness. We therefore used one of our inservice programs to lead them through a three-part Orderliness Exercise: (1) Orderliness in Life and Nature, (2) Aspects of Orderliness, and (3) Orderliness Assessment (see Figures 8.3–8.5 on pp. 158, 160, and 161, respectively).

FIGURE 8.3
PART 1 OF ORDERLINESS EXERCISE: ORDERLINESS IN LIFE AND NATURE

This is an exercise for understanding the deeper, more wholistic nature of orderliness.

Global Theme: *Orderliness is present everywhere.*

These exercises should first be done with the entire adult community. They should be done "lightly" (in a constructivist/discovery fashion that allows for diversity of insight and contribution) to begin with, until the concept of orderliness makes sense. Only after that should exploratory, discovery experiences on orderliness be designed for children.

Instructions

1. Find something in nature that expresses and symbolizes order to you. Simply observe it. Explore it with all your senses. Keep coming back to what you have selected. Process your experience and observations alone and with others. Notice how what you are looking at moves and changes continually even while it keeps its identity and form.

This exercise will help you acquire a felt meaning for the profound nature of order.

2. Use this global theme to begin to explore orderliness in nature and science (e.g., "families" such as phylums and categories, growth patterns and the notion of unfoldment over time), in poetry, in drawings and classical paintings, and in music. Link this theme to our own (i.e., human) growth and development over time.

Use this exercise to begin understanding how "orderliness is present everywhere" and how to introduce the concept of orderliness as a universal, integrated, thematic concept touching every facet of life and the curriculum. As you explore the multifaceted aspects of orderliness, begin to see how you can help children understand the joy of living in an orderly world.

The introductory activities involved an experience with nature, as shown in Figure 8.3. First, we processed Part 1 and discussed it. Then we followed the first exercise with Part 2 on aspects of orderliness (Figure 8.4). We introduced, discussed, and explored various aspects of orderliness with the staff. We sought to demonstrate that the key to real orderliness is to realize that orderliness operates in several different ways at the same time. All the participants shared their thinking and became part of the process of discovery and deeper understanding.

Again we processed. We shared some of our experiences as one participant recalled being in one class where the teacher had printed in huge letters on the board: "DO NOT WRITE ON DESKS!" and moments later was sitting in another class where each desk had a piece of paper taped to the top of the desk. The paper said: "Write Here!" With such examples, we helped the school, and in the case of Park View, the teachers, to see how they and students could benefit from common procedures and common beliefs that were coherent. We were not asking everyone to do things in lockstep; our goal was coherence, not conformity. Living on the edge of possibility requires a type of orderliness that embraces and facilitates creativity and diversity.

Teachers held similar discussions during the week and in the process groups even when we were not present.

Part 3 of the Orderliness Exercise consisted of supplemental activities and an Orderliness Assessment (see Figure 8.5). We discussed issues and procedures that finally gave a more prescriptive picture of what teachers can do and how to evaluate their actions. What they had acquired by this time was a sense of meaning and purpose. They also knew that they were free to take charge of the Orderliness Assessment in any way that served their unique purposes.

We reflected on the order of these activities: We could have given the participants the assessment first; but in the best traditional teacher manner, they would have implemented the directions and, in our terms, changed their basic notions of rules and order very little.

FIGURE 8.4
PART 2 OF ORDERLINESS EXERCISE: ASPECTS OF ORDERLINESS

1. A sense of community

A safe and supportive community is vital. It consists of a close-knit group of people who share some common goals and values and who have a built-in capacity to respect each other, even in the midst of profound disagreement.

2. A set of norms and guidelines

These are the behaviors that are generated and accepted by everyone. Although they may be negotiated from time to time, the bottom line is that they guide some of the basic and everyday ways in which people behave.

3. Routines

There is real power in routine. Routines operate in the office, in transport (e.g., the way that buses work), in the ways in which classes change, in the timetable, and elsewhere. The important element here is for everyone to adhere to agreed routines as much as possible, just to maintain the sense of rhythm in the way that things work. However, too many routines can become counterproductive because they tend to become "automatic"; so keep them meaningful.

4. Celebrations

These bring life, as well as order, to a community. They mark special occasions, rites of passage, ways of beginning and ending, and specific and important moments. They are more than just routine activities. They need to be accompanied by a real felt sense of their importance. Examples include a renaissance fair presented by students, parent/student nights, and theatrical and artistic exhibits.

5. Mutual respect

Orderliness emerges out of mutual respect—and contributes to it. The more we genuinely appreciate others for who they are, and the more they appreciate us, the stronger the community becomes, the easier it is to develop and implement basic rules and routines, and the more authenticity we find in celebrations and rituals. Mutual respect among all people at all levels is a vital part of the cement that binds a community together and makes orderliness possible.

FIGURE 8.5
PART 3 OF ORDERLINESS EXERCISE: ORDERLINESS ASSESSMENT

Meet with everyone and review the strength and commitment of your community. Basically review what it takes to participate in your community. What does everyone need to know to be an active participant in all phases of the community?

Carry out assessment after participants have experienced the basic brain-based learning inservice program and group/community processing and explored a global theme for orderliness.

Remember that orderliness is never separate from the "whole"—the quality of your entire community. Orderliness without community spells "rules" to be broken. Your global theme should continually be "woven" in to help children understand that they are engaged in something that makes sense.

Take a moment and examine the following:

We have often discussed the "invisibles," the unique teacher values, assumptions, and expectations and the hidden connections between people that guide and lead to the establishment of certain rules and procedures in our school and classrooms. How do our individual rules and invisible assumptions match those of other teachers? What do we do collectively? Invisibles are the critical foundation for an orderly community. Imagine designing an integrated authentic experience with four colleagues. How might the "invisibles" result in a lack of orderliness and become stumbling blocks? How would "coherent" invisibles help you to make the project enjoyable?

In the next section, explore each of the five areas and take notes on discrepancies and commonalities in current procedures and values. Your ultimate objective is to give students a sense of living in an orderly, "coherent" world where things make sense.

1. Rules and routines
Working in groups

- What are the basic rules (e.g., group size, time when meeting, and reason for meeting)?
- Where do the groups meet regularly (e.g., around tables, on rug, or outside)?
- How are roles assigned within groups (e.g., rotate scribes or leaders)?

Notes on discrepancies and commonalities:

Individual work

- For what purposes is individual work done (e.g., reading, research, personal reflection, or analysis)?

FIGURE 8.5—*continued*
PART 3 OF ORDERLINESS EXERCISE: ORDERLINESS ASSESSMENT

- What are the basic rules?
- Where is the work done on a regular basis (e.g., in individual seats, reading or relaxation "corner," pillow mount, or library)?

Notes on discrepancies and commonalities:

Maintenance and protection of school community

- Are students responsible for maintaining school grounds? Their desks and "special places"?
- How can everyone help to make the school beautiful?
- Can they plant things? Can they "harvest"? When and how? What are the rituals? Who is in charge?

Notes on discrepancies and commonalities:

2. Places and things

Have students explore the ways in which places, things, and resources are organized. Examples include library resources, an understanding of what goes on at the nurse's station (or what to do when not feeling well), where the telephones are, how to reach the custodian and what is involved in the custodian's work, and how the cafeteria works (include the kitchen and how the kitchen "nurtures" the school).

3. Celebrations and rituals

- What are the celebrations and rituals?
- How can the following celebrations take place so that everyone enjoys them: flag raising and salute, large school gatherings, special projects, and dealing with visitors?
- Who records the celebrations? When and how (e.g., videotape or newsletter)?

Notes on discrepancies and commonalities:

4. Orderliness in the community

Explore the ways in which orderliness can be experienced personally. Can it be a way to organize meetings? When would be a good time to reflect on the degree of orderliness in class and in the school generally? How could it best be done?

5. Orderliness as a curriculum theme

In how many ways can the idea of orderliness be introduced into curriculum and instruction? In what ways can it be used as a link between subjects and teachers?

What We Observed: Commonalities and Differences

At the end of our orderliness exercise, we found a significant agreement and shared understanding at a simple level. People did become more honest, courteous, and respectful, for instance. At Dry Creek, we had clear evidence that the elements identified in Figure 8.4 were in place.

When teachers applied the notion of orderliness to children in the classroom, however, we observed some fundamental differences in understanding the essential idea, as evidenced by characteristic requirements and behaviors. We thought we began to see evidence of three powerful mental models at work:

• *Mental Model 1: Teachers used rules to maintain order.* Despite what these teachers might tell us, their classrooms and their interactions with students indicated that they believed that the primary purpose of orderliness was the traditional notion of order through discipline. Students needed to be quiet, well behaved, and obedient. This approach was enforced through clear codes and strict discipline. It showed up, for example, in the frequent use of punishments (such as citations) and rewards (such as stars) for specific behaviors.

• *Mental Model 2: Student interactions were permissible within a context that staff controlled.* Students were permitted some choice of teacher-sanctioned interactions and behavior, subject to a code and fairly tight supervision. One illustration was the use of cooperative groups that teachers formed and monitored. The groups worked when the teacher decided, and had to become silent and attentive when the teacher decided.

• *Mental Model 3: Children demonstrated the capacity to both relate and self-regulate, based on a largely implicit culture of autonomy and self-restraint.* The expectation was that even in long-term and complex situations, students would maintain an adequate degree of cooperation and respect for others. Disciplinary backup was evident, but it was secondary to the overall atmosphere. One good example was a 3rd grade class member who felt that her group needed

163

more time on a project. She autonomously conducted her own survey of the issue with the rest of her group before presenting the proposal to the teacher. We also began to see how this kind of orderliness was facilitated by the type of instruction that accompanied it.

In effect, our work on orderliness, and seeing the differences between those who thought in terms of law and order and those who thought in terms of patterns of coherence that self-manifest, helped us begin to see fundamental differences in the qualities of the mental models that people have. Sometimes different mental models simply reflect different beliefs. But often, something more is at work. We began to look for this added element as we worked with other aspects of instruction and curriculum. Indeed, these differences began to be paramount in our minds. We introduce them in Section 3 of this book and fully expand them in our forthcoming ASCD book, *Unleashing the Power of Perceptual Change: The Potential of Brain-Based Teaching* (in press).

Implementing Low Threat/High Challenge

We used the understanding gained in the process groups and our exploration of downshifting and orderliness as the foundation for developing in teachers an understanding of how learning is inhibited by threat and enhanced by challenge. We introduced the handout shown in Figure 8.6 (see p. 165) and used it as the basis for brainstorming, discussion, and modeling.

We needed teachers to understand that creative and complex thinking required that students take chances and risks and that they would not do that in a classroom where outcomes were known beforehand, where efforts were tied to a right answer and rewards, and where punishments and evaluations were tied to grades. Moreover, a teacher's ability to create low threat and high challenge in the classroom depends on the teacher's grasp of orchestrated immersion and active processing. Consequently, only much later were we able to translate these conditions into an approach to classroom teaching.

FIGURE 8.6
CONDITIONS THAT SUPPORT BRAIN-BASED TEACHING/LEARNING

• Outcomes are relatively open-ended.

• Emphasis is on intrinsic motivation.

• Tasks have relatively open-ended time lines or time lines appropriate to the purpose of the task.

• Tasks are challenging but not too difficult.

• Support for preferred work mode (group or alone) is available.

Integrating all these elements was possible only through the work of the process groups on relaxed alertness, orchestrated immersion, and active processing of experience; a great deal of creativity, negotiation, pairing, and sharing among staff; and continuous feedback and workshops by us. The next chapter describes this ongoing process.

9

Implementing Immersion and Active Processing

At Dry Creek and Park View schools, we worked with the staff in many ways to explore the concepts of orchestrated immersion and active processing. In this chapter, we illustrate some of our processes and further introduce the wide range of ways in which people interpreted the same experiences and words.

Orchestrated Immersion in Complex Experience

The brain principles (see Chapter 5) show that people function in a multiplicity of different ways at any one time. In "complex experiences," different sensory modalities, including sight, sound, and touch, need to be combined intelligently for the purpose of learning. Because learning engages the entire physiology, the whole body needs to participate to some extent. Emotions need to be engaged. The locale memory system—the system that registers autobiographical experiences and is motivated by novelty—needs to be involved in intelligent ways. Stimuli from the peripheral environment need to support specific content. Timing needs to alternate so that in addition to dealing with a situation or problem consciously here and now, the brain is also primed to continue functioning at an unconscious level afterward. These things are impossible to do one at a time with a checklist. Immersion in rich, natural experiences that automatically engage as much of the learner's capacity as appropriate or necessary is what we are after. Orchestration is the design of experiences in a sufficiently rich way for all the different elements to be naturally engaged. And because the brain is a complex adaptive system, within that design must be the potential for self-organization.

To give teachers an initial sense of what immersion in complex experience might look like, we gave them a copy of Figure 9.1 (from *Making Connections*, Caine and Caine 1994a, p. 33) and explored it.

FIGURE 9.1
COMPARISON OF TRADITIONAL AND BRAIN-BASED TEACHING

Area	Traditional Teaching	Brain-Based Teaching
Source of Information	Simple (two-way—from teacher to book, worksheet, or film—to student).	Complex (e.g.,social interactions, group discovery, individual search and reflection, role-playing, and integrated subject matter).
Classroom Organization	Linear (individual work or teacher directed).	Complex (e.g., use work stations; individualized projects; and thematic, integrative, and cooperative methods).
Classroom Management	Hierarchical (teacher controlled).	Complex: designated status and responsibilities delegated to students and monitored by teacher.
Outcomes	Specified and convergent. Emphasis on memorized concepts, vocabulary, and skills.	Complex. Emphasis on reorganization of information in unique ways, with both predictable and unpredictable outcomes; divergent and convergent; and increase in natural knowledge that is demonstrated by ability to use learned skills in variable contexts.

After processing this list, we searched for a realistic understanding of what complex experience might mean.

Complex Experience from the Perspective of Layers of Experience

One powerful idea is that of "layers of experience." Ideas acquire more meaning when they play themselves out at many levels. Sports provide an excellent example. Games may be played in the classroom or in special classes, such as physical education. An additional layer can be found in the social relations between students, which is often influenced by their sporting interests and prowess. A "coach" or a type of apprenticeship relationship can constitute a further layer. Beyond that is the layer of the school's engagement as a whole, with displays of trophies and the large marquis in the front of the building, which tends to announce games. Sports may be discussed by families, with parents going to events and supporting their children. The media devote space and time to sports, with overlapping stories that range from the local to the international. Finally, at least one underlying construct remains, the notion of *game,* which is almost universally understood and can provide opportunity for everyone to participate. All these aspects of experience are layers that point to the power, meaning, and purpose of sports.

We suggested that the same model be used for all learning. Therefore, something that is to be learned should not be restricted to an exercise in class, but should be meaningfully linked to as many areas of student lives as possible, including home, the broader world, friends and peers, and the whole school. The teacher does not have to design an activity for each layer but rather begins to think initially how what students are to learn is meaningful to their lives. These other areas of our lives are where we find possible layers of experience, and the more we can engage them, the more real and vital the learning. In essence, we have to be able to replicate for geometry, music, and geography what we do with sports. We suggested, therefore, that we could begin the task of orchestration by taking a topic and making it more complex in terms of the number of layers of interactions that could be introduced.

An experience is complex, we therefore suggested, when it is a part of many interacting levels of participation (see Figure 9.2).

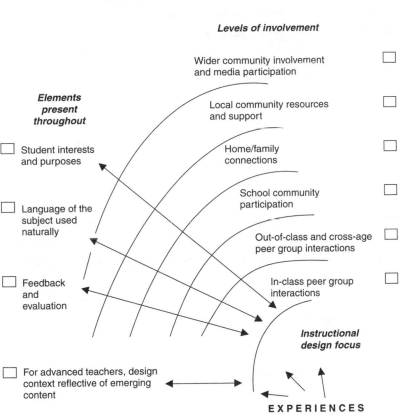

FIGURE 9.2
ORCHESTRATED IMMERSION IN COMPLEX EXPERIENCES

Commentary
1. This is a design tool and checklist of the elements of authentic experience.
2. Several elements and layers should be present, some extensively.
3. The goal: Seek coherence and connectedness between the layers and other elements.

Again, we wanted our illustrations to be suggestive, not prescriptive. We wanted the teachers to implement the ideas in their own ways. In some respects, the results were gratifying. One 5th grade teacher at Dry Creek organized a simulated space flight replete with NASA audiotapes, a classroom filled with planets and stars, and many hands-on experiments that real astronauts would have to perform. A K–2 teacher had students replicate parts of the rain forest (later ordered to be demolished by the fire department as a safety hazard) with incredible detail. In another school, a team of teachers replicated a city in which they embedded mathematics, including algebra and geometry. Yet others had activities that ranged from developing a genuine stock exchange to simulating historical events.

We also presented the idea of layers of experience in workshops around the United States. What was interesting and confounding was that although some teachers found these activities easy to organize, others looked at the diagram in Figure 9.2 in simplistic terms. One teacher, for instance, felt that the local community and resources were involved if she purchased some materials at a local store. This view of what connecting with the local community meant can be contrasted with another school where the 6th grade students were writing and editing one entire page of the weekly community newspaper. Once again, we were confronted with the different ways that individuals interpreted our suggestions for teaching.

Thematic Instruction and the Integration of the Curriculum

The relationship between thematic instruction and the integrated curriculum has been explored in many different contexts (e.g., Fogarty 1993). We defined a theme as an idea around which information can be organized—partly like a carton in which many grocery items can be carried. A *theme* is a way of combining elements of the curriculum, and it can be useful in instruction. Education uses many approaches to thematic instruction; in our workshops, we provided materials to teachers to familiarize them with some of what is being done.

Our approach was to take the idea of "layers" and use it as a way of organizing the understanding of themes. Specifically, we suggested that differentiating between topics, concepts, and global themes would be useful:

- *Topic* refers to the prescribed or selected curriculum content (e.g., explorers, photosynthesis, and division). It consists of incontrovertible facts or skills.

- *Concepts* are underlying ideas that give a prescribed topic meaning. For example, explorers are engaged in search and discovery, photosynthesis is an example of combining different kinds of elements to create food, and division is a method of partitioning. Once one or more underlying concepts have been identified, analogies, metaphors, or illustrations in other content areas that can enrich and help to make more sense of the concept are easy to find. Exploration, for instance, is what scientists, historians, and psychologists all do in their different ways. Division is important in cooking, social studies, economics, and geography.

- *Global themes* are big ideas that link, connect, or transcend any subject or group of subjects. Examples that we used are the pithy readings mentioned in Chapter 7: "Everything comes in layers" and "Order is present everywhere." Ultimately, these ideas become an organizing philosophy or approach to reality and spell out a sense of orderliness that links the scientific world to one's personal reality and experience. As these ideas become internalized, they become tools to enable a student to approach any new subject or field with the knowledge that the area is never completely new. A student can always know that she has some organizing ideas for beginning to understand anything.

What We Did

We worked with teachers in an attempt to communicate these different levels of understanding. For example, one of our themes is that "Change is present everywhere." In addition to referring to the work that we were doing to generate orderliness in the school community and relating that to the idea of change, we included exercises that we hoped would lead the way toward adopting the theme in the classroom. Figure 9.3 shows one exercise that we used.

FIGURE 9.3

EXERCISES TO DEVELOP AN UNDERSTANDING OF GLOBAL THEMES FOR SUBSEQUENT CLASSROOM USE

Step 1

Examine the global theme: "Change is present everywhere." Take some time to process the theme in groups and individually. How is it true? Where is there an exception?

Step 2

Use the theme "Change is present everywhere," and explore it within the various disciplines. Identify where or how this idea is true in nature and astronomy, biology, geology, and science in general. Also explore it in poetry, drawings and classical paintings, music, literature, mathematics, and other subject areas.

Step 3

Take the same global theme and begin to link it to your own (human) growth and development over time. How might the idea be true for your own physiological changes, as well as perception and behavior? How does it reflect what happens in families and relationships?

Summarize what Steps 1–3 tell you about change.

Step 4

Experiment with the idea of change being present everywhere to find out how to introduce the concept of change as a universal, integrated, thematic concept touching every facet of life and the curriculum. As you explore the multi-faceted aspects of change, begin to see how you can help students experience the joy of living in a world that is both dynamic and orderly. Your goal is to have them deeply understand change to the point where they see that both their own changes and the world's changes make sense.

What We Observed

We found dramatic and fundamental differences in the ways that teachers reacted to and used these ideas:

• *Many teachers simply did not have a grasp of the differ-ence between facts and concepts.* Although some spoke about the "concepts" being taught, even so-called "higher" concepts were often treated as bits of information to be memorized. A concept is an underlying idea that gives a fact meaning. That many teachers did not understand this key idea was actually quite shocking to us. This lack of understanding helped explain the variable responses that we were observing and became a thrust for much of what we researched and describe in the rest of this book.

Here, for instance, are some anonymous responses to a post-work-shop questionnaire asking what "struggles" teachers had experienced:

○ "Identifying the concepts."

○ "What is a concept?"

○ "I am still trying to understand the 'concept' idea and how to integrate it."

○ "It is important to see how concepts can be taught through an integrated manner. To do this, we need to be able [to make] connections between many different topics."

These differences in understanding are played out in the way themes are used. For those who see nothing but *facts,* a theme is a gimmick to aid memorization. "Family" can be used as a device to help memorize the "family of chemicals," for example. This is only one approach to helping students remember. For those who are working with concepts, the facts are secondary and will be automatically stored, to a large extent, when the concept is understood.

• *Many teachers who had a good grasp of the central role of concepts had enormous difficulty in appreciating the deeper levels at which concepts can be connected.* At one level, this difficulty shows up in finding analogies for some types of concepts. It did not occur to them, for instance, that the issues of probability taught as "chance" in a math lesson also connected to how chance played itself out in multiple ways in history, archeology, and literature. At another level, they had difficulty in relating concepts to everyday life choices. Thus, many (and perhaps most) of their students do not understand how chance and probability act as opposite forces to choice and purposive action. They do not understand that probability is active in their everyday lives, not only in rolling dice.

Teachers need to learn how to reach across subject matter to access meaning, because we have focused and fragmented our thinking on the basis of topics and subjects. Thus, a teacher working creatively with masks was startled when asked about whether students understood that we often wear masks in our everyday interactions. Such an idea would obviously wait until students could take a course in psychology. The problem is that if teachers cannot see broader connections as relevant, they will not only fail to facilitate broader thinking in students, but they will also not be able to facilitate student-initiated learning tied to personal meaning and purposes.

• *A few teachers had a wonderful grasp of the dynamic nature in which big ideas are woven into the fabric of everyday experience and how this interweaving can be implemented in instruction.* For example, a 5th grade teacher was planning to teach her class about electricity. She followed the curriculum and wanted to upgrade what she did last year. Her new global theme for the year was "Everything is separate and connected." As she brainstormed with colleagues, one suggested inviting the custodian to participate. These colleagues knew that 2nd graders had been working with dollhouses and thought that the custodian could teach the 5th graders how to wire a building in a simple way (he used to be an electrician). Then he could help oversee the 5th graders as they wired the dollhouses of the 2nd graders. Since Dry Creek was going have an open house in a few weeks, perhaps the dollhouses could also be put on display, the 2nd graders could show them off, and the 5th graders could explain to parents what they had done. This example (not yet implemented) was discussed by some teachers during one of our inservice programs with Dry Creek.

The Integrated Curriculum

As we work with teachers, it becomes clearer and clearer to us that many apparently sound strategies become techniques that are not well grounded in theory or understanding. The idea of the integrated curriculum is one. The problem is that integration has become a label for finding different ways to mix subjects; one assumption is that such integration is automatically better than focusing on individual subjects, and another is that a single subject cannot be taught in a way that involves adequate integration of other ideas. Both assumptions are unwarranted, and both stem in part from some confusion about the links between complex experience and the combination of subjects or disciplines.

One solution we adopt, as described previously, is to explore the organizing aspects of themes and big ideas. Another is to ask teachers to focus on what we call "global experiences" and to generate an integrated curriculum from the vantage point of experience, rather than to look for experiences to fit a preplanned set of topics. (We were, of course, confronting our theory of learning—particularly the creation of dynamical knowledge. Our teachers needed deeper processing and understanding.) Here are the two methods we used:

• ***Method 1: Using Student Interests as a Frame of Reference.*** We suggested that teachers should always be on the lookout for something in which a student is passionately interested—sports, computers, financial issues, interpersonal issues, movies, music, and politics are some examples. The point is that student interest in a specific issue can be the frame for organizing and integrating the curriculum in a powerful and realistic way that enhances rather than diminishes student interest and understanding. This point is beautifully illustrated in a quote from one of the first graduates of Peninsula, a school in California that has worked with these ideas for many years:

> Mrs. _____ was a genius at bringing out our natural skills. That's how she built self-confidence; finding how we could excel at things. I was very good at math, very good at science. I was not interested in history. I was not interested in learning writing skills. She had a very neat way of showing that those two were related—that history of science, history of math, and writing about it were tied together (Fadiman 1988).

• **Method 2: The Wheel of Experience.** This is a more systematic process but is probably the most effective method that we have used. The teacher uses what we call a "design wheel" to develop a wheel of experience (see Figure 9.4). This technique allows for all kinds of associations to emerge.

FIGURE 9.4
DESIGN WHEEL

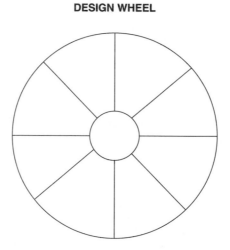

The teacher begins by selecting some moderately long-term and complex activity or issue that is appropriate for her class. (Of course, several teachers working together or an entire school can also make the selection). This activity or issue is labeled and placed in the center of the wheel.

Next, each mandated or prescribed subject in which the activity plays a role is labeled and placed in one of the segments in the outer circle. The teacher now brainstorms various ways that the several subjects may be connected in some way to the selected issue, activity, or idea. Two examples follow:

Example 1: If we place "probability" in the center of the wheel, then we can place other subjects in which probability plays a role around the center (see Figure 9.5 on p. 177).

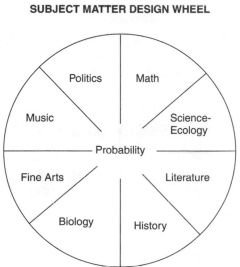

FIGURE 9.5
SUBJECT MATTER DESIGN WHEEL

Teachers can now explore the notion of probability in many ways. At the same time, this approach creates opportunities for students to expand their own interests within designated academic fields without losing track of the core concept.

Example 2: An alternative approach is to use more of a "free-association wheel": Teachers and eventually students brainstorm the many ways the skill or concept in the center can be explored (see Figure 9.6 on p. 178).

We found that the design wheel, when used by teachers brainstorming together, was the best vehicle that we had for making the integrated curriculum practical and for creating experiences for learning. Even though it was powerful, however, we consistently found that teachers interpreted it at different levels of complexity. Most found it easiest to find different types of experience in which one idea might play itself out. Others began to see how one idea could manifest in some way in what appeared to be different subject areas. Our biggest challenge continues to be to get teachers (in their minds) beyond the fragmentation and separation of subjects and disciplines to see how to allow student, rather than teacher, purposes, to lead the way. Similarly, having teachers construct intellectually rich experiences out of which students "extract" the information is also challenging—and requires a profoundly different way of thinking.

FIGURE 9.6
FREE-ASSOCIATION WHEEL

Active Processing of Experience

Complex experience and relaxed alertness are critical; but if we want learning to improve significantly, then we have to help students capitalize on experience. Merely having a complex experience does not guarantee that much will be learned from it. The embedded ideas and skills must be brought to the surface, articulated, and demonstrated. Moreover, this investigation, inquiry, examination, and challenge must be ongoing while students are engaged in complex experiences.

Educators have devised many approaches to what we call *active processing*. One is "responsive elaboration" (Roehler, Duffy, Conley, Herrman, Johnson, and Michelsen 1987), a teacher's ability to "generate spontaneously . . . unplanned metaphors, images, analogies, examples, explanations, scaffolding, and prompting" (p. 4).

Active processing must be more than just a culminating activity. Because it is ongoing and can be embedded everywhere, active processing is perhaps the most challenging aspect of brain-based learning.

Active Processing Deals with Outcomes and Assessment

We provided teachers with possible student performance outcomes for brain-based learning (see Figure 9.7 on p. 180).

These performance outcomes spelled out some of what brain-based learning was meant to accomplish. In our terms, such performance revealed students who can think, behave, and engage in lifelong learning, and who know how to find and use information for almost any purpose.

What we found was that teachers' capacity to introduce and implement these outcomes varied enormously. Some teachers paid lip service but largely discounted the outcomes. Some reduced them to versions of what was already being done. Others used the outcomes as a lever into new ways of thinking. A few teachers realized that if they were to take the outcomes seriously, they would have to make significant changes in how they ran their classes. This type of change was gratifying. Even more gratifying, however, were those teachers who began to introduce outcomes such as those described as natural by-products of the changes in their teaching. In effect, the "outcomes" became aspects of the ongoing life of the class. For such teachers, active processing was becoming natural. That change was not the case for most teachers, however.

Active Processing Is a Way of Exploring the Ramifications of Experience

We went into some depth on how one might help a student learn from experience. In the early days of our program, we supplied a set of strategies. The idea was that teachers would explore these in their process groups and come to an understanding of them. A fairly complex idea was behind the list of strategies. We were hoping that teachers would see that every discipline carries with it some basic mode of thinking that can be applied to every other discipline. Thus, active processing is not just a way of thinking. It is actually a way of using and therefore learning about the essential nature of the different disciplines that comprise the curriculum.

FIGURE 9.7
GUIDELINES FOR STUDENT PERFORMANCE OUTCOMES FOR BRAIN-BASED INSTRUCTION

Instructions

1. Please look at the following list of visible and tangible student performance outcomes. These behaviors should be visible to someone visiting your classroom or could appear in your professional portfolio as evidence of your students' having achieved genuine learning in a brain-based classroom.

2. Decide which of the following items belong in Perceptual Orientations 1, 2, and 3. This will help you understand how to teach them. (Remember that outcomes for Perceptual Orientations 2 and 3 will be indirect and the result of students' processing their experiences).

3. Pick the 10 performance outcomes you will commit to for the next 3 months. These will become the focus of continuous active processing. Once you have selected the 10 outcomes, begin now or in your groups to brainstorm experiences that would result in evidence of such student learning.

Students will demonstrate through oral expression, written work, diagrams, drawings or design, journals or portfolios, peer teaching, performance, or demonstration, their ability to

  1. Use the formal language of the discipline studied.

  2. Define concepts of a discipline and connect them to life.

  3. Take risks in thinking and creative work.

  4. Express opinions and defend their views on issues.

  5. Speculate, explore alternatives, and pose hypotheses.

  6. Make predictions and assess the results.

  7. Explore multiple possibilities.

  8. Recognize cultural nuances.

  9. Fill in gaps in understanding, using their own initiative.

  10. Use clues and evidence to support conclusions.

  11. Relate form to function.

  12. Identify elements of a structure that has a particular purpose.

Figure 9.7—continued
GUIDELINES FOR STUDENT PERFORMANCE OUTCOMES FOR BRAIN-BASED INSTRUCTION

13. Revise, reshape, and deepen earlier understandings of a concept.

14. Challenge a thought or opinion, demonstrating agreement or disagreement.

15. Endorse something or a particular concept or approach or question it.

16. Retell specific details.

17. Elaborate or expand on an idea.

18. Make connections between what they learn from the text or formal experience and their own prior beliefs.

19. Express a major understanding about, or insight into, a subject.

20. Express a major insight into their own behavior or the effect their behavior has on others.

21. Express an insight into life.

22. Use professional standards for the medium used (e.g., oral comments are in complete sentences, and words of the discipline are used correctly; graphs are accurate; and artwork meets high standards).

23. Discuss a subject in terms of its effectiveness.

24. Express an understanding of beauty, elegance, and harmony.

25. Be able to identify the basic structure of something and name its basic processes and functions.

Figure 9.8 (see p. 182) summarizes procedures that we supplied to teachers. In our inservice programs, we would deal with just a few elements at a time. We should add that this is our own list. We use these processes in our practice and encourage others to use them in action as much as possible.

Teachers took to creative elaboration (Item 2 in the table) like proverbial ducks to water. It was essentially an imaginative and entertaining way to work with practice and rehearsal. However, they found the more complex processes difficult to include. Even though the other processes were addressed in several process group meetings, most teachers could not find a way to adequately relate the questions

FIGURE 9.8
PROCEDURES USED IN ACTIVE PROCESSING

Active processing of experience

Definition: Active processing is the consolidation and internalization of information and procedures by the learner in a way that is both personally meaningful and conceptually coherent.

Active processing is the key to perceiving patterns and making sense of experience. The brain/mind naturally searches for meaning, tests experience, reacts to novelty, and seeks control. Active processing expands on natural capacities and processes.

Experts and professionals always process experience

- Lawyers ask critical questions.
- Doctors rely on keen observation and diagnosis.
- Architects must relate form to function.
- Therapists look and listen for hidden meanings and patterns.
- Athletes monitor skill, performance, and attitude.

WAYS TO PROCESS EXPERIENCE	
Process	**Activities**
Enhanced attention and sensory observation	1. Assist students to relax. 2. As them to describe a simple object out loud in rich sensory detail. 3. Ask them to examine and describe smaller parts of the object. 4. Use basic space/time relations. 5. Discuss: "Understanding is in the details."
Creative elaboration	1. Repetition in rounds and in groups. 2. Games. 3. Puzzles. 4. Songs. 5. Exaggerated imitation and modeling. 6. Visualization.
Relating to personal experience and what is already known	1. What does it remind me of? 2. What do I already know about it? 3. Is it bigger? Smaller? Nearer? Further? Higher? Lower? Similar? Different?

FIGURE 9.8—*continued*
PROCEDURES USED IN ACTIVE PROCESSING

WAYS TO PROCESS EXPERIENCE	
Process	**Activities**
Seeking broader and deeper meanings	1. What is the main idea? 2. Does any other subject or idea explain this? 3. What symbols are being used? 4. What are the essential metaphors? 5. Compare and contrast ideas and procedures in different domains and subject areas. 6. Does this idea connect with any general principle of life?
Critical thinking and questions	1. What/where/who/how/when—specifically? 2. What are the hidden and obvious assumptions? 3. What specific inferences are being made? 4. Ask follow-up questions. 5. Look for counter examples.
Exploring system features	1. How does it work? 2. What is the basic structure? 3. What are the basic processes and functions? 4. Where are the beginnings and the endings? 5. What features rely on what other features? 6. How many layers are there? 7. Is it a closed or open system? 8. What are the inputs and outputs? 9. Where is there feedback or feed forward?
Generating alternatives	1. Find new analogies and metaphors. 2. Turn ideas and procedures upside down, back to front, and inside out. 3. Call on imagination, adventure, intuition, and play. 4. How would other cultures or roles interpret this? 5. Express opinions and ideas in different art forms. 6. Search for artistic representations of ideas and impressions. 7. Explore the presence of beauty, ugliness, dissonance, coherence, harmony, and elegance.

FIGURE 9.8—*continued*
PROCEDURES USED IN ACTIVE PROCESSING

WAYS TO PROCESS EXPERIENCE	
Process	**Activities**
Reflecting on personal feelings, choices, and actions	1. What am I feeling about this? 2. What do I want to do with it or with respect to it? 3. What did I do? 4. How did it work out? 5. What could I have done differently?
Closure	1. What is the bottom line? 2. What is the final decision, for now? 3. What does this really mean? 4. When is there nothing more that I can do? 5. Can I let go when there is nothing more that I can do?

Teaching active processing

1. Adjust for the level of your students.
2. Use immersion and modeling.
3. Make active processing real.
4. Use active processing everywhere.

and processes to their work in the classroom. This inability both puzzled and frustrated us.

Only after some time did we realize that the capacity of a teacher to help students process experience actually depended on the teacher's ability to *design* experiences in the first place. Introducing questions and challenges that guide a student into alternative and deeper ways of doing what he is doing is possible primarily when the student is working on an experiment or writing about an ongoing project. Moreover, one can often elicit core insights only during an experience, such as at the precise moment that a chemical reaction takes place in a test tube or some behavior is seen in animals. We came to see that when teachers need to oversee and manage everything that is going on in the classroom, they have neither the time nor the opportunity to walk around and interact in sufficient depth with individuals and small groups. One implication was that teachers needed more aides or smaller class sizes. Another was that they needed to have self-organizing or self-managing classes so that they could be free to rove. They could also train students to ask provocative questions during the experience.

A second key to developing a mastery of active processing became evident to us as we walked through classrooms with our video camera. Natural questions to ask students were "What are you doing?" and "Why? What is it for?" In fact, we formulated a set of five simple questions:

1. What are you doing?
2. What is the purpose?
3. Can you explain it?
4. What would happen if . . . ?
5. Do you know why . . . ?

After asking these questions for some time, it dawned on us that they were a simple, but powerful, basic platform or *scaffold* for teachers to use.

The questions work at several levels. One is *unobtrusive assessment*. Every time the questions are asked, a small bit of information is provided about what the students know and can do. Many answers to these questions add up like dots that ultimately provide an extremely detailed picture of student competence and understanding. Second, the questions open the door to *guiding the learning*. When a student offers an explanation, a further question can be asked. When a problem is solved, students can be led to more complex problems when the teacher asks, "What would happen if . . . ?" Indeed, this type of questioning is at the heart of the Socratic method as it is used in law schools, when students analyze cases.

Finally, we found that these questions were a *natural gateway to enrichment and integration of the curriculum*. For example, an experiment with the displacement of an object by water can be supplemented with the question: "Did you know that the ancient Greeks tried to do exactly what you are doing thousands of years ago?" or "Could you conduct this experiment on the space shuttle? Why or why not?" or "In what way is the displacement of objects like the displacement of people?" or "There is a work of art that shows displacement in a very unusual way. Can you see how it relates?"

A final point that we found exciting was that as teachers mastered the art of processing activities, their questions became the way to engage student motivation and led naturally to the introduction of richer and more complex thinking, projects, and experiences. They could focus students' attention on details, call forth expertise, and help them to see more global connections. We were therefore finding for ourselves what many others have suggested: *The right sorts of questions and questioning techniques naturally energize the entire learning and teaching process.*

Example of Relaxed Alertness, Immersion in Complex Experience, and Active Processing in Operation

In our second year with Dry Creek, we felt we had a major breakthrough with respect to teaching. As part of our inservice program, we invited three lead teachers to present to their colleagues math and science programs implementing brain-based instruction. Although we (Renate, Geoffrey, and Sam) had visited several weeks earlier (we are located 450 miles away) and had helped them with their presentation focus, the teachers were still apprehensive because this was the first time that they would be formally presenting their unique translation of brain-based math and science; and they knew they would receive feedback from their colleagues and from us.

On the day of the program, the *challenge* level was extremely high but was beautifully balanced by the enormous support the teachers received from all the participants. The mere fact of their willingness to present generated appreciation. The quality of the four presentations varied, showing a mixture of brilliant creativity, good student-centered exploration, and some fairly sophisticated but orthodox delivery of material.

After those presentations, we spent some time with three of the presenters as a group, asking questions and inviting them to reflect on the experience. This discussion proved to be the source of great insight—and inspiration—to all of us.

The three presenters were then invited to address the school as a whole and to share anything that seemed important to them. This opportunity gave them a chance to put together their own emerging understanding. The presentations were also a catalyst for the staff as a whole, many of whom grasped for the first time the instructional and curriculum approach that we had been working toward. For the first time, we were speaking the same language, both literally and perceptually. One teacher expressed it best: With tears in her eyes, she said, "I see it now, it's not this bit or that bit—it's the whole thing."

Results

Ultimately, brain-based teachers are different. Their strength is in making use of other formal resources and instructional programs for teachers, but they do not practice any one approach exclusively or exhaustively. Rather, they use their understanding of relaxed alertness, immersion in complex experience, and active processing as the organizing concepts that guide them. The central concern is for the teachers to become better equipped to know what new strategies to adopt and how to adopt them. Thus, the teachers translate new approaches and inservice program content into their own learning community, using the theory as a guide. Here is an example of how one teacher at Dry Creek documented the change in her approach to reading:

> In the second year, we had students pretty interested in reading, but we were open to learning more. The district had adopted the Houghton Mifflin Literacy program. We tried their approach, and students were enjoying reading but were not learning how to read better. We had someone on our staff from Reading Recovery, and she helped us by giving us some reading strategies that really worked. These strategies gave students a self-sustaining system that allowed them to read on their own (Teacher at Dry Creek Elementary School).

What happens with genuine brain-based learning and teaching is that the teachers make use of critical training and information, but adapt them to their community and student perceived needs. Thus, strategies from Reading Recovery were helpful, but only up to a point. The Houghton Mifflin series was used, but only those parts that made sense for this particular class.

As in the preceding example in reading, we are observing teachers making critical decisions about what outside materials to incorporate and when to use them and for what purposes. Teachers ignored the guided reading specified by the literacy program, for example, and instead developed what they called "Literacy Circles," where students participated with "lots of discussion" and critical thinking and reflection.

Guidance from brain-based learning came in the sense that teachers recognized that they needed to invoke student purposes and meanings in the form of student choices. Keeping the classroom community positive and students free to take risks was also critical. Teachers introduced essential reading strategies and techniques to help students master the basic skills essential to allowing them to take further risks and deal with higher challenges. Students participated in understanding the need for these skills. Having students master the basic "self-sustaining skills" from Reading Recovery helped teachers focus on and emphasize challenge, not remedial comprehension.

Where a teacher understood how active processing worked, we found it present everywhere. Again, in the case cited previously, active processing was used widely:

> Students are continuously asked to invoke complex and critical thinking. Students are not only encouraged to talk about a story but are invited to make inferences and reflect on alternatives. In order to heighten recall and practice their own storytelling, students are asked to remember a story by highlighting five significant events and then tell the story to students in another class. They are encouraged to practice storytelling with each other and give each other feedback. This provides practice and rehearsal and includes suggestions for improvement from each other. They also ask for feedback from the class to whom they read the story (Teacher at Dry Creek Elementary School).

Evidence of Student Academic Success

Using the brain-based approach to reading outlined here, student reading scores at Dry Creek moved from the 50th percentile in 1st grade and the 49th percentile in 2nd grade in February 1993, to the 60th percentile in 1st grade and the 55th percentile in 2nd grade in May 1995, to the 79th percentile in 1st grade and the 74th percentile in 2nd grade in February 1996. Math scores also increased, although not as dramatically. Both schools reported greater engagement of student involvement in learning, and assignments and projects were completed more frequently.

Grade point averages at Park View have increased by one whole point for all students on D-track. Failure rates have moved from 20 percent to below 8 percent for the students enrolled in brain-based classrooms. This success rate occurred despite the fact that 28 percent of the students in D-track were special needs students who were mainstreamed. Impartial assessment by the principal, vice principal, and other teachers insisted that such success was not mere grade inflation but due to rigorous teaching tied to high standards. Our own observations (although we are obviously vulnerable to the challenge of bias) supported this observation. We decided to see if these grade changes persisted after students left Park View.

Park View is the only feeder school for the junior high school that teaches the same group of students in the 8th and 9th grades. If students' grades in D-track were not inflated, then those students should be able to perform at higher levels in the junior high school as well. We therefore looked at grade point averages for students in the 8th grade to see if D-track students performed significantly better. Of the four tracks from Park View that served as the single feeder school for the junior high, 34 percent of the students with a grade point average of *B* were from D-track. Of all students with a grade point average of *B+*, 39 percent were from D-track. And fully 40 percent of the students with a grade point average of *A* were originally in D-track. These results are statistically significant: The appropriate percentage of D-track students should be approximately 25 percent.

We also found something else that, although not conclusive in and of itself, has fascinated us. In California, students can volunteer to take a standardized exam in algebra called the "Golden State Award." Over the past two years, the number of students choosing to take the exam and receiving the award has doubled, with the largest number of volunteers originating from D-track. Of those students awarded the Golden State Award (those scoring highest in algebra), 45 percent came from D-track. The other 55 percent is distributed among the other tracks *at an average of 18 percent per track.* Since one of the changes we look for in students who use brain-based learning is a change in self-efficacy (see Chapter 11), the fact that more students volunteered from D-track than from the other tracks strikes us as significant. The higher scores are obviously due to a combined effort between D-track teachers and the junior high teachers, but still reflect on learning at Park View. It is also important to add that D-track uses primarily "Math Renaissance" in the 7th grade. Math Renaissance is a brain-based approach (with limitations). It emphasizes teaching by using experiences and some active processing. In any event, brain-based learning is a far cry from teaching individual skills and "to the test"; given time, it gets genuine results.

Changes on Standardized Test Scores

In California, students take the California Test of Basic Skills (CTBS). Although we had told teachers that they should not expect to see changes in standardized test scores for the first year, and were rather casual about this in the second year, we expected to see changes in the third year. Some indications of change have appeared at Dry Creek, particularly in the 1st and 2nd grades and in the multiage classrooms. These classes happen to be where our most advanced brain-based learning teachers are housed; we have therefore focused on this group.

At best, the CTBS shows steady progress upward in math and writing. We also know that special education and special needs students have benefitted. However, since all students are mainstreamed at both schools and both Dry Creek and Park View have 20 percent to 30 percent of such students, separating scores is proving difficult.

Results of CTBS scores at Park View have been difficult to document in a meaningful manner. Park View includes only 6th and 7th grades;

and testing is only done in the 6th and 8th grades. This timing means that CTBS testing for Park View students is done only in the 6th grade, after approximately six months of instruction. This is not enough time to effect change on an exam that is so specific. By the time students are in the 8th grade, they have had six months of instruction from another teacher that would confound the results, and D-track teachers could not take full credit for any change, positive or negative. By all other measures, positive things are happening here, but as yet, we cannot point to standardized test scores as a measure of success.

Active Processing

We have to acknowledge that the active processing at Park View and Dry Creek both may still be too weak. We have only begun to focus on it this year. Active processing includes the continuous and ongoing questioning and challenging of critical ideas. It invokes the scientific process and reflection. It also includes practice and rehearsal of vocabulary, concepts, and ideas. But it never includes teaching skills only useful for taking a standardized test. Everyone is looking forward to documenting better CTBS scores, especially since future funding and other benefits depend on standardized test scores. Teachers, however, report seeing their students thinking things through, working harder, and producing better and more creative work.

Ultimately, we strongly suspect that a different test may be needed for the kind of teaching we are advocating. Something like the CLAS test (modified) that was eliminated in California may fit our schools much better. In the meantime, the schools' students are bringing in the Golden State Award and getting better grades even two years down the road. Their students can read, love to read, and love learning. These results will have to serve as an indicator to everyone that their hard work is paying off.

Here, for instance, is some writing from a 6th grade Dry Creek student reflecting on the strongly brain-based program in the K–1–2 program at her school:

All about the amazing K-1-2 class

On February 1, 1996, my class and I went to Mrs. Berry's classroom to observe how they function in math. Some of the things I saw were pretty neat. . . . I saw little kids with confidence in themselves when working with a hard problem. I also saw kids that put lots of effort in[to] their work, but I think the most important thing was the teachers and the [older] kids explaining the problem to the [younger] kids, and teaching the class to add and subtract with beans and buttons.

I heard the adults communicating with the kids in a fun, coloring, building, talking kind of way. I also heard a very patient teacher with a lot of perseverance in her class.

Now you're probably wondering, did you learn anything and how did you feel? . . . Let's see, I learned that the kids need a lot of space to do their work. I learned that kids get distracted very easily, but can learn things easily too. Lastly, I learned that little kids are smarter than they look.

Now, let's see, what did I feel? . . . I remember I felt two things and they are this: Those kids are in a very caring environment, and they are learning stuff I didn't learn until 3rd grade. They'll be pretty smart kids.

Well, I only smelled one thing and it is this. I smelled something fishy because why did they have a more advanced education than us?

Well, what I've been trying to say or what I think is the most important thing is a wish. I wish that I could have had their education when I was their age (student at Dry Creek Elementary School).

SECTION 3

What We Learned

This section revisits community and describes problems that emerged as the change process took hold.

We introduce three instructional approaches that became apparent. Each has its own identifiable parameters, which served to clarify both teacher resistance and teacher change. This description can be extremely helpful in creating a clearer picture of our goals for instructional change.

Beyond the three instructional approaches, we also found three "perceptual orientations." We found that teachers at Perceptual Orientation 3 did not just teach differently, they were intrinsically different types of people.

It is Perceptual Orientation 3 that we originally had in mind when we wrote Making Connections: Teaching and the Human Brain.

The problem of change is grounded in conflicting mental models. The orientations shed light on the nature of these differences.

We conclude the section with a brief summary of the book and a glimpse into the future as we see it.

10

Monitoring the Learning Communities

*Schools differ greatly in the extent to which they can be charac-
terized as caring communities, and there is considerable agreement among teachers and students in their perceptions of this
characteristic of schools. [In addition,] school community is significantly related to a large number of desirable outcomes for both
students and teachers.*
> —Battistich, Solomon, Watson, and Schaps 1994, p. 15

What is a "community"? From the beginning of our work with
brain-based learning and teaching, we knew that community was vital,
and we sought to understand what it entailed. Much of what we
discovered is supported by others, such as Mary Driscoll (1994), who
spells out what a cohesive school community is like:

A system of values that are shared and commonly understood
among the member of the organization;

A common agenda of activities that marks membership in the
organization;

Teachers [who] engage in collegial practices . . . [so] that they
perceive other teachers as sources of help and support when faced

with academic problems . . . [and] this broadly based connection
with other teachers is also manifest in their relation with students
(pp. 4–5).

Driscoll goes on to introduce other important elements. These
include parents as members of community; an assessment of community in smaller units (such as classrooms); and, as important as any
other item, respect of teachers, administrators, students, and "classified"
staff (such as maintenance personnel) for each other.

In our work with the two schools, Dry Creek and Park View, which
we discuss in this book, we did not have the resources to evaluate
community in a systematic and long-term way. We have a great deal
of anecdotal information and extensive survey data, however, that
together illustrate Driscoll's concepts and give a good sense of the
nature of the community that developed in both schools.

Becoming a Learning Community: First Three Years at Dry Creek

Although the atmosphere at the end of our first workshop was
excellent, we sensed a considerable amount of trepidation. Almost all
attention for the first few weeks was focused on the creation of the
process groups. We had selected some volunteers to be facilitators in
the early stages, and most participants in the first workshop had chosen
the facilitator with whom they initially wished to be.

Despite such preparations, the beginning was not easy. Even
though most people had agreed to this journey together, we all had to
deal with many "invisible" issues: from volunteering time and spending
time on something not directly related to required "work" and planning,
to not being in the right group or in a group with the "wrong" people,
to working out routines and leadership roles. The first hurdle, in fact,
was for each group to find its own way to implement the process and
to come to believe that the process actually made sense. In this current
of anxiety, we found ourselves on the phone a great deal. In systems
terms, we had generated some *disequilibrium*. Generally, our goal was

to support the group process and to constantly reassure people that no outcomes were sought and nothing else "had" to be done.

The early stage is aptly described by Cindy Tucker, the principal:

> At this point, we're in the process of becoming a learning community. Our study groups are meeting regularly, and after some adjustments and refinements, everyone has a home. There are layers upon layers of feelings, some interesting conversations, questions and comments, insights and connections. I think we're right on track with the change process as we experience a mixture of exhilaration, exhaustion, determination, uncertainty, reluctance, and passion.

Perhaps the most exciting early result was the jelling of the groups. Within two months, each group had become connected: Most people, even those who had rarely associated with each other, had closely bonded. For example, one person stated that the group's meeting time had become "sacred." The groups continued to meet in staff "free" time; and when staff were given the option to be rotated to other groups after six months, they rejected the option unanimously.

During this time, participants began to have substantial insights into the nature of learning and teaching, powerfully reflected in the anonymous survey that the principal conducted after about three months. Here are some comments:

> Aha! There's not really just one right way for students to do an assignment.

> I'm remembering myself as a child.

> It's great getting to know group members in a new way.

> I'm aware that I'm doing too much direct teaching. I should facilitate more.

> Although I read the book [*Making Connections*] over the summer, I didn't internalize it. Actively processing in a social context is increasing my learning and making me realize how important it is that we do this with kids.

I see the importance of patterning. The brain does not easily learn things that are not logical and have no meaning. We must help students to see meaning of new information.

The result appeared to be exactly what we wanted. On the one hand, we saw genuine excitement as staff began to appreciate the nature of learning by doing some learning of their own. On the other hand, the staff were bonding and developing a sense of community and coherence that provided a powerful social fabric within which learning and self-reference could take place.

The New Sciences Come to Life

At this point, we began exploring the new sciences in earnest. We were becoming acquainted with terms and constructs. As we wrote at the time, "There seems to be an intuitively felt 'good fit' between some of the constructs of complexity theory and the way in which our process is playing itself out in Dry Creek" (Caine and Caine 1994b). We saw many points of possible connection even if our explorations were still naive and tentative.

We began by asking questions. We knew that the school as a whole needed to make a decision in those early weeks about whether to proceed with brain-based learning. We wondered if that reflected a "bifurcation point." Was this an example of a system far from equilibrium? The school staff were already aware of a need for major change, and we had introduced an organizational structure—small, cross-functional groups—that was unlike anything that most staff members had experienced. Would the school revert to what it had always been, or would it evolve into something more complex and more orderly? We found that the latter occurred—the school seemed to evolve.

By the end of six weeks, an enormous change occurred. A significantly new type of order and orderliness permeated the entire school. After the groups bonded, we discovered a substantial improvement in the climate or atmosphere of the school and in the entirety of the social relations within it. For example, the custodians freely visited the staff room, engaged in banter with teachers on an equal footing, and were becoming recognized as de facto and effective counselors of children. Teachers began to exchange ideas on an ongoing basis; and to this day, we are struck by how intellectually rich much of the teacher discussions are at both schools. Change was reflected in small touches, such as adding tablecloths and plants in many classrooms. We saw more positive interactions between parents and office staff, and between children in class and on the playground. One of the custodians was treasurer and recently became president of the school's Parent and Teachers Association.

The concepts that run in tandem with the idea of bifurcation points are *emergence* and *self-organization.* Although a great deal of effort was spent on "inducing" the change, there was something about such change that was not "managed." It was *not* simply the result of a vote taken after a debate. Rather, the critical factor was the jelling of the individual groups. This process was an emotional/intellectual process that just *happened,* then was translated into the school as a whole. It seems to correspond with Doll's (1993) view on self-organization and the curriculum:

> It seems plausible to posit that perturbations can work as a positive force when the atmosphere or frame in which they are perceived is comfortable enough that pressure is not produced to "succeed" quickly, when in this atmosphere the details of the anomaly can be studied (maybe even played with), and when time (as a developmental factor) is of sufficient duration to allow a new frame to emerge. While the emergence itself is spontaneous, a gestalt switch, the period of time before emergence seems to require almost a nurturing of the anomaly (p. 166).

Other ideas began to cascade through our discussion. Was the excitement that the staff felt during their learning something like the edge of chaos or what we now call "the edge of possibility"? In the order that we were finding and the pattern of insights that the staff were having, was there evidence of what are called "attractors"? We had introduced the notion of "thematic attractor" in *Making Connections* (Caine and Caine 1991). Was our theory somehow operating as an attractor, and if so, how did that work? How relevant was the notion of fractals? A central idea, deriving from fractal geometry, is that every complex system consists of multiple layers that in many respects are self-similar. The shape of a coastline, for instance, is approximated in the shape of one bay, which is approximated in the shape of little inlets. In a school, it is intuitively appealing to suggest that in many respects, the ways that teachers treat children is similar to the ways that administrators treat teachers, which is similar to the ways that school boards treat administrators. Many layers of parallel and simultaneous operation are present. Our own feeling was that if a new and more complex order emerged from the study groups, it ought to be observable in part in a set of self-similar relationships at different orders of magnitude. Change would, therefore, be visible in individuals and in the system at multiple levels. It should show up in the way that administrators deal with teachers, in the way that teachers deal with custodial and secretarial staff, and in the way that all staff interact with students.

Evidence of Wholeness

We felt that we really were observing evidence of an emerging sense of wholeness and interrelationship. We had been convinced early on that the spirit that we were looking for would be particularly nourished and sustained by the participation of those who are not full-time teachers. We found such evidence. As one office staffer stated toward the close of our second workshop with Dry Creek:

> This program has given me a sense of worth (I can't really put into words what I'm trying to say), self-esteem, more confidence in myself. To be able to express myself in front of a group was very frightening, but all three of you have made it very nonthreatening.

> I am writing this on the third day during a coffee break because I just realized my mind has not wandered while all the workshops were in progress. This is a big thing for me because this reminds me of school, which I did not like. . . .

I have never felt like a part of the whole (THE GLOBAL WHOLE) as I have since we started the process. If I can give one student this experience I will feel like I have accomplished something. . . .

It has been the experience of my life.

Over the next two years, in fact, even after the support staff no longer participated in process groups with teachers, the support staff provided some of the best evidence of a fundamentally new sense of school community. For example, in our second year, the support staff decided to work together to create a museum to feature their own backgrounds and lives. They did this in conjunction with the California Department of Parks. Michael Tucker, a curator with the department, assisted in this project. The resulting museum was both professional and personal, and the support staff described the project as immensely satisfying and fulfilling. The school, staff, and community shared a great deal of pride in it. And it became a vehicle for introducing many students to real-world art displays and museums. Since that time, teachers and students have used the display area for other exhibitions. Meanwhile, the support staff began another project—raising funds to provide technology for the school. All these examples embody brain-based learning and demonstrate possibilities that a learning community generated.

Finally, the administration and teaching staff made a deliberate, systematic attempt to embed some principles of brain-based learning into the everyday life of the school as a whole. Here are two examples. Early in our work, we introduced the notion that music and art are effective in maintaining a good classroom environment (not to mention enhancing spacial intelligence). To our delight, not only every classroom, but also the central office and the offices of the principal and the assistant principal began to show evidence of this idea. Soft music (often classical), posters of works of art (primarily the impressionists), and flowers or plants began to appear everywhere. We had also been working with global themes—big ideas that could apply to any and every subject and to any and every classroom. These were the ideas we introduced as *process principles* in the early stage of the group process. We found individual teachers each selecting a global theme for their classroom. In addition, the principal and her assistant invited the staff to select a big idea for the school; and that theme helped frame everyday school business. The theme for 1994 was "Orderliness is present everywhere." This theme was not an exhortation for law and order and for punitive measures, but an expression of the fact that life has pattern, rhythm, routine, and meaning and that the classroom and the real world both reflect that order.

In short, people at the school spent a great deal of time creating a coherent community where common practices, routines, and celebrations provided continuity. The community also worked to understand the meaning of orderliness and coherence, which includes the connectedness everyone feels for each other. The goal was to create a community that was connected by genuine caring within an intellectually challenging climate.

We did not set out to increase test scores (which, at this stage of the process, we regard as a politically necessary evil). We set out to change a school and to change teaching in accordance with brain-based learning, in the belief that students would be more fulfilled and would perform at a much higher level as a necessary result.

To the delight of all concerned, Dry Creek won a California award as a distinguished school toward the end of our first year together. The award was not based on standardized tests scores (these were still low), but on the school's commitment to the ideas expressed in the California Elementary Task Force Report *It's Elementary* (1992), which is highly compatible with brain-based instruction. Dry Creek was also the subject of a film and interviews by the National Education Association (NEA) for presentation on the Learning Channel in October 1994.

The school began to show academic improvement toward the end of the third year of our working together: Students who have been in the school since the beginning of the program have shown steady improvement in standardized test scores (see Chapter 9). Many of the changes went beyond what could be captured on standardized tests, however. Some of the most impressive changes have taken place in special education students. Following is an interview with a parent of an autistic child. The interview was conducted in our absence for the NEA video mentioned earlier:

Interview with a Parent of an Autistic Child

What was your first reaction when you found out Dry Creek was going to implement this new type of teaching called BBL [brain-based learning]?

Well for me, for my child, it wasn't only BBL. It would be the first time that she would be fully included in a typical classroom for most of the day. So I was very excited about it. I didn't know anything about BBL at the time, but just the thought that she would be in a typical classroom excited me very much. I believe that schools are really in crisis, so I was excited to learn about a new approach.

Now, your daughter is a special case. We'll talk about that and how this has affected your daughter.

The changes I've seen in my daughter are really quite dramatic. I have a background in speech and language pathology so maybe that's why I see many, many changes there. But she is approaching people and speaking and asking people questions, which I didn't see very often before outside of family. That was really exciting to me. Also, I see that she's using a greater variety of sentences, her expressive vocabulary is really growing, and she just seems to be blossoming. I'm really excited about the changes I see in her. I attribute most of it to what is going on here at the school.

Can you tell me how you think BBL has helped her grow?

I think part of it is the way BBL has helped my daughter blossom—it seems to be very accepting and looks at each child as a whole child. To me, it goes right along with my philosophy, and I believe it looks at her as an individual who is intelligent, has potential, and that's something I don't always see. I feel that, I know that at this school there is an energy here that is unlike any school I've been in. I attribute that to the way that I see staff here really pulling together and believing in BBL. My opinion is that part of the key to success is that the staff here is firmly committed to this approach, and I think that's partly why it's successful. As far as other ways that I see growth and ways that BBL has affected my daughter is that it seems to me that she is becoming more of a critical thinker. With her particular challenge, which is autism, that is tremendously exciting to me.

You said it's exciting. Tell me how you feel about seeing your daughter change like this.

She comes home from school and she's excited and happy. I know she feels accepted. She's challenged. Yet things are tailored to her. For me, the situation at the school is I feel very nearly ideal for her. I really hate to see the day when she has to leave this school. I want to see this approach in all schools.

Reality Check

While we were beginning to see genuine success at Dry Creek, we introduced Cindy (the principal) and Kris (her assistant) to *Leadership and the New Science* (Wheatley 1992); their enthusiastic response was that clearly some parallels between the ideas expressed in the book and what we were all experiencing were present.

Their enthusiasm, however, introduced a note of caution. Who and what exactly was responsible for the change at Dry Creek? How much of it was due to our participation, and how much was due to Kris and Cindy? The bottom line is that the entire process would have been too difficult, if not impossible, without Cindy and Kris's outstanding and continued leadership. These people had a deeply embedded intuitive sense and belief in our process; they monitored, supported, dialogued, and worked hard. The need for them to work so hard, however, was sobering. Was this really the *self-organization* of a learning organization, we asked, if so much energy was needed from the leaders of the school and from us?

We decided to ask parents if they were seeing a difference in their children. Sixty-five percent of the parents responded to our question-naire; of these, only three responses were negative. Our question was simple: "Would you recommend Dry Creek to another parent coming to the district?" Parent responses focused around three pivotal points:

1. *Evidence that the school is seen as a healthy community.*
2. *Evidence that parents are noticing instructional changes.*
3. *Impact on children with special needs.*

We limit the responses we quote here to those that refer to brain-based learning directly or indirectly. We have edited sparingly and indicate when we have made changes for the purpose of clarity. We have grouped the responses on the basis of the point they reflect. (Note that Dry Creek is abbreviated "DC.")

Supportive Responses

1. Evidence that the school is seen as a healthy community:

[Letter 1]
Both of my daughters have attended DC for two years. Throughout this time, I have seen them blossom. The teachers and the staff are always willing to talk to you and help you in any way possible. I have volunteered throughout the school for two years. During this time I had [direct] experience of their teaching abilities. Their approach to teaching is different than any other I've ever seen. The children are challenged and enjoy learning and have the ability to help ones that are younger than they. The staff and curriculum is the best that I have been exposed to and would highly recommend them to any parent considering sending their child.

Sincerely,
(unsigned)

[Letter 2]
What I love most about DC is that the children are a part of how things are run. They seem to gain so much self-esteem from being part of running the school. The hands-on learning is great. They all really seem to enjoy school. They never seem to get bored

because they are so involved. I would recommend the brain-based instruction to everyone. . . .

I believe the teachers and staff at DC are truly caring and dedicated to their pupils. The program they're implementing on brain-based learning is a wonderful learning tool, and I feel fortunate that my children are a part of this. I honestly feel it is a better way to teach the children and that they're actually grasping what they're learning and not just memorizing facts for a few years. I love (and my children do as well) the Friday sings. . . . Another thing I like is the way the teachers make a presentation of some kind at the PTA meetings so we the parents can better understand the approaches they're taking with our students. I just wish more parents would attend.

(unsigned)

[Letter 3]
The children are allowed to make choices while completing the required work showing that there is always more than one way to solve a problem.

DC also emphasizes individuality and teamwork. Here the younger children are permitted to study with and benefit from the experiences of the older children.

(unsigned)

2. Evidence that parents are noticing instructional changes.

[Letter 1]
K—, my daughter, is in the 1st grade. This is a combined classroom. There are K–2nd [grade] children in her class. Boy, does this make a difference! K— has learned to read so quickly, it's amazed me. She knows a lot about our environment and anatomy for a 6-year-old. I know these subjects seem like high school subjects, but when they're taught by DC, the kids listen and understand.

I am thankful for DC's ethics and goals. They have trained, disciplined, and loved my children in a way that I was incapable of. You won't find a better school, anywhere.

Sincerely,

[Letter 2]

I have had children attending DC since 1980 and have seen many changes, but none have been as "positive" as the new teaching procedures. Staff and students alike are enthusiastic in teaching and learning. Students are more responsible for their actions, which has also increased self-esteem. Students also work more in "groups," which teaches them how to associate with others. Students learn and retain more as they are able to apply what they learn in every day living.

(unsigned)

[Letter 3]

Something that is not real apparent is the curriculum that incorporates all the subjects and blends science with reading math and art (the brain-based instruction). My kids enjoy their school work, they think its fun! Thank you.

DC Staff

(unsigned)

[Letter 4]

Math is an area that has amazed [me] with brain-based learning. In watching these children, I have learned a new way of looking at math, and all of a sudden it clicks as to how it all works. It is so much easier to learn, and it stays with them longer because it makes sense and it's understood. Our son learned multiplication in 1st grade, and I feel it's because of how it was explained to him.

I've also enjoyed watching the children build life-size animals. They take the time to research the animal, its characteristics, lifestyle, habitat, etc., before they build it. These are things they remember. Last year I was [there when] children [were] building a whale. While stuffing it with paper, they were naming the organs that each piece represented. I love all the creating that goes on in these classes and enjoy learning with them. The best part is that they're learning just by having fun.

All in all, with brain-based instruction, I feel that the learning possibilities are endless. I'm so glad our children are at a school that cares enough to provide this type of instruction.

(E's mom)

3. Impact on children with special needs:

[Letter]

To answer the question, I would say that DC has an excellent staff for caring, understanding, your child's feeling, and a parent's concern. All the teachers that I've had to deal with have been a proud and wonderful experience for my children and me. Example: My son R— has ADD [attention deficit disorder] and ADHD [attention deficit hyperactivity disorder], which is a very troubled and hard child to work with. In kindergarten, he had Mrs. — . She and I worked together to help [him]. She was always there and tried hard. Now in the 1st grade, he has Mrs. — again, another kind and understanding teacher. They both took the time even to read up and learn to cope with my son's problems. If not for Mrs. — , I would not have gotten the help or even know what ADD and ADHD were. Cindy Tucker—what a woman. To handle all these children and then R— , too. I commend you. This is a great school. But I don't want to share.

Always and Forever . . .

(unsigned)

On the Down Side

[Letter]

With the new year-round school schedule, the kids seem to be out of school as much as they are in school! School is closed one to two weeks per month, with the exception of three months (Feb., May, and Aug.). [Author's note: This is inaccurate.] The kids' study skills and commitment have plummeted because (I believe) the continuity has vanished. It's like [dieting] for two weeks and then eating anything you want for a week or two. Children need more structure. I also don't believe this prepares the children for life in the real world. When you have a job, you don't go to work, take vacation, work, vacation, work. . . . You work, work, work, work, and then you've earned vacation time.

My daughter has attended DC for three years now, and I have yet to see a book brought home (other than library books). Oh, I am mistaken—she did have one reading book in 5th grade. No math books, no science, history, English—NONE! Where are the books? Is this why homework is so minuscule? I have friends in three different counties, and all of their children had to build a mission and write a report on missions in 3rd grade. My daughter never had to write any reports until 5th grade and that was it—one report. Spelling is about the only homework that is brought home weekly.

Becoming a Learning Community: Park View

As with Dry Creek, our early impression was of a surprising lack of community. In fact, Park View had different ideas about how to proceed with restructuring and where brain-based learning fit. We began with all the D-track teachers and some teachers from A-track and other tracks. (See Chapter 7 for a description of the tracks at Park View.) In the early stages, the D-track group was hungry for a sense of community; and that was what the teachers focused on, even though members were concerned that brain-based learning might just be "one more thing." As one teacher said: "I'm not sure how I feel about this, but I feel that it is something that I have to do."

Indeed, teachers in D-track were so interested in community that the theory and implementation were probably treated at a surface level. One teacher, however, recollected:

[The continued interaction] tied us together to make a common commitment for ourselves and our kids. In the process groups, we had struggles and breakdowns but we made that commitment to keep this going. It is a part of any relationship.

We are not sure why the process did not work for some of the other teachers. Some staff suggested that perhaps they didn't feel that they were getting the direct help they wanted. One teacher stated: "All we do is talk and reflect. I don't get it."

Another staff member suggested:

> We in D-track had choices and we were able to use what we learned to move in and out of process. In other groups, there was no flexibility or ability to move in and out of process. [There were a few who were heavily invested in direct teaching.] Perhaps the other groups wanted to show that they were doing something. D-track also started out by wanting to "show" something, but began to change over time.

In systems terms, we think we saw several factors operating within the school as a whole:

1. There was a significant lack of consensus from the beginning, a difference that seemed to be based on some quite different values and purposes.

2. The system was perturbed as a result of the restructuring grant, our inservice programs, and other factors. This situation tended to exacerbate earlier differences.

3. The larger system self-organized around traditional ideas by isolating the brain-based learning group. The system sought to preserve itself and directed a significant degree of hostility toward the brain-based learning group.

4. Meanwhile, the smaller brain-based learning group jelled at a level that the members had rarely experienced elsewhere. We had the emergence of a learning community with this group that paralleled what had happened at Dry Creek.

We observed both significant individual renewal and a sense of something larger, to which all belonged. The following quotes are from three teachers reflecting on the group process and Renate's work and inservice programs:

[Comment 1]
This gave me the opportunity to identify the emotions and the intuitiveness of teaching. It has also made me a stronger person to continue on this journey.

[Comment 2]
I didn't know enough about it. I came in because I saw it as a vehicle to solidify relationships with my track and in order to mainstream my kids.

[Comment 3]
There is a recognizable difference that is lasting and genuine within D-track. We had become angry. But now we've shifted to empowering ourselves and not blaming others for the elements we want to change. We became more responsible. It was a genuine shift in how we saw ourselves and the school. Our desire was not to manipulate the school, but to take ownership for and of ourselves.

At Park View, we also found a growth in insight about learning and the needs of kids. Here are some comments reflecting the glimpses we had seen at Dry Creek:

[Comment 1]
Part of growing came with sharing with others—the people. Now I see where I have short-changed the kids. This opens more doors for me. I don't feel alone. For years I have felt alone.

[Comment 2]
We need to live on the edge of possibility. On the edge of creativity.

[Comment 3]
I'm there to nurture and facilitate, but I'm not doing "IT." We used to put up beautiful bulletin boards in elementary schools, but that was showing *us*; now the class shows itself.

Interim Results at Both Schools

We have found several indicators of improvement at the level of community and culture in both schools, through unsolicited comments, increases in parent involvement, and fewer discipline problems—evidence of the "relaxed alertness" of brain-based learning.

Unsolicited Comments

Both student and parent comments at both schools are highly positive. Visitors to Dry Creek, where the state of the community can be more readily identified (the entire school is involved), remark repeatedly on the uniqueness of the community. Approving comments have come from the following diverse groups: substitute teachers, visitors from other schools, parents, the staff sent by NEA to film the school in action, and even outside contractors who work on the school plant.

Demonstrated Increase in Parental Involvement

Evidence pointing to positive change includes the number of parents attending PTA meetings at Dry Creek and the number of parents attending parent/student/teacher conferences in D-track at Park View. At Dry Creek, where 37 percent of the students qualify as Title I, attendance at Title I meetings has increased from zero to more than 40 parents.

At Park View, parental attendance at student-led teacher/parent conferences is now above 75 percent.

Fewer Discipline Problems

At Park View, the number of student disciplinary referrals on D-track has dropped dramatically, as have suspensions (from 20 percent to 5 to 8 percent). Dry Creek has had a significant drop in vandalism and student disruptions. This drop has changed for the worse in recent times, as we describe in Chapters 11 and 12, and has led to some rethinking on our part.

* * *

In general, the environments created by those engaged in brain-based learning reflected what we had in mind when we spoke of "relaxed alertness." Our observations suggest that the process we introduced can make a significant difference, and that it is possible to develop a rich and deep sense of community among those who may have rarely interacted or communicated with each other. The traditional system of schooling, however, has deep roots and is capable of disrupting what might otherwise be regarded as impeccable communities. We began to see that happening and wanted to understand what we saw.

Despite the overwhelmingly glowing reports at Dry Creek, somewhere during our third year together, two things began to puzzle us. The first had to do with the teachers (see Chapter 11) and the second with the system (see Chapter 12).

11

Teachers—Change and Nonchange

During the third year of our work with the two schools, we perceived that some fundamental patterns in teacher behavior simply were not changing. We had been seeing these patterns in a variety of contexts and finally began to observe them systematically. In Chapters 7 and 8, we describe what we did in terms of actual instruction; and we indicate that we continually "bumped up" against some fundamental differences in how teachers interpreted our instruction. For example, we found different ways in which teachers construed the notions of orderliness, layers of experience, and the relationship between facts and concepts. Teachers also had differing degrees of comfort with active processing. What is interesting is that our observations confirm the view of Roehler et al. (1987):

> Not all teachers find it easy to do this kind of spontaneous thinking
> . . . [and] the degree of metacognitive control a teacher has over
> knowledge about reading instruction seemed to distinguish be-
> tween teachers who can do it (responsive elaboration) and those
> who cannot (p. 4).

We began to look at what teachers were doing in relationship to their mental models—how their interpretations and actions reflected deeper and more basic assumptions. In fact, we found clearly observable overall instructional differences that played themselves out. These approaches influenced how teachers related to us, what they perceived we were doing, and how they sought to implement what we were all working on.

Observing Differences in Teaching

We have already touched on the difference between *mental models* and *espoused models*. The espoused model refers to the more or less formal explanations we give for our actions. Those explanations may or may not reflect our theories in use or mental model. Espoused models are often elaborate. They can also be used to frame what we do in a "better" or more sophisticated light.

Mental models are theories-in-use. They drive what we actually do. As Robert Keidel (1995) writes:

> We make decisions based on the way we frame life. We decide—and design—as we think (and feel). In other words, human organization reflects cognitive organization (p. 5).

In the spirit of the new sciences, people are participant-observers who experience a world that is shaped, in large measure, by what they deeply believe. As we worked with teachers at both schools, we came to see that the differences between teachers reflected more than just differences in skill.

Patterns of Difference: Approaches to Instruction

If our mental models are our theories-in-use at the moment of behavior, then what teachers believe about the teaching-and-learning process and their behaviors or actual instruction would have to form an observable pattern. Others have reached the same conclusion. Argyris, for instance, makes a distinction between what he calls Model I and Model II teacher behavior. In Model I, "the teacher unilaterally designs the teaching environment and controls it" (Argyris, in Hyman and Rosoff 1984, p. 39).

In Model II, the approach is bilateral: "[Teachers] design situations or environments where participants can be origins and can experience high personal causation . . . tasks are controlled jointly. . .[and] protection of self is joint enterprise and oriented towards growth (Argyris, in Hyman and Rosoff 1984, p. 41).

We began with a sense of these differences, and they have been strongly confirmed and expanded. The nature of these differences in teachers' approaches to instruction began to be visible as we worked with teachers and observed in classrooms. We have since translated these clusters of differences into what we call "approaches to instruction." We have labeled them Instructional Approaches 1, 2, and 3. The details, and more specific benchmarks and indicators of the differences in approaches, are dealt with in more depth in another book to be published by ASCD in 1997. The book is entitled *Unleashing the Power of Perceptual Change: The Potential of Brain-Based Teaching*, and it describes the changes in thinking and teaching that we identified over a period of four years.

Indicators of the Instructional Approaches

We needed indicators of the differences in teaching. We have identified five aspects of instruction that appear significant, but we suspect that there are more:

1. The objectives of instruction
2. The teacher's use of time
3. Sources for curriculum and instruction
4. How teachers define and deal with discipline
5. How teachers approach assessment

No single indicator practiced in isolation determines someone's instructional approach. It is the "buy-in" to a particular practice that leads us to suspect that we are observing a general pattern.

Instructional Approach 1

In observing teachers using this approach, we saw practices that paralleled the more mechanistic view of learning and teaching at one end of a continuum. Instructional Approach 1 relies on top-down thinking and the control of information.

In terms of systems thinking, these teachers were trying hard to maintain equilibrium within a system that was naturally complex and dynamic. Not trusting or understanding how to facilitate and harness the natural chaos that comes with a system that is dynamically organized, they tried to control it like a well-ordered machine. For example:

• *The objectives of instruction.* The teaching objectives focus almost entirely on the acquisition of prespecified, correct information, facts, and skills.

• *The teacher's use of time.* Time allowed for mastering skills and concepts tends to be closely guided by an artificial time schedule determined by someone other than the learner.

• *Sources for curriculum and instruction.* Instructional sources include the designated curriculum guide, handbook, or other appropriate authorities. Primary sources for instruction are texts, manuals, lectures, and demonstration videos that teachers select and present. Teachers separate content into designated subjects that are themselves taught as a series of fragments and topics.

• *How teachers define and deal with discipline.* Discipline is almost always seen as those procedures necessary to deal with behavior that disrupts instructional delivery and teacher control.

• *How teachers approach assessment.* Assessment is based on the ability of students to replicate precisely what teachers or instructional sources have presented.

Instructional Approach 2

Instructional Approach 2 is considerably more complex and so-phisticated than Instructional Approach 1. It is still primarily a com-mand-and-control mode of instruction, with many of the same beliefs and practices as in Instructional Approach 1, but with critical differ-ences. In particular, it uses complex materials, it can incorporate powerful and engaging experiences, and teaching is often with an eye to creating meaning and not just presenting materials for memorization. For example:

• **The objectives of instruction.** The teaching objective is still a highly focused set of outcomes, tending to combine prescribed curricu-lum with "packaged" instructional materials, such as the *Full Option Science System* materials (Lawrence Hall of Science 1992). The emphasis is on teaching with "designed experiences." In terms of brain-based learning, the goal is acquiring scholastic or technical knowledge and emphasizes the understanding of ideas and concepts.

• **The teacher's use of time.** The approach to time has shifted somewhat. That students are engaged in activities and these activities cannot be tightly controlled without creating a sense of frustration frequently leads teachers to begin to look for greater chunks of time.

• *Sources for curriculum and instruction.* The instructional sources are expanded to include the use of groups, discovery, and some types of technology. Teachers include preplanned opportunities for student exploration and exchange that can range from the trivial to the fairly sophisticated. Teachers also may use peer teaching and introduce thematic instruction and the integrated curriculum, but these tend to be highly structured and teacher controlled.

• *How teachers define and deal with discipline.* The approach to discipline has not changed much. The deciding factor again is that teachers design activities using a coherent plan of instruction; and students must know how to cooperate with those objectives. Teachers tend to see noncooperation with the teaching plan and designated activities as disruptive and as a problem to maintaining necessary discipline. Self-organization in students is evident when tasks and activities become provocative and touch student purposes and meanings.

● *How teachers approach assessment.* Assessment includes some form of performance. Teachers tend to experiment with some types of authentic assessment. They use paper/pencil tests, along with instructor-controlled performance assessments and evaluations. Teachers often provide opportunities for problem solving, projects, performance, and some student choice of problems to solve or questions to answer. Both teachers and students often develop complex rubrics for evaluation.

Instructional Approach 3

At the other end of the continuum is the type of teaching we had envisioned as brain based. At the two schools, this kind of teaching was more fluid and open. It included elements of self-organization, as classrooms gathered individually or as a unit around critical ideas, meaningful questions, and purposeful projects.

Instructional Approach 3 is much more learner centered because genuine student interest is at its core. It is also highly organic and dynamic, with experiences that approach the complexity of real life. The language and methods of teachers who use Instructional Approach 3 are often felt to be suspect and nontraditional by others. Teachers using this approach view students as active meaning makers who are trying to make sense of their world. Teachers using Instructional Approach 3 can employ, but have broken away from, the delivery model of teaching. Their approach emphasizes the ways that people naturally learn:

● *The objectives of instruction.* We call the objective in this approach "expansion of dynamical knowledge or perceptual knowledge." For Instructional Approach 3, the curriculum should become knowledge that the students can use naturally in their everyday lives.

• *The teacher's use of time.* Time becomes flexible and is tied directly to learner needs, driven by complex individual and group projects.

• *Sources for curriculum and instruction.* These sources are multiple. Instructors and students develop partnerships, embedding prescribed curriculum in student-centered processes and capitalizing on student interests.

• *How teachers define and deal with discipline.* The traditional approach to discipline has been discarded and replaced by a sense of order based on learning and instruction tied to common meanings and purposes.

• *How teachers approach assessment.* Authentic assessment of all types is employed. Students participate in evaluating their own process and progress. Outside experts and peers also conduct assessments. Teachers occasionally use paper/pencil tests for surface knowledge. However, assessment primarily focuses on two issues:

      1. What does the student understand, and in how many ways can this understanding be demonstrated?
      2. What can the student do on the basis of this understanding, and how can this knowledge be applied in real-world and dynamic experiences?

It seemed to us that most of the current work done on restructuring and teacher change is actually directed at Instructional Approach 2. Given the instructional level at most schools, such work strikes us as an appropriate goal at this time.

As we shared the instructional approaches with the teachers at the two schools, we heard a collective sigh of relief. We, too, felt relieved, because we interpreted their reaction as positive and a breakthrough that would lead to their teaching with all the approaches, including Instructional Approach 3. Surprisingly, Instructional Approach 3 was used only in some cases. What we had not foreseen adequately was the strength of operative mental models that did not allow teachers to go beyond Instructional Approach 2. The ability to shift from one approach to another as needed is ultimately what we were after, but most teachers were literally "stuck" in their mental models. We discovered just how difficult breaking out of one's mental model can be.

Perceptual Differences that Underlie the Instructional Approaches

A teacher's ability to use different instructional approaches depends on her "world view" or system of belief. We first began to understand this relationship when we observed that some teachers could use all three approaches as needed. Other teachers seemed to be restricted in the approaches that they could implement. Ultimately, we found that what we came to call "perceptual orientations" were fundamentally different for teachers who felt comfortable with Instructional Approach 3. We spell out our research and enlarge on the differences in *Unleashing the Power of Perceptual Change: The Potential of Brain-Based Teaching* (Caine and Caine, in press).

We see four qualities or dimensions as core elements of the perceptual orientations:

- A sense of self-efficacy grounded in authenticity.
- The ability to build relationships that facilitate self-organization.
- The ability to see connections between subjects, discipline, and life.
- The capacity to engage in self-reflection to grow and adapt.

They are almost certainly aspects of more comprehensive world views, but that larger exploration is beyond the scope of this book. What we suggest here is that the four dimensions we identify are sufficient for grasping the essential deep differences in perception that govern the ability to implement and understand the different instructional approaches.

From Power to Self-Efficacy Grounded in Authenticity

Teachers at Perceptual Orientation 3 have moved from seeing power as primarily invested in others or outside forces to having a sense of self-efficacy, where power and decision making reside predominantly within themselves. They believe in their own ability to affect change. In some sense, however, a person can be empowered and still be a tyrant. We saw in teachers with Perceptual Orientation 3 an additional quality, which we describe as being grounded in authenticity.

Carl Jung talks of the "mask" or persona that we project to others. It is meant to continually convince ourselves and others that we are what we say we are. This way of looking at ourselves is related to the notion of the "espoused model," or the explanations most of us give to ourselves and others for what we do. Authenticity, on the other hand, is associated with a lack of artifice and hence defensiveness. Orientation 3 teachers tend to self-disclose more readily and face reality even when it hurts. Without any conscious plan on our part, almost every teacher who moved into Perceptual Orientation 3 thinking while we were working with the two schools went through some form of personal transformation involving "facing self," seemingly unrelated to the process. We all need our illusions, of course, and Perceptual Orientation 3 thinkers are no different. It is therefore a matter of degree.

From Control to Building Relationships That Facilitate Self-Organization

Here are two responses of Perceptual Orientation 3 teachers to the question: How do you ensure student empowerment?

[Kindergarten Teacher]
Student empowerment is, in part, a by-product of child-centered, self-selected activities and long-range projects that cross curriculum. A teacher must also be in tune with what sparks genuine interest in their students and be willing to drop preplanned agendas and go where students want to go. You have to listen to their ideas and let them try to make it work. You must put them in the position of "teacher" as often as possible. You must pose broad questions, accept all answers and encourage students to

demonstrate the how and why of their ideas—how do you know
that will work? Why do you think that will work?

[High School Teacher]
Tricky. Nonverbal as well as verbal feedback tells me a lot. On the
other hand, I no longer subscribe to the belief that students should
run the curriculum and we should only study what they wish to
study. A good and effective teacher should be able to interest and
empower students in concepts, ideas, and units that they didn't
know could interest them. After all, that is one of the key roles of
the teacher.

The approach of teachers with Perceptual Orientation 3 to control
has shifted dramatically. They understand the relationships between
information and experience, between learning and context, and between students and teacher. That is why they can facilitate self-organization within the classroom and the school. Discipline is a secondary
concern because it is a natural consequence of learning organized
around meaningful projects and activities. Orderly processes are understood and collectively agreed on. Routines and procedures are
established and respected. Student responsibilities are everywhere,
from keeping an orderly classroom and school, to helping others
evaluate their work and challenging each other.

Expanded Cognitive Horizons

Here are two more responses of Perceptual Orientation 3 teachers:

[High School Teacher]
I incorporate the notions of preview and review with my teaching.
I emphasize the role of connections, including the connections of
content. I emphasize multiple perspectives and multiple solutions
in the problem-solving process.

[High School Teacher]
I have always felt like a sponge. Sometimes [my ideas] come to
me in a bookstore while browsing, often on trips to historical sites,
[and] frequently while reading the newspapers. I read four newspapers a day. Lately, I have been getting some fantastic ideas over

the Internet. For example, I was able to take oral histories from a WPA project from the 1930s and wed this with maps and diaries from still other sources on the 'Net.

Perceptual Orientation 3 teachers have a bigger picture in several different ways, which collectively makes possible dealing with content at high levels. They understand the differences between facts and concepts and the different levels of meaning. They tend to be expert in some domain and have a "felt meaning" for additional disciplines and the ways in which subjects and disciplines interpenetrate each other. They tend to have a rich grasp of process. Finally, they have a sense of wholeness and interconnectedness. As a result, they can see more connections among and between subjects, disciplines, and life.

Self-Reference and Process

Here is a response from another high school teacher:

[High School Teacher]
I reflect on my teaching as I teach and make modifications as I proceed through each period. I regularly assess my choice of examples and attempt to read the faces of my students and reflect on the type of responses and questions that I get from my students.

Perceptual Orientation 3 teachers have a significant capacity to self-reflect, understand mindfulness, and have reflective intelligence. They see themselves as true lifelong learners. They do not see themselves as needing to have the right answer, but pride themselves in knowing how to "turn the question around" so that students see finding answers as their responsibility. Above all, they see themselves as constantly and necessarily learning.

Teacher Transformation

For us, brain-based learning depends on teachers' being Perceptual Orientation 3 thinkers, with the capacity to use all three instructional approaches as needed. Figure 11.1 shows the versatility of such teachers.

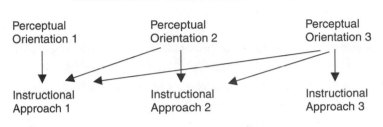

FIGURE 11.1
COMPARISON OF PERCEPTUAL APPROACHES

Perceptual Orientation 1   Perceptual Orientation 2   Perceptual Orientation 3

Instructional Approach 1   Instructional Approach 2   Instructional Approach 3

There is a fundamental difference, however, between acquiring new strategies and changing one's world view. The first is closer to being trained; the second involves transformation. Our impressions of much of the current work on teacher development and restructuring is that it operates at the level of developing new modes of doing things, but not at the deeper level of becoming the sorts of people who can do things differently. One reason why so much in education does not change is that people implement new strategies from the point of view of their current mental model—an aspect of their orientation.

We are not discounting the importance of introducing new modes of doing things and of mastering new strategies. Indeed, sometimes the best way to change personally is to do something different, experience the new and unusual consequences, and then have to reconcile those new experiences with prior experiences and beliefs. For example, consider a teacher who tends to use a stand-and-deliver approach and is persuaded to attempt some version of cooperative learning. The teacher then finds that students have mastered some ideas that he did not teach. That teacher has an opportunity to confront some deeply held prior beliefs. Transformation can occur when prior beliefs are identified and examined. When we introduced new strategies, we hoped that teachers would confront their own such beliefs. The objective was for the strategies to open up possibilities that could then be explored in the process groups.

We had a felt sense that a basic shift in perception was what mattered most in the long run. This shift became clearer to us in our work with Dry Creek, Park View, and elsewhere, as hitherto invisible perceptual patterns began to emerge. The task for us now is to work with educators on the transformational process of acquiring more complex and richer modes of perception. Ultimately, our view is that the educators who will thrive and will be needed most in the 21st century will be at Perceptual Orientation 3. They will need to have self-efficacy to deal with a fluid, yet frequently dysfunctional, system. They will need to have mastered the art of facilitating self-organization by students and others. They will need to have sufficiently broad cognitive horizons to be able to integrate new ideas and new information and to facilitate their introduction into ongoing and dynamic student experience. They will need to be able to face and know themselves and interact authentically with the people with whom they deal. And they will need to engage in the deep reflection and self-reference that makes constantly growing and adapting to a rapidly changing world possible.

12

Reality Test—Dry Creek and the Larger Picture

Over time, as we began to focus on instructional and curricular issues at Dry Creek, the school began to lose some of the excitement and dynamism that had been present in the early days. In part, that leveling off is a regular phenomenon and something with which we are familiar. Novelty itself is a spur in the early stages of learning any new system. Pockets of considerable excitement still existed, though, and the sense of community was exceptional. But we were seeking something more. We had begun to identify what we meant by living on the edge of possibility, and something was missing.

Reversion from Process to "How To's"

We began to look at what had changed at the school. Most important to us was the fact that all but one of the process groups (the repeating one for new members of staff) had become study groups. They were focusing on "how to" improve their instruction. We felt the primary reason for this change was an increasing sense of urgency from the administration, district, and staff to increase student achievement on standardized measures.

This focus on results and how to's had begun toward the end of our second year with a district-mandated literacy program. For example, a superb K–2 teacher was distressed because the district had issued some guidelines for what she had to do on a daily basis in her classroom. Because she was sincere and wished to comply, this direction was totally stifling her capacity to be creative and function in the new ways that she had been learning.

Instead of taking time to reflect on how they were implementing brain-based learning and connecting with their entire process as a school, teachers were using much of the time to talk about how to implement the district mandates. We have to add that many were also frustrated by some of our suggested procedures and strategies, such as the way we introduced active processing (as described in Chapter 9). The consequence was that they began to explore more traditional techniques and strategies, and many began to lose the element of personal reflection and the focus on learning so critical to moving toward a mental model of brain-based learning and teaching.

We found that all the teachers and administrators were under pressure to introduce specific "new" methods and procedures into their teaching. Some of the best teachers felt dispirited as they abandoned creative and challenging approaches and adopted a one-hour-at-a-time schedule doing enforced reading and literacy activities. Some aspects of writing were improving at the cost of the whole child and student involvement in the excitement of learning. Teachers went back to direct teaching and "covering" the subject (reading), not embedding the reading skills in sophisticated ways, using student meaning and purposes.

System Realities

The bottom line was that the larger system was still alive and well. The sense of community had changed, but much of the traditional structure was still in place; and it was still stable in some of the old ways. The age-grade structure was still largely in place. Curriculum mandates were still coming down the line and overpowering new and emerging understandings. Special programs were advocated irrespective of the philosophy of brain-based learning. Technology was barely extant. Students had one room set aside for computers, and most of these were ancient. Administration was still too top down in nature, notwithstanding the attempts of the principal and her assistant to engage and empower the staff. At the same time, modes of assessment were being changed. The school had invested a considerable amount of effort in working with the California CLAS test, which was then eliminated. Thus, we had a stable bureaucracy combined with at least two different sets of changes—from the formal system and from us.

A Shift in Leadership

In the second half of 1995 (our fourth year together), further events at Dry Creek precipitated a minicrisis. The school was deeply saddened when the principal, Cindy, accepted a position at another school much closer to her home. She had powerful personal reasons for the change, and by and large, the whole school supported her decision. Her leaving, however, created a sense of instability in the community. Her departure was followed by a period of waiting to see who would replace her, and during this time, the community experienced further instability. A temporary principal was appointed; and Kris, the assistant to the principal, applied for the job as new principal. These events required that she be away from the school not only for interviews but also for other critical duties she had taken on. The school was left with far less direct leadership. The teachers and staff had also lost their commons room during this same time. Because of the school's growth, the room had to be used as a classroom until temporary buildings could be added. The community therefore had no common meeting place and had found nowhere to be together.

Fortunately, because Kris had impeccable credentials, she was selected as the new principal. This was also one more time where the support of the Rio Linda School District needs to be commended. Nevertheless, this time has proven to be a genuine test for all of us. Here are some results of the shift in leadership:

• The loss of Cindy strained relationships. In interviews with small groups of teachers and the staff, we found that things had deteriorated from their perspective to the point where two of the best teachers said they were seriously thinking about leaving the profession.

• Discipline problems reemerged on the playground, at lunch, and in a small number of classes—problems that had dissipated during our three years together. Moreover, teachers expressed major disagreements on how to handle discipline. Some teachers advocated a strong "law-and-order" approach. Others felt that this approach was totally inconsistent with the spirit toward which we had been working. The clash revealed itself in the issuing of citations for misbehavior (much like a police officer issues parking fines or tickets for speeding) by one group and the self-imposed task of protecting those cited by the other.

Most of the discipline problems focused on a small number of students (about 20). The same students consumed most of the time of the resource personnel, as well as that of the principal and the office staff. Much of the burnout and frustration can be laid at the door of dealing with this small subset of students.

• When Cindy first became principal of the school, she adopted an intensive hands-on approach, which she then implemented with the assistance of Kris. When Cindy resigned, Kris found herself doing the work of two people. She then solicited support from one exceptional teacher to be an assistant, thus taking this teacher out of the classroom (much to the latter's distress). The duties of the office staff also changed, as they began to handle more of the discipline and counseling issues, even though these responsibilities were not their prescribed jobs.

• One major problem for us was that although the first shift in community had been freeing and joyful and had engendered more respect of staff for each other, the shift had not been accompanied by ways of dealing with conflicts and profound differences. An old aura of "niceness" still had a hold. Thus, the staff found dealing with differences and conflict directly and effectively difficult.

Bureaucracy: Larger System Constraints

Because Dry Creek is part of the larger system, many problems continue. Here are some examples:

• Resource people other than office staff each have a supervisor outside the school. Part of their salary is tied to a set of specific conditions about what they can do, whom they can work with, and so on. Hence, under the literal terms of their employment, these people feel that they are not permitted to do much pooling of resources or to work with students who are not designated as having special needs, even if by so doing they could improve their results and reduce the burden on the school as a whole.

• In 1996, California released some funds to reduce class sizes in Grades 1 through 3, from 33 and higher to 20. Such activity, of course, was a boon. Dry Creek reacted very quickly by hiring new teachers. Space, however, had to be found. As a result, every free area, including stage and faculty common rooms, became classrooms. Thus, staff have no place where they can mingle freely during their breaks. This situation hurts the collegial nature of the school.

We have found that the preceding examples are characteristic of many schools and districts.

Near, But Not Yet on, the Edge of Possibility

Many educational reports have emphasized how difficult school change can be, and we were experiencing that difficulty. It seemed to us that at a deep level, the system was being shaken and disrupted, and yet had in place structures and processes that were designed to resist change. In some respects, the system was becoming more fluid and dynamical, yet a stable system was being shaken to the point of fragility.

New Brain-Based Initiatives

Our mood during this time has been mixed. Though we wanted some things to happen differently, we expected that a crisis or series of crises would have to occur if real change was going to happen. The disturbances were, in many respects, welcome opportunities.

Renewal of Process

When the spirit of self-reflection and personal process appeared to be dying, we proposed forming a new group with teachers who felt that they wanted to be challenged further. Our plan was to use *Leadership and the New Science* (Wheatley 1992) and "A Post-Modern Perspective on Curriculum" (Doll 1993). First, the proposal was to go back to the original process of self-reflection, and for the group as a whole to examine what was happening in the school in the light of these ideas.

Second, at the same time, several new staff members had arrived, and one of the teachers agreed to facilitate a process group for the new staff members and for any other members who had been with the school for some time and wished to go through the *Mindshifts* process again.

Third, some classified and nonclassified staff had jointly decided that the school's technological poverty was unacceptable. They wanted to work together in a group to develop a plan and acquire the technology needed, and Geoffrey worked with them. They have already had a small measure of success, though the school is still hopelessly underequipped in information technology.

The cumulative impact of these three new groups has been substantial. Two have been functioning as process groups, beginning with a moment of quiet and then moving to the ordered sharing. They have also engaged in extensive personal reflection on the basis of their own learning. And the conclusion has been primarily a joint sigh of relief—a sense that we were going back to what worked and were rediscovering the spirit that we had created. Here, for instance, is part of an unsolicited letter from one of the teachers:

We may have lost our "field" when we lost our process groups. It "feels" different already as we come together under the old process group framework. These groups must help the S-matrix theory. [Sometimes diagrams represent a way of modeling the dynamic lives of high-energy particles. See Wheatley 1992, p. 69.] Participation is crucial for adults and students. I'm working on being more of a participant. It's helping me with — [a student not experiencing success].

"Neighborhoods"

At least one major problem revolved around teacher change. As mental models shifted, different perceptions ensued. Perceptual Orientation 3 thinkers became impatient because they felt restraints on their growth. Perceptual Orientations 1 and 2 thinkers felt different kinds of pressures to get it "right" without understanding the process.

After a visit in January 1996, we suggested (following a proposal we had made a year earlier) that teachers might reorganize into smaller communities that they later called "neighborhoods." The idea was that teachers with the same mental models and orientations work with the same set of children from kindergarten through 6th grade. We felt that the neighborhoods would form around the instructional approaches. We further suggested that each neighborhood be responsible for all the children within its domain, including discipline. At the same time, the policy of issuing citations for misbehavior was seen as conflicting with a brain-based approach and would be abandoned in most, and possibly all, neighborhoods.

In some ways, the new arrangement has led to a great sense of relief and a release of pressure. Staff has finally become aware that they could be using the same language and yet mean entirely different things. Such changes have also provided permission and opportunities for those who share beliefs and ideas to work together. Many teachers were happy to take such opportunities, even when they occasionally had to change the grade levels and the configurations of their classes (from single grade to multigrade).

Finally, we have again invited the support personnel—everyone except full-time classroom teachers—to form their own group (currently called "the hub"). The idea is that they find ways to pool information about the children with whom they are working, share resources, and work together to solve common problems.

Most people have welcomed the new configuration, but it has brought new challenges. For instance, some teachers have had to be added to neighborhoods somewhat arbitrarily. Thus, disagreements occur between some teachers working together for the first time, and over different ways of using or working with support and classified staff.

All of this means that Dry Creek is in a state of flux. Disequilibrium is real, but disequilibrium does not mean that the edge of possibility has been reached. What is exciting is that, notwithstanding all the challenges, the school is now on a firm footing, and clear evidence shows that teachers and staff are becoming more empowered.

Implications for Systems Generally

The entire restructuring issue seems to originate from a clash of mental models and larger perceptual orientations, and perhaps the biggest problem is an inability to communicate.

In our travels and work, we have found many people who resonate with our ideas. Almost all of them have studied the changes in our collective understanding of learning, read our books or other books on brain research and teaching, and been involved in some type of intellectual and professional systemic change program over time. Almost universally, the primary frustration they experience focuses on their inability to communicate with colleagues or members of the public who have more traditional views or, in our terms, different orientations.

Differences Between Perceptual Orientations 1 and 3

• Perceptual Orientation 1 thinkers want to know what to do—what the steps are—while Perceptual Orientation 3 thinkers tend to be happy with words and actions, such as "flow" and "process."

• Perceptual Orientation 1 thinkers search for ways that students can "accumulate" knowledge—while Perceptual Orientation 3 thinkers examine ways to "facilitate emergent knowledge" or "complex thinking." Thus, the construction of meaning is a Perceptual Orientation 3 focus, whereas memorization is a Perceptual Orientation 1 focus.

• Perceptual Orientation 1 focuses on specific, identifiable, and quantifiable outcomes that can be tested for. Perceptual Orientation 3 favors complex outcomes that are best assessed, manifested, and observed in real performance in complex contexts.

• A major tension exists in attitudes to time, planning, and the sequencing of ideas, skills, and activities. Perceptual Orientation 1 focuses on building blocks and a planned series of instructional steps that lead to the formation of a skill or concept in a predetermined way. Programmed learning is an example of this approach. This type of sequencing depends on the teachers being totally in control.

For Perceptual Orientation 3, sequencing is fundamentally different. For example, the timing of activities and interventions is governed, to a large extent, by student interests and the ways in which understanding is developing in the student's mind. This kind of timing cannot be fully planned or anticipated. Perceptual Orientation 3 thinkers, however, would likely help students understand sequencing when students are creating a presentation, putting together a creative product, writing, or organizing a certain scientific project. For Perceptual Orientation 3 thinkers, the biggest dilemma is knowing how to explain teaching that occurs within a living, moving context where everything is naturally together, always changing, and teacher facilitated but rarely teacher directed.

When Perceptual Orientations 1 and 3 thinkers get together, they find that they are speaking a different language, have different world views, and generally find relating to each other extremely difficult. What is a rich and productive experience for Perceptual Orientation 3 thinkers is a waste of time for Perceptual Orientation 1 thinkers. What is creativity and discovery for Perceptual Orientation 3 thinkers is noise and disorder to Perceptual Orientation 1 thinkers. What is a sense of wholeness and interconnectedness to Perceptual Orientation 3 people is re-garded by Perceptual Orientation 1 thinkers as flaky and phony. And the inquiry and self-reference that is the stuff of life to Perceptual Orientation 3 thinkers is all too often seen as unnecessary self-indul-gence by Perceptual Orientation 1 people. Perceptual Orientation 2 thinkers can often see both views and are frequently caught in the middle.

Perceptual Orientation 3 teachers have sufficient self-efficacy to make complex decisions on their own, are flexible enough to recognize and organize curriculum around student meanings and purposes, have both disciplinary knowledge and broader understanding indicative of broader cognitive horizons, have internalized a sense of wholeness, and know how to work with process and how to reflect on their experiences. Teachers with this orientation are simply different people. They don't just *do* different, they *are* different.

Differing perceptions lead to different realities. The differences in perceptual orientation help explain some of the major disagreements that people have about what seem to be common topics. Look at the controversy surrounding the language arts strategies of "whole language" and "phonics." We explore the differences in depth in the next section ("Differing Perceptions Regarding Whole Language and Phonics").

Differing Perceptions on Whole Language and Phonics

Whole language has become enormously popular in the United States. Yet it has also been extremely controversial. Thus, the whole language movement has recently been berated in California for gener-ally reducing language proficiency, as evidenced by performance on standardized tests. A "back-to-phonics" approach has, therefore, been advocated. This approach refers to a method of teaching reading by associating letters and combinations of letters with the appropriate speech sounds.

The issue is a superb illustration of a clash of orientations in many interconnected ways. Specifically, what we are seeing is a common phrase, "whole language," being interpreted and applied in fundamen-tally different ways and understandings. From our perspective, the question is not about "whole language" but about whose version of whole language we are talking about. Whole language practiced by a Perceptual Orientation 1 thinker is profoundly different from whole language practiced by someone with Perceptual Orientation 3. Relating the evolution of whole language to the instructional approaches and perceptual orientations may be helpful:

• *In the Beginning.* As it was originally conceived, whole language relies on a Perceptual Orientation 3 approach and, when done with appropriate sophistication, is a superb example of what we mean by Instructional Approach 3.

Whole language centers authority in the teachers, not in material or any administrative guidelines. The thrust is to embed and integrate all aspects of language in a dynamic way that utilizes natural capacities and propensities of students. Thus, many "methods" and "strategies" may be involved, but never in a rigid, prescriptive way.

What teachers, administrators, and community members should note is that *whole language does not exclude phonics.* It incorporates and moves beyond phonics, but the specific components that constitute a language all continue to be important. The word "whole" does not mean and should not be construed to mean that specific details and skill components are irrelevant. These components are embedded in a larger and more complex process, requiring Instructional Approach 3. This approach is extremely labor intensive and uses such elements as multiple social configurations, individual student interests, group discussions, and teacher/student or student/student journaling.

• *What Has Happened.* Pure phonics instruction fits Perceptual Orientation 1 thinking and practice. Such instruction is fairly fragmented (focuses on a "bit" at a time), is quantifiable, and reflects observable results gained in relatively small and discrete time periods. One also does not have to deal with the whole person, complex interactions, or "process" to teach phonics.

When people who are comfortable with this approach seek to use whole language instruction, they construe whole language in a limited way. In one example we observed, "whole language" meant that students should read 12 books instead of 5. In some districts, "whole language" is translated as reading programs that are stratified with specific objectives for each grade or category. Here, "whole" meant that everybody is accounted for or included.

Perceptual Orientation 1 thinkers who are given instructions to "teach" whole language will be frustrated and will tend to translate it into a more fragmented, quantifiable approach. Because they tend to follow the rules loyally, they may also abandon their emphasis on skill development and attempt to do things they don't understand. They will then abandon their own sense of expertise for teaching skills, and students benefit neither from basic skill acquisition nor from complex learning based on experiences embedded in natural or meaningful wholeness. Thus, the intended complexity of whole language is abandoned for a more linear interactive format. Much of what is meant to be "whole" is lost, and instruction becomes mediocre at best—particularly in classrooms where the pupil-teacher ratio is 35 to 1. *No one should be surprised that such confusion fails to yield consistently high scores in reading.*

From our perspective, both phonics and the use of literature make sense. The exclusiveness, however, strikes us as unnecessary. As a matter of fact, how can phonics and rich literary experiences help but enrich each other? Children need both specific skills and complex experiences that introduce and firmly establish a joy of reading and of text in general. Moreover, the degree of emphasis will vary from child to child. Brain-based learning teachers need to be able to use anything and everything to help a child learn. They also need to know what is appropriate. They need to be at Perceptual Orientation 2 or 3. At Perceptual Orientation 1, teachers are better off using more linear approaches, such as phonics, and focusing on isolated skills. This focus can lead to moderate success on standardized tests. We should add, however, that in terms of long-term needs and the degree of literacy required in the age of information, phonics without the whole will be hopelessly inadequate.

A Word on Park View

Park View had issues similar to those emerging at Dry Creek, but much earlier in Park View's life with us. The D-track, for instance, functioned to some extent as the type of "neighborhood" that Dry Creek is establishing. At Park View, hostility between the tracks had been going on for some time. And, as mentioned earlier, there was a change of principals early in our work together.

Within D-track itself, however, we have seen a great deal of self-efficacy. The D-track teachers were officers in the union, on leadership committees, and generally involved in task groups that affected their own programs and the overall fate of the school. On a more personal level, the difference in inservice programs was also profound. At Dry Creek, we visited for short, intensive periods and seldom ended up in debates with teachers or were subjected to critical questioning. Conversely, at Park View, teachers worked with Renate more intensively and began to be more confident about what they could and could not do. They also led initiatives to change instructional time and saw ways to incorporate district guidelines without violating a brain-based approach. Teachers at Park View, therefore, had many more difficulties with the system but were much more empowered. This difference between the teachers at Dry Creek and at Park View had worried us for some time because we had identified self-efficacy as a critical part of becoming a genuine brain-based teacher. In fact, this issue goes right to the core of restructuring and teacher transformation, as we discuss in the next chapter.

At Park View as well, the clash between mental models and perceptual orientations is evident and at the core of differences and system tensions.

13

The Edge of Possibility

But where the dialogue is fulfilled in its being, between partners who have turned to one another in truth, who express themselves without reserve and are free of the desire for semblance, there is brought into being a memorable common fruitfulness which is to be found nowhere else. At such times, at each such time, the word arises in a substantial way between men who have been seized in their depths and opened out by the dynamic of an elemental togetherness.

—Martin Buber, *The Knowledge of Man*

Our original intent in working with Dry Creek and Park View was to assist in restructuring the two schools by applying the theory of brain-based learning. We wanted to build strong communities within which adults could change, and we wanted to change educators' mental models of teaching and learning. We expected teachers to shift their own beliefs about learning and teaching; and we expected these new views to drive changes in their teaching to be compatible with what we had identified as brain-based learning.

To achieve these changes in teaching, we designed process groups:

1. Teachers met at least three times a month for 1½ hours.

2. Teachers read *Making Connections* (Caine and Caine 1991, 1994a), worked with *Mindshifts* (Caine et al. 1994), and reflected on and processed their own understandings. That is, they learned how to learn continuously.

3. Teachers were encouraged to change whatever they wished on the basis of their new understandings.

4. The process groups acted as a powerful learning community, modeling respect and mutual trust.

5. Teachers were asked to see themselves as continuous learners in all facets of their lives.

Teacher Change

In our work with the two schools, we wanted teachers to change from an almost universal belief in an "information-delivery" approach to teaching to one that was flexible, creative, and open to students' search for meaning. We wanted this change to emerge as a consequence of their taking on board a learning theory and a theory of practice grounded in research on learning and the neurosciences. Such teaching means that students would be engaged in purposeful tasks generated primarily by their own interest. At the same time, we expected teachers to continuously "embed" the necessary basic and more sophisticated skills—from correct spelling and grammatical text to critical thinking and scientific inquiry. Ultimately, we wanted teachers to facilitate the acquisition of new, dynamic knowledge in natural "whole" settings. We were looking for a type of teaching that would simulate the world in which this generation will ultimately live—the computer/communications age governed by a new view of science and our universe.

In the process, our own understanding was continually challenged; and our goal changed somewhat. We came to a deeper appreciation of how difficult changing a school in its entirety can be. We also learned that shifting mental models involved a much more extensive perceptual change than we had initially envisioned. The shift to what we had identified as brain-based teaching required teacher transformation in some demanding ways. Therefore, we sought to understand the dynamics of systems, to further understand how mental models manifest themselves in actual behavior, and to grasp what personal changes were needed to shift out of a deeply entrenched way of thinking about learning and teaching. Our goal ultimately focused on understanding and identifying the essentials necessary for system and teacher transformation.

After four years of work with both schools, we believe we were moderately successful in helping teachers move out of an information-delivery approach and become Perceptual Orientations 2 and 3 thinkers.

Dry Creek

At Dry Creek, almost everyone was at Perceptual Orientation 1 when we began, except for the principal, Cindy, and her assistant, Kris. Currently, Perceptual Orientation 1 is still the home of a few teachers; but most are now more or less comfortable within the "zone" of Perceptual Orientation 2. In addition, about five individuals are probably Perceptual Orientation 3 thinkers. They demonstrate higher self-efficacy, have significant capacity to let go of control in the classroom, have significantly expanded their cognitive horizons, and are spontaneously processing information most of the time.

Park View

At Park View, everyone who was in the original group (D-track) began at Perceptual Orientation 1. Of the original group of 14 participants, 6 fell by the wayside over the years, leaving 8 teachers who have been in the program from the beginning. Of these, at least 6 staff members are Perceptual Orientation 3 thinkers.

As evidence of teacher change, we have collected videotaped lessons (including pre- and postbrain-based learning), audio and video interviews, personal remarks made during spontaneous encounters, and discussions over a $3\frac{1}{2}$-year period. We also have received written responses to our research questionnaire. With the exception of one or two teachers, they all say that the entire process is extremely difficult and that the process is continuing. Also, without exception, all participating teachers say that they can never go back. Even though some of them long for the simplicity and predictability of the past, they state that they cannot let go of the expansion of their own creativity and the freedom to explore the edge of possibility with their students. They also agree that they have a common language with each other that is easy and almost intuitive and that this common language does not translate to interactions with most of their other colleagues.

At Park View, not everyone has been able to make learning, not teaching, the primary focus; but a significant number have. Neither do all teachers see learning as a process instead of memorized and surface knowledge. Across the board, however, classrooms are more experiential and more interesting for students. In the classes of Perceptual Orientation 3 teachers, students and teachers exhibit reflection, critical thinking, and taking responsibility. Self-organization is evident and most clearly demonstrated where students spontaneously organize around provocative projects or ideas and where teachers act as facilitators, continually helping students expand and process what they are learning. Discipline problems, as they are commonly referred to, are absent. The emphasis is on creating community. Orderliness and coherence are a natural part of such classrooms, as teachers and students let the tasks and learning drive their behavior. Thus, students know what the basic routines are and how to work in groups, in pairs, individually, or in assembly. The purpose of the activities or tasks also determines what the time schedules are, when to link with sources outside school, and how to find and use appropriate materials and resources.

Following are two observations from students in Renate's Educational Psychology class at California State University, San Bernandino, who visited Park View:

[Observation 1]
My classroom observations at Park View Middle School were extremely important to me. All of the lectures and books in the world would not have communicated brain-based learning as well as those observations. Seeing the way that the teachers interacted with the students and the way that the students responded to the material was impressive. It was clear that quality learning was going on there.

[Observation 2]
From my observation, [the Park View teacher] allowed the students to flow with this project. She consulted on time and gave encouragement to the students, but each student expressed control and a sense of accomplishment. The student I talked to told me that it felt good to work on a project from beginning to end without the teacher. It was their own ideas and group work that gave them the feeling of doing something and doing it right. [The teacher] stayed in the background and shared in the [decision-making process].

From a traditional viewpoint, these classes look frightfully "loose"; yet they are fundamentally compatible with a computer age environment where information can be gathered in an infinite number of ways. In fields as varied as poetry, art, physics, and biology, as well as personal understanding based on communication skills and reflection, students not only learn the newest information about their physical universe, but they also learn about themselves. They gain a strong sense of self-efficacy and identity.

Whole School Change

We would love to be able to say that if schools do all the things that we have suggested, the emergence of a higher-level learning organization is guaranteed. Unfortunately, such change is not the case—and the call for a strategy that can always be replicated is misguided. Process and theory *can* always be introduced, but the workings out are always unique.

Results Can Be Influenced But Not Guaranteed

There are at least three possible consequences for schools that venture into disequilibrium and open themselves to the process that we describe. These consequences occur at what can be called "bifurcation points" (see Figure 13.1 on p. 246). What can be predicted is that there will be many moments of possible transition, moments bathed in uncertainty and ambiguity. Disequilibrium might lead to reverting to traditional practice, disintegration, or evolution:

1. *The process might die out, and the school revert to former practices.* In this scenario, the stable state is just too much to deal with. The burdens imposed by the district, the burnout experienced by those who wish to do more, the resistance of those who are comfortable where they are, and other factors mean that the process as a whole dies on the vine. A school may have pockets of enthusiasm, schools within schools, small "neighborhoods" of students, and teachers that are dynamic enough to be relatively self-sustaining. But as a whole, the school will not be much different several years down the road.

2. *The school might evolve.* In this scenario, a critical mass is reached such that a fundamentally more complex mode of operation emerges. New configurations allow staff to work together in different ways, students to engage in complex projects, time to be organized, assessment and evaluation to be conducted, technology to be infused throughout the system, resources to be allocated, and so on. These configurations usually do not happen in a planned way, but emerge as a consequence of the dramatically changed beliefs and ways that participants interact. The model that we described of Lakeview School in Chapter 3 is one such example. The Creative Learning Plaza that we described in Chapter 2 is a mode of operation planned from the beginning, but the district had to allow its introduction.

3. *The school might disintegrate.* In this scenario, the competing demands, needs, beliefs, and values are so powerful and differences so deeply entrenched that the school will fall apart.

These alternatives are possible for a district, school, subsystems within a school, and individuals. The process and the theory induce and prepare participants and the system for these moments. Capitalizing on and "managing" these bifurcation points are the real mastery of transformation.

FIGURE 13.1
BIFURCATION

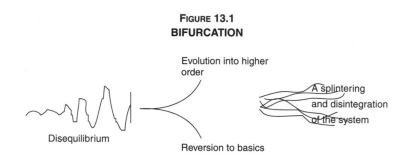

How Can We Assist Schools in Evolving to the New Complex Form?

As strong supporters of public education, we find ourselves caught in what for us is the peculiar belief of supporting the charter school movement. Our reasoning is simple. Many schools have the capacity to transform themselves. However, the larger system is immensely strong and pervasive.

There is a point beyond which a school by itself cannot go. We believe that significant relief from the bureaucratic structure is needed. Schools need to be freed from many constraints to have the opportunity to pool their resources and reconfigure themselves. Teachers and educators need to be free to transform themselves into Perceptual Orientation 3 thinkers. And Perceptual Orientation 3 thinkers need to be free to create learning communities that promote learning compatible with this age of possibility. For this reason, notwithstanding the problems involved, we support the charter school movement in principle.

Problems exist because many parents and members of the community are invested in Perceptual Orientation 1 thinking. That thinking simply will not lead to the emergence of a Perceptual Orientation 3 school. Consequently, as a school moves toward charter school status, we recommend that members of the community be invited to participate in the small process groups, similar to those we advocate for school staff. The crux of the matter is that the fate of the school is decided by prevailing community beliefs about learning and related issues.

The Practice of Facilitating Self-Organization

We believe that some guidelines for practice are emerging. Here, we are in the paradoxical situation of advocating openness of process and yet advocating an approach to process. Nevertheless, every intentional approach to change requires some theory of practice and some rails to run along.

1. Self-Organization Happens

We begin with the idea that complex adaptive systems self-organize as a matter of course. They may, however, assume stable states and resist further change until conditions change. A bureaucracy, for instance, has embodied within it a belief system that reflects mechanistic and hierarchical thinking. Nevertheless, bureaucracies themselves are the products of self-organization around those basic beliefs.

2. To Induce Change, Recognize or Introduce Disequilibrium

The current educational climate has begun to perturb all schools to some extent. The boundaries between the school and the outside world are opening: "Outsiders" can now see into and influence what happens in schools. Education has also lost or is losing control of content, as students, teachers, families, and others go on-line and begin to experience the power of information technology.

These changes are automatically felt, sensed, or recognized in various ways by participants in the systems. They then begin to think about what the changes mean for them. That is, everyone always engages in some type of self-reference. As we discussed in the preceding chapter, there will be varying degrees of awareness and openness, denial and image building. Thus, people will interpret the situation differently. Some will confront change. Some will retreat and seek to barricade themselves. Some will welcome change. Different ways of doing all of the above are possible. All involved, however, will interpret the situation in terms of their deep beliefs and values, their mental models of how the world and education should work.

3. Build Community

The indispensable foundation for facilitating the emergence of a higher-order system is to create a deep sense of community that most members intrinsically value. Creating this sense was the first thrust of our small-group process. As much as possible, we wanted people to be able to function in a nonhierarchical, mutually respectful way. This type of community is important for several reasons:

• People need something to replace the old system and hold on to while the system itself is disturbed. That is, we are capable of creating an alternative center of order, built not on structure but on relationship, while the structure itself is called into question. Evidence of this action is seen in our process groups, where the bonding between people is so tight that the groups seek to preserve themselves.

• The groups are havens of safety, and a feeling of safety is absolutely essential when people are going to be called on to make major changes and take extreme risks. Downshifting is as much a problem for adults as it is for students. The demands and conflicts in the larger community seem to us to be downshifting almost all those involved. The process groups, in our experience, help to neutralize downshifting and create the conditions in which self-efficacy can grow.

• The groups become a way of generating new types of relationships. As Wheatley remarks, "Relationship is all there is" (*Leadership and the New Science* 1993). In schools, most staff members function in a state of semi-isolation, and their connections with each other tend to be extremely limited and at arm's length. Self-organization is optimized when relationships are both real and rich. The process groups are our vehicle for developing the sorts of relationships that facilitate appropriate change.

We should add that it is vital to regularly bring the groups together and to employ in the larger group practices developed in the smaller process groups. When that integration does not occur, a bunker mentality can emerge: The small group is "home," and its members do not identify with the larger community. At Dry Creek, we worked on this integration from the beginning. At Park View, the movement out into the larger community has now become a focus for the D-track teachers.

4. Maintain Self-Reference and Adult Learning—The Energy of Change

Above all else, a learning community is one in which learning is the norm. The dynamism of constant, in-depth learning is the engine of transformation. All our experience confirms that maintaining the self-reflective process is critical. In the process groups, each person publicly discloses personal insights and learnings. In so doing, individuals support others to do the same and find ways to "go deeper" themselves. We are convinced that this community-based, self-reflective process is what begins to generate the "field of learning" that permeates the larger system and that itself is then felt by and influences others.

Every group that "worked" engaged in self-reflection. At Park View, this spirit pervades D-track. At Dry Creek, the spirit was in the early process groups, the groups for new staff members, and the group that formed to study complexity theory itself. It is now returning to the neighborhoods. Business groups that we associated with operated in a similar manner and confirm our impressions.

5. Examine Basic Assumptions, Especially Those About How People Learn

Self-organization takes place around the core values, beliefs, purposes, and meanings that actually drive people. When we engage in self-reference, these core beliefs direct us, even if we have limited awareness of what those beliefs are. Thus, the thrust of self-reference is to examine the appropriate set of core beliefs. This principle guided us from the beginning, and we still hold it dear. Our approach was to use *Mindshifts* (Caine et al. 1994) as a tool for reflecting about learning.

What we learned, and simply did not appreciate for a long time, is that some additional skills need to be acquired for examining one's own assumptions (see Gerard and Teurfs 1995a):

• *Active listening and constructive questioning.* The art, here, is to pay full attention to what is being said without investing in anything other than eliciting what a person really means. Through active listening, people gain a sensitivity to inappropriate pushing and probing, so that no one feels obliged to debate or disclose what is considered personal and private. People develop a heightened awareness of the time and patience needed for the many layers of meaning—embedded in what someone says—to surface. Such articulation becomes immensely valuable.

• *Reflectiveness and self-reference.* The key to testing your own assumptions is the ability to listen to yourself. As Isaacs (1993) says, "Listen to the listener." This ability includes being aware of the nature of your responses to what others are saying and being aware of what drives your responses. What people find is that a realm of unconscious processing is present. Most of us are not aware of it, and yet the unconscious processing can be quite emotional.

• *Communication without investing in a specific response.* To genuinely communicate with people who have different opinions, and to be able to learn from them as well as assist them in learning from us, we need to communicate effectively without advocacy. That is, we need to be open to a range of possible responses, including acceptance or rejection of our opinions and indifference to our opinions. This type of communication is sometimes characterized as putting what one needs to say "on the table" or "in the center of the group" as a contribution.

• *Conflict resolution.* Most organizations avoid confrontation and healthy discussions that bring conflict out into the open. Yet how can we communicate at any other than superficial levels if we do not know how to deal with conflict? Authenticity, one of the characteristics of Perceptual Orientation 3 thinkers, is compromised.

In some respects, in our work with the two schools, we did not pay enough attention to these skills; nor did we employ them adequately in the early stages of our work. For example, in the dispute at Dry Creek about the nature of discipline, one key (in retrospect) would have been to inquire as to the assumptions about learning, downshifting, and relationships that fueled the different opinions. It is not enough to hold and express opinions, no matter how strong. The key is to examine the cement that binds our opinions to us. When we do that over time, and in a safe space, we begin to engage in the type of learning that allows mental models to change. At that point, new core beliefs emerge, around which the system can self-organize.

The exploration of fundamental assumptions is also at the heart of the real identity, the real purpose, and the real vision of the school. When we process at deeper levels, a genuine sense of identity can begin to emerge, which then serves to fuel and focus ongoing self-organization.

6. Upper-Level Management and Decision Makers Must Participate

Our experiences suggest that upper-level management's total participation in the change process is absolutely critical for change to be real. It does not matter how aware they are. They *must* be active participants in the group process. They must not only work on their own assumptions, but others must *see* them doing this work. Our work with business groups was illuminating in this regard. Employees who become Perceptual Orientation 3 thinkers are more empowered and want to make broader decisions—at which point the power, hierarchy, and paternalism of the system become perturbed. At the onset of the Information Age, technological access, and the work of process groups, the mystique surrounding those higher on the ladder becomes "thin" and is open to challenge. As Senge, Wheatley, and others strongly suggest, managers and executives need to become comfortable with multiple roles—sometimes leading, sometimes following.

The practical implication for schools is that the principal should be an active participant if the school as a whole is to change. It is much easier to build smaller Perceptual Orientation 3 thinking communities (such as D-track) than it is to change an entire school.

7. For an Entire School to Change, a Majority of the Staff Must Be Willing Participants

There are two elements to this conclusion. First, those who participate must be volunteers. We have found, to our cost and dismay, that when people are "induced" to participate, the process is undermined. Some nonvolunteers express anger, others camouflage their feelings, and others sabotage the process. At the same time, the volunteers do not feel safe and become unwilling to deal with issues in depth. Those in the process groups must *choose* to be there.

In addition, a majority of staff need to be on board and actively involved. Extensive work has to be done from the beginning so that if a school embarks on a self-referential process, it has chosen to do so as a whole and because there is something at stake that most members feel is important.

8. There Is a Way to Begin

In a school where change is both desired and feared, one way to begin is with an experimental "arm" at the school. Our work in D-track at Park View is an example. We suggest that a group of teachers who wish to explore a new approach work together as a unit, with every grade level in the school represented. Parents who wish to have their children participate would be sought as well. In effect, this "arm" might resemble a charter school within the larger school. We see this group as a living laboratory, from which all learn, and which can be extended to the larger school as understanding and support grow.

Impressions of the Future

One aspect of the future is certain: The information explosion in the neurosciences informing our understanding of learning and teaching—and the technology expansion—will not stop. The genie will not go back into the bottle. We cannot stop the increase in social disequilibrium, nor can education be shielded from it.

Societal Trends

Our impression is that society as a whole has become extremely volatile and is poised directly on the edge of chaos—and possibility. Education is being pulled into the turbulence. As that happens, our further impression is that a bifurcation point is emerging—a bifurcation based on the pull of competing beliefs and desires (see Figure 13.1). We see at least three general tendencies that will also play themselves out in the future of education:

• Among many communities and schools, people are clearly expressing a strong yearning for the security and assurance of yester year. This longing seems to be one of the values that undergirds the "back-to-basics" movement. The intense protest about the lack of basic skills in many of the students who graduate from high school is accompanied by a desire for more courtesy and a respect of a traditional notion of family, and a need for controlling the process of education and socialization. Thus, some values that we endorse (such as courtesy and competence) are sought by relying on the power of the system, fragmentation of the curriculum, tight control, and the virtual elimination of process. These activities are characteristic of a Perceptual Orientation 1 approach to education, an approach that has powerful supporters and promoters in many quarters.

• Much of the mainstream work in restructuring seems to be moving toward more dynamic teaching and learning. Cooperative learning, thematic instruction, community involvement, authentic assessment, the FOSS "designed experience" materials, and other developments seem to us to endorse richer student experience. However, these areas tend to still be embedded in a hierarchical system emphasizing control, site based or community based though it may be. Thus, much current change is grounded in Perceptual Orientation 2.

• Many schools and communities, on the other hand, are experiencing great waves of change. These societal changes—and upheavals—affect schools *whether we like it or not*. Changes in technology, entertainment, flow of information, reconfiguration of basic institutions, and a host of other developments are leading to the emergence of many modes of communication and information transfer, and therefore, to many possible modes of education. Examples include different sorts of apprenticeships; schools and colleges as marketplaces; distance education; self-paced, computer-based instruction; interactive international projects; and the proliferation of home schooling and other alternative education arrangements. The possibilities that we describe here tend to be associated with empowerment rather than power, self-organization rather than control, interconnectedness rather than fragmentation, and reflection and metacognition rather than a focus on planning. In our terms, an education system grounded in Perceptual Orientation 3 is emerging, irrespective of the resistance that it meets.

These strands interact. Thus, in its spread, home schooling is a major new player on the scene. Home schooling is part of the system disruption, yet it is often an expression of a back-to-basics philosophy.

Communicating with the Fractal Public

The strands and patterns that we describe have a fractal quality. Hints of bifurcation are everywhere. They can be found within individual schools. They can be found between schools within single districts. They can be found within local communities. They can be found in the business community. They can be found at governmental levels.

Many politicians, parents, administrators, teachers, people in business, and others have deeply internalized Perceptual Orientation 1 thinking and the instructional approach that accompanies it. Moreover, many members of the public see themselves as experts in teaching and learning, based on Instructional Approach 1, and judge all teaching and school through those lenses.

As a result of this societal orientation, many current educational reforms, such as the use of FOSS science materials, Math 2000, Math Renaissance, authentic assessment, and other programs characteristic of Instructional Approach 2, are tantamount to the "New Math" of the '60s for many people. Parents often do not understand why such programs are better than what they had in school. Even if they did poorly in school, these parents believe in the system. One reason why outcome-based education is looked at suspiciously is that the old predictables of traditional tests and teacher- and text-based knowledge are not a critical part; and an emphasis on "outcomes" does not resonate with public memories of their own school days.

Teaching approaches based on constructivism, engaging multiple intelligences, and honoring different learning styles and apprenticeships can strike Perceptual Orientation 1 thinkers as even more "soft," unfocused, and unrelated to passing tests and getting high grades.

At the same time, many developments in technology, corporate consulting, and business are essentially based on Perceptual Orientation 3 thinking. Thus, a significant and growing element of the public is willing and able to conceive of education in terms of Perceptual Orientation 3; these people and groups are willing and able to both supplement and compete with the traditional system.

In a climate with such opposing forces, communication with members of the public is difficult; but we have some suggestions. First, brain-based learning places much emphasis on the quality of the community. We have a saying: "Community is everything." We need to involve and include as many people as are willing and able. Our society is already too downshifted. Building trust and relationships is therefore critical.

Second, knowing about both the instructional approaches and the perceptual orientations has helped enormously as we work with the public. There is a danger, however: Just identifying the different approaches and orientations can lead to judgmental labeling and contribute to more blaming, categorization, and attempts to impose control. The information and differences with which we are dealing must be dealt with collaboratively and through mutual exploration.

Third, if we want parents and the community to endorse Perceptual Orientation 3 thinking and teaching, then we will need to do more than talk to them—we will have to *show* them and give them direct experiences. One way is to have parents and the community experience sophisticated interactive software. Adults seeing a program like Dinosaur (from Microsoft), Red Shift—Multimedia Astronomy (from Maris Multimedia Limited, England), or Who Built America? (from The Voyager Co., New York) can become instant converts. Parents can see how children of the future—and right now—can have access to knowledge and information their generation didn't dream of. Already, technology can provide students with learning that makes the information-delivery kind of teaching look desperately outmoded. At the least, they might understand the challenges educators are grappling with, why or how teachers are needed, or when teachers have to get out of the way.

Fourth, we are comforted by sophisticated attempts at local and international levels. An example on the local level is Jamie Vollmer's Local Control Project (see Bibliography for address). This project is an intensive grassroots effort throughout Iowa and elsewhere to communicate about new needs and approaches to education by working with large numbers of service and church organizations. An example at the international level is spearheaded by John Abbott (1994), head of Education 2000 in the United Kingdom. Abbott is working on an extremely ambitious program called the "21st Century Learning Initiative," now located in Washington, D.C. With the sponsorship of organizations such as the Johnson Foundation, he is bringing together leading synthesizers and practitioners in educational change and related fields from around the world. According to Abbott (personal communication, Oct. 1966),

> The 21st Century Learning Initiative's essential purpose is to facilitate the emergence of new approaches to learning that draw upon a range of insights into the human brain, the functioning of human societies, and learning as a self-organizing activity. We believe that this will release human potential in ways which nurture and form democratic communities worldwide, and will help reclaim and sustain a world supportive of human endeavor.

The Spirit of Democracy

In a time of volatility and disequilibrium, the system will self-organize around the prevailing core values and beliefs. Change will occur. It will be substantial. And the education system will coevolve with the larger context within which it interacts. Our challenge is to identify a set of beliefs that are sufficiently broad to allow for unity and diversity. At the risk of being trite, we believe these beliefs embody the spirit of democracy:

> The music comes from something we cannot direct, from a unified whole created among the players—a relationship holism that transcends separateness. In the end, when it works, we sit back, amazed and grateful (Wheatley 1992, p. 87).

We need to work together and to respect each other. We know that to do otherwise, to attempt to impose control on the dynamic processes that are taking place, will lead to consequences both unpredictable and unsettling. Transformation cannot be imposed. Nor, in times of turbulence, can it be prevented.

Ultimately, however, our own preference is for Perceptual Orientation 3 thinking to prevail. We believe that education should emphasize the joy and enchantment that are intrinsic to human growth and the experience of relationship. A point is reached when separating personal growth from professional lives is dysfunctional. There is a connection between who we are as persons and who we are as learners and educators. We further believe that the focus on growth and fulfillment will lead to the substantially improved educational practice and higher standards being called for. Our own practical thrust (see *The Reenchantment of Learning*, Crowell, Caine, and Caine, in press) continues to be the reciprocal professional and personal development of the person. We will continue to work for the emergence of Perceptual Orientation 3 thinkers and systems. Such work means, for instance, that we need to assume that every person is significantly more intelligent than we initially think. It also means that we need to assume that everything, without exception, is connected to everything else in more ways than we can currently conceive of.

Unity and Diversity

We welcome the diversity and dynamism of current change, though we strongly regret the confrontational nature of much of the discourse. The direction that education takes depends ultimately on the set of values and compelling beliefs that prevail. Thus, what we end up with depends as much on how all of us conceive and reconceive ourselves as it does on what we ask others to do.

Ideally, we need a set of common and compelling ideas, meanings, and purposes within which the different orientations can flourish. The basic shift can be described quite simply. At the core of the traditional system is a set of beliefs that can be expressed as follows:

Only experts create knowledge.

Teachers deliver knowledge in the form of information.

Children are graded on how much of the information they have stored.

We suggest that the changes needed to radically improve education will emerge naturally once the larger community begins to subscribe to a different set of beliefs. Thus, we invite educators and the public to take seriously the following:

Dynamical knowledge requires individual meaning making based on multiple sources of information.

The role of educators is to facilitate the making of dynamical knowledge.

Dynamical knowledge is revealed through real-world performance.

Bibliography

Abbott, J. (1994). *Learning Makes Sense*. Hertfordshire, United Kingdom: Education 2000.

Abraham, F.D., and A.R. Gilgen, eds. (1995). *Chaos Theory in Psychology*. Westport, Conn.: Praeger.

Agnati, L.F., B. Bjelke, and K. Fute. (July 1992). "Volume Transmission in the Brain." *American Scientist* 80: 362–373.

Aguayo, R. (1990). *Dr. Deming: The American Who Taught the Japanese About Quality*. New York: Simon and Schuster.

Alexander, C.N., and E.J. Langer, eds. (1990). *Higher State of Human Development*. New York: Oxford University Press.

Allen, P.M. (1993). *Nonlinear Dynamics and Evolutionary Economics*, edited by R.H. Day and P.E. Chen. New York: Oxford University Press. Allman, W.F. (1994). *The Stone Age Present*. New York: Touchstone.

Amabile, T. (1983). *The Social Psychology of Creativity*. New York: Springer-Verlag.

Anderson, C.W., and E.L. Smith. (May 1985). "Teaching Science." In *The Educators' Handbook: A Research Perspective*, edited by V.E. Koehler. New York: Longman, Inc.

Apple, M.W.E., and J.A. Beane, eds. (1995). *Democratic Schools*. Alexandria, Va.: ASCD.

Armstrong, T. (1994). *Multiple Intelligences in the Classroom*. Alexandria, Va.: ASCD.

Aron, E., and A. Aron. (1986). *The Maharishi Effect: A Revolution Through Meditation*. Walpole, N.H.: Stillpoint Publishing.

Arthur, W.B. (1994). Keynote presentation at 4th Annual Chaos Network Conference, Denver, Colorado.

Ashton, P.T., and R.B. Webb. (1986). *Making a Difference: Teachers' Sense of Efficacy and Student Achievement*. New York: Longman, Inc.

Bandura, A. (April 20, 1992). "Self-Efficacy Mechanism in Sociocognitive Functioning." Presentation at the annual meeting of the American Educational Research Association, San Francisco.

Barnhart, C.L., and R.K. Barnhart, eds. (1979). *World Book Dictionary*. Chicago: World Book—Childcraft International.

Battistich, V., D. Solomon, M. Watson, and E. Schaps. (1994). "Students and Teachers in Caring Classroom and School Communities." Paper presented at the annual meeting of the American Educational Research Association, New Orleans.

Becker, E. (1968). *The Structure of Evil*. New York: The Free Press.

Begley, S. (February 19, 1996). "Your Child's Brain: How Kids Are Wired for Music, Math, and Emotions." *Newsweek*, pp. 57–61.

Benson, G.D., and W.J. Hunter. (December 1992). "Chaos Theory: No Strange Attractor in Teacher Education." *Action in Teacher Education* 14, 4: 61–67.

Blair, B.G., and R.N. Caine, eds. (1995). *Integrative Learning as the Pathway to Teaching Holism, Complexity, and Interconnectedness.* Lewiston, N.Y.: The Edwin Mellen Press.

Blair, J., and P. Konley. (April 22, 1995). "Something So Right at One Public School." *Los Angeles Times*, p. 87.

Boettcher, W.S., S.S. Hahn, and G.L. Shaw. (1994). "Mathematics and Music: A Search for Insight into Higher Brain Function." *Leonardo Music Journal* 4: 53–58.

Bohm, D. (November 6, 1989). "On Dialogue: Meeting of November 6, 1989" (booklet). Ojai, Calif.: David Bohm Seminars.

Bonstingl, J.J. (1992). *Schools of Quality: An Introduction to Total Quality Management in Education* (rev. ed. 1996). Alexandria, Va.: ASCD.

Bopp, J., M. Bobb, L. Brown, and P. Lane. (1984). *The Sacred Tree: Reflections on Native American Spirituality.* Lethbridge, Alberta, Canada: Four Worlds Development Press.

Bower, B. (1995). "Images of Intellect: Brain Scans May Colorize Intelligence." *Science News* 146: 236.

Boychuk, B. (December 22, 1995). "There's No Such Thing as a Free Federal Program." *Los Angeles Times*, p. B9.

Brauth, S.E., W.S. Hall, and R.J. Dooling, eds. (1991). *Plasticity of Development.* Cambridge, Mass.: The MIT Press.

Briggs, J.P., and F.D. Peat. (1985). *Looking Glass Universe: The Emerging Science of Wholeness.* Great Britain: Fontana Paperbacks.

Briggs, J., and F.D. Peat. (1989). *Turbulent Mirror: An Illustrated Guide to Chaos Theory and the Science of Wholeness.* New York: Harper and Row.

Brown, J.L., and E. Pollitt. (February 1996). "Malnutrition, Poverty, and Intellectual Development." *Scientific American* 274, 2: 38.

Caine, R.N., and G. Caine. (1991). *Making Connections: Teaching and the Human Brain.* Alexandria, Va.: ASCD.

Caine, R.N., and G. Caine. (1994a). *Making Connections: Teaching and the Human Brain* (rev. ed.). Menlo Park, Calif.: Addison-Wesley Publishing Company.

Caine, R.N., and G. Caine. (April 1994b). "Patterns of Wholeness: Can Complexity and Systems Theory Help Us Understand Restructuring of Schools?" Paper presented at the annual conference of the American Educational Research Association, New Orleans.

Caine, R.N., and G. Caine. (April 1995). "Reinventing Schools Through Brain-Based Learning." *Educational Leadership* 52, 7: 43.

Caine, G., R.N. Caine, and S. Crowell. (1994). *Mindshifts: A Brain-Based Process for Restructuring Schools and Renewing Education.* Tucson, Ariz.: Zephyr Press.

Calvin, W.H., and G.A. Ojemann. (1994). *Conversations with Neil's Brain: The Neural Nature of Thought and Language.* Reading, Mass.: Addison-Wesley Publishing Company.

Campbell, S. (1995). "A Sense of the Whole: The Essence of Community." In *Community Building: Renewing Spirit and Learning in Business*, edited by K. Gozdz. San Francisco, Calif.: New Leaders Press.

Cannon, A. (February 4, 1996). "The Mood of America." *Austin American-Statesman*, pp. D1–D5.

Capra, F. (1966). *The Web of Life.* New York: Anchor Books.

Capra, F. (1988). *The Turning Point: Science, Society, and the Rising Culture.* New York: Simon and Schuster.

Capra, F. (February 1995). *From the Parts to the Whole: Systems Thinking in Ecology and Education.* The Professional Development Briefs: Fourth Annual Colloquium, Burlingame, Calif.: California Staff Development Council (CSDC).

Capra, F. (March 1995). "Creating Community Through Ecoliteracy: An Ecological Model for School Innovation and Reform." Paper presented at the annual conference of the Association for Supervision and Curriculum Development, San Francisco.

Carr, C. (1994). *The Competitive Power of Constant Creativity.* New York: American Management Association.

Casey, K. (1995). "The New Narrative Research in Education." In *Review of Research in Education,* edited by M.W. Apple. Washington, D.C.: American Educational Research Association.

Chalmers, D.J. (December 1995). "The Puzzle of Conscious Experience." *Scientific American* 273, 6: 80–86.

Chapman, G. (January 11, 1996). "'Friction-Free' Economy Rhetoric Holds a Time Bomb." *Los Angeles Times,* p. D2.

Chapman, G. (February 22, 1996). "Jumping On—and Off—the Technology Bandwagon." *Los Angeles Times,* pp. D2–D5.

Churchland, P.S. (1986). *Neurophilosophy: Toward a Unified Science of the Mind/Brain.* Cambridge, Mass.: The MIT Press.

Cleveland, J., J. Neuroth, and S. Marshall. (November 1995). *Learning on the Edge of Chaos: Complex Adaptive Systems Theory and Human Learning, First Draft.* Lansing, Mich.: On Purpose Associates.

Clifford, P., and S.L. Friesen. (September 1993). "Teaching and Practice: A Curious Plan." *Harvard Educational Review* 63, 3: 339–358.

Cochran-Smith, M., and S.L. Lytle. (March 1990). "Research on Teaching and Teacher Research: The Issues That Divide." *Educational Researcher* 19, 2: 2–9.

Collier, G. (1973). *Inside Jazz.* London: Quartet Books.

Colvin, R.L. (May 5, 1995). "Teachers Speak out in Favor of Reading Aloud." *Los Angeles Times,* p. 3.

Colvin, R.L. (December 8, 1995). "Eastin's School Reform Plan Scaled Back." *Los Angeles Times,* pp. A1–A40.

Combs, A.W. (1991). *The Schools We Need: New Assumptions for Educational Reform.* Lanham, Md.: University Press of America.

Combs, A.W., R. Blume, A. Newman, and H. Wass. (1974). *The Professional Education of Teachers.* 2nd ed. Boston: Allyn and Bacon.

Combs, A.W., A.C. Richards, and F. Richards. (1988). *Perceptual Psychology.* Lanham, Md.: University Press of America.

Combs, A.W., and D. Snygg. (1959). *Individual Behavior. A Perceptual Approach to Behavior.* New York: Harper and Row.

Crowell, S. (1989). "A New Way of Thinking: The Challenge of the Future." *Educational Leadership* 47, 1: 60.

Crowell, S., G. Caine, and R.N. Caine. (in press). *The Reenchantment of Learning.* Tucson, Ariz.: Zephyr Press.

Csikszentmihalyi, M. (1990). *Flow: The Psychology of Optimal Experience.* New York: Harper Perennial.

Csikszentmihalyi, M. (1993). *The Evolving Self: A Psychology for the Third Millennium.* New York: HarperCollins.

Curwin, R.L., and A.N. Mendler. (1988). *Discipline with Dignity.* Alexandria, Va.: ASCD.

Damasio, A.R. (1994). *Descartes' Error: Emotion, Reason, and the Human Brain.* New York: Avon Books.

Darling, D.J. (1996). *Zen Physics: The Sense of Death, the Logic of Reincarnation.* New York: HarperCollins.

Darling-Hammond, L.E., ed. (1994). *Review of Research in Education.* Washington, D.C.: American Educational Research Association.

Day, R.H., and P.E. Chen. (1993). *Nonlinear Dynamics and Evolutionary Economics.* New York: Oxford University Press.

DeAngelis, T. (September 1995). "A Nation of Hermits: The Loss of Community." *The APA Monitor* 26, 9: 1.

De Bono, E. (1970). *Lateral Thinking.* New York: Harper and Row. DeChardin, P.T. (1976). *The Heart of Matter.* New York: Harcourt Brace Jovanovich.

Deci, E.L., R.E. Driver, L. Hotchkiss, R.J. Robbins, and I.M Wilson. (1993). "The Relation of Mothers' Controlling Vocalizations to Children's Intrinsic Motivation." *Journal of Experimental Child Psychology* 55, 2: 151–162.

Deci, E.L., and R.M. Ryan. (1987). "The Support of Autonomy and the Control of Behavior." *Journal of Personality and Social Psychology* 53, 6: 1024–1037.

Deci, E.L., A.J. Schwartz, L. Sheinman, and R.M. Ryan. (1981). "An Instrument to Assess Adults' Orientations Toward Control Versus Autonomy with Children: Reflections on Intrinsic Motivation and Perceived Competence." *Journal of Educational Psychology* 73, 5: 642–650.

Deci, E.L., W.H. Spiegel, R.M. Ryan, R. Koestner, and M. Kauffman. (1982). "Effects of Performance Standards on Teaching Styles: Behavior of Controlling Teachers." *Journal of Educational Psychology* 74, 6: 852–859.

Del Prete, T. (1990). *Thomas Merton and the Education of the Whole Person.* Birmingham, Ala.: Religious Education Press.

Dennett, D.C. (1991). *Consciousness Explained.* Boston: Little, Brown and Company.

Dewey, J. (1938). *Experience and Education.* New York: Collier Books.

Dewey, J. (1944). *Democracy and Education.* New York: The Free Press.

Dewey, J. (1962). *Reconstruction in Philosophy.* Boston: The Beacon Press.

Diamond, M.C. (1988). *Enriching Heredity: The Impact of the Environment on the Anatomy of the Brain.* New York: The Free Press.

Dienstbier, R.A. (January 1989). "Arousal and Physiological Toughness: Implications for Mental and Physical Health." *Psychological Review* 96, 1: 84–100.

Dolan, W.P. (1994). *Restructuring Our Schools: A Primer on Systemic Change.* Kansas City: Systems and Organizations.

Dole, J.A., and G.M. Sinatra. (April 1994). "Beliefs and Conceptual Change: Research in Social and Cognitive Psychology." Paper presented at the annual meeting of the American Educational Research Association, New Orleans.

Doll, W.E. (1993). "A Post-Modern Perspective on Curriculum." *Advances in Contemporary Educational Thought.* New York, Teachers College, Columbia University.

Doll, W.E. (1995). "Ghosts and the American Curriculum: Search for a Neopragmatic Cosmology." Unpublished paper for Eidos Institute, St. Petersburg, Russia.

Driscoll, M.E. (April 1994). "School Community and Teacher's Work in Urban Settings: Identifying Challenges to Community in the School Organization." Paper presented at the annual meeting of the American Educational Research Association, New Orleans. (Available from New York University).

Dryfoos, J.G. (1994). *Full-Service Schools: A Revolution in Health and Social Services for Children, Youth, and Families*. San Francisco: Jossey-Bass.

Duffy, T.M., and D.H. Jonassen, eds. (1992). *Constructivism and the Technology of Instruction: A Conversation*. Hillsdale, N.J.: Lawrence Erlbaum.

Eccles, J.C. (1989). *Evolution of the Brain: Creation of the Self*. London: Routledge.

Eccles, J.C. (1994). *How the Self Controls Its Brain*. Berlin: Springer-Verlag.

Edelman, G.M. (1992). *Bright Air, Brilliant Fire: On the Matter of the Mind*. New York: Basic Books.

Egan, K. (1989). *Teaching as Story Telling: An Alternative Approach to Teaching and Curriculum in the Elementary School*. Chicago: University of Chicago Press.

Egol, M. (1994). *Information Age Accounting: Catalyst and Enabler of the Self-Organizing Enterprise*. New York: Arthur Anderson.

Eisler, R. (1987). *The Chalice and The Blade*. San Francisco: Harper and Row.

Ekman, P., and R.J. Davidson, eds. (1994). *The Nature of Emotion: Fundamental Questions*. New York: Oxford University Press.

Elbow, P. (1986). *Embracing Contraries: Explorations in Learning and Teaching*. New York: Oxford University Press.

Elmore, R.F. (December 1995). "Structural Reform and Educational Practice." *Educational Researcher* 24, 9: 23–26.

Fadiman, D. (1988). *Why Do These Kids Love School?* (videotape). Menlo Park, Calif.: Concentric Media.

Fellmeth, R.C. (July 5, 1995). "California: A Society That Cuts Child Welfare but Boosts Jails." *Los Angeles Times*, p. B7.

Fernlund, P.M. (1995). "Teaching for Conceptual Change." In *Integrative Learning as the Pathway to Teaching Holism, Complexity, and Interconnectedness*, edited by B.G. Blair and R.N. Caine. Lewiston, N.Y.: The Edwin Mellen Press.

Fiske, E.B. (1992). *Smart Schools, Smart Kids: Why Do Some Schools Work?* New York: Simon and Schuster.

Flanigan, J. (January 10, 1996). "With Its New Lab, Caltech Has a Formula to Survive Uncertainty." *Los Angeles Times*, pp. D1–D11.

Flores, B.E., E. Garcia, S. Gonzales, G. Hidalgo, K. Kaczmarek, and T. Romero. (1986). *Holistic Bilingual Instructional Strategies*. Phoenix, Ariz.: Exito.

Flores, B., P.T. Cousin, and E. Diaz. (1991). "Transforming Deficit Myths About Language, Literacy, and Culture." *Language Arts* 68, 5: 369–379.

Fogarty, R.E., ed. (1993). *Integrating the Curricula: A Collection*. Palatine, Ill.: IRI/Skylight Publishing, Inc.

Francis, D. (1995). *Wild Horses*. New York: Jove Books.

Freeman, W.J. (1995a). "The Kiss of Chaos and the Sleeping Beauty of Psychology." In *Chaos Theory in Psychology*, edited by F.D. Abraham and A.R. Gilgen. Westport, Conn.: Praeger.

Freeman, W.J. (1995b). *Societies of Brains: A Study in the Neuroscience of Love and Hate*. Hillsdale, N.J.: Lawrence Erlbaum.

Fullan, M.G., and S. Stiegelbauer. (1991). *The New Meaning of Educational Change*. New York: Teachers College Press.

Gablik, S. (1991). *The Reenchantment of Art*. London: Thames and Hudson.

Gardner, H. (1985). *Frames of Mind: The Theory of Multiple Intelligences* (rev. ed. 1993). New York: Basic Books.

Gardner, H. (1991). *The Unschooled Mind: How Children Think and How Schools Should Teach*. New York: Basic Books.

Gardner, H. (1993). *Multiple Intelligences: The Theory in Practice*. New York: Basic Books.

Garmston, R., and B. Wellman. (April 1995). "Adaptive Schools in a Quantum Universe." *Educational Leadership* 52, 7: 6.

Gates, W.H. (1995). *The Road Ahead.* New York: Viking.

Gateva, E. (1991). *Creating Wholeness Through Art.* Aylesbury, Bucks, United Kingdom: Accelerated Learning Systems, Ltd.

Gazzaniga, M. (1985). *The Social Brain: Discovering the Networks of the Mind.* New York: Basic Books.

Gazzaniga, M. (1992). *Nature's Mind: The Biological Roots of Thinking, Emotions, Sexuality, Language, and Intelligence.* New York: Basic Books.

Gell-Man, M. (1994). *The Quark and the Jaguar.* New York: W.H. Freeman and Company.

Gendlin, E.T. (1962). *Experiencing and the Creation of Meaning.* Glencoe, Calif.: The Free Press of Glencoe.

Gendlin, E.T. (1981). *Focusing.* 2nd ed. New York: Bantam Books.

Gerard, G., and L. Teurfs. (1995a). *The Art and Practice of Dialogue* (audiotape series). California: The Dialogue Group.

Gerard, G., and L. Teurfs. (1995b). "Dialogue and the Learning Organization." Paper presented at Session M20 of the National Conference of the American Society for Training and Development, Dallas.

Gilovich, T. (1991). *How We Know What Isn't So: The Fallibility of Human Reason in Everyday Life.* New York: The Free Press.

Glatthorn, A.A. (1994). *Developing a Quality Curriculum.* Alexandria, Va.: ASCD.

Goerner, S.J. (1994). *Chaos and the Evolving Ecological Universe.* Langhorne, Pa.: Gordon and Breach Science Publishers.

Goerner, S.J. (1995). "Chaos and Deep Ecology." In *Chaos Theory in Psychology,* edited by F.D. Abraham and A.R. Gilgen. Westport, Conn.: Praeger.

Goguen, J.A., and R.K. Forman, eds. (1994). "Journal of Consciousness: Controversies in Science and the Humanities." *An International Multi-Disciplinary Journal,* Vol. 1, UK and USA: Imprint Academic.

Goleman, D. (1995). *Emotional Intelligence: Why It Can Matter More Than IQ.* New York: Bantam Books.

Goodlad, J.I. (1984). *A Place Called School: Prospects for the Future.* San Francisco: McGraw-Hill.

Goodlad, J.I. (1990). *Teachers for Our Nation's Schools.* San Francisco: Jossey-Bass.

Goodlad, J.I., R. Soder, and K.A. Sirotnik, eds. (1990). *The Moral Dimensions of Teaching.* San Francisco: Jossey-Bass.

Goodman, K. (1986). *What's Whole in Whole Language?* Portsmouth, N.H.: Heinemann.

Goodman, K., and Y. Goodman. (1979). "Learning to Read Is Natural." In *Theory and Practice of Early Reading,* edited by L. Resnick and P. Weaver. Hillsdale, N.J.: Lawrence Erlbaum.

Gozdz, K., ed. (1995). *Community Building: Renewing Spirit and Learning in Business.* San Francisco: New Leaders Press.

Gruneberg, M.M., and P.E. Morris. (1979). *Applied Problems in Memory.* London: Academic Press.

Hanh, T.N. (1976). *The Miracle of Mindfulness!: A Manual on Meditation.* Boston: Beacon Press.

Harman, W. (1988). *Global Mind Change: The Promise of the Last Years of the Twentieth Century.* Indianapolis: Knowledge Systems, Inc.

Harman, W. (September 1992). "The Shifting World View: Toward a More Holistic Science." *Holistic Education Review* 5, 3: 16-17.

Harste, J.C. (1989). *New Policy Guidelines for Reading: Connecting Research and Practice.* Urbana, Ill.: National Council of Teachers of English and the ERIC Clearinghouse on Reading and Communication Skills.

Hart, L. (1983). *Human Brain, Human Learning.* New York: Basic Books.

Herrnstein, R.J., and C. Murray. (1994). *The Bell Curve: Intelligence and Class Structure in American Life.* New York: The Free Press.

History-Social Science Curriculum Framework and Criteria Committee. (1987). *History-Social Science Framework.* Sacramento: California State Department of Education.

Hobson, J.A. (1994). *The Chemistry of Conscious States: How the Brain Changes Its Mind.* Boston: Little, Brown and Company.

Hooper, J., and D. Teresi. (1986). *The 3-Pound Universe.* New York: Dell Publishing Company.

Houston, J. (1982). *The Possible Human: A Course in Enhancing Your Physical, Mental, and Creative Abilities.* Los Angeles: J.P. Tarcher, Inc.

Houston, R.W. (1986). *Mirrors of Excellence: Reflections for Teacher Education from Training Programs in Ten Corporations and Agencies.* Reston, Va.: Association of Teacher Educators.

Hyman, R., and B. Rosoff. (1984). "Matching Learning and Teaching Styles: The Jug and What's In It." *Theory into Practice* 23, 1: 35–43.

Isaacs, W.N. (1993). "Taking Flight: Dialogue, Collective Thinking, and Organizational Learning." *Organization Systems* 22: 24–39.

It's Elementary. (1992). Elementary Grades Task Force Report. Sacramento, Calif.: California Department of Education.

Jacobs, H.H., and L. Nadel. (1985). "Stress-Induced Recovery of Fears and Phobias." *Psychological Review* 92, 4: 512–531.

Johnson, P.H. (November 22, 1995). "High School Students Mount Global Bid to Design Space Shuttle Pit Stop." *Los Angeles Times*, p. 4.

Jones, B.F., A.S. Palinscsar, D.S. Ogle, and E.G. Carr, eds. (1987). *Strategic Teaching and Learning: Cognitive Instruction in the Content Areas.* Alexandria, Va.: ASCD.

Journal of Consciousness Studies. Thorverton, United Kingdom: Imprint Academic.

Kaplan, P. (April 8, 1996). "School's out—CD ROM's in." *Los Angeles Times*, p. D9.

Kauffman, D.L. (1980). *Systems 1: An Introduction to Systems Thinking.* Minneapolis, Minn.: S.A. Carlton.

Kauffman, S.A. (August 1991). "Antichaos and Adaptation." *Scientific American* 265, 2: 78–84.

Kauffman, S. (1995). *At Home in the Universe: The Search for the Laws of Self-Organization and Complexity.* New York: Oxford University Press.

Keidel, R.W. (1995). *Seeing Organizational Patterns.* San Francisco: Berrett-Koehler.

Kelso, J.A. (1995). *Dynamic Patterns: The Self-Organization of Brain and Behaviour.* Cambridge, Mass.: The MIT Press.

Kierstead, F., J. Bowman, and C. Dede, eds. (1979). *Education Futures: Sourcebook 1. Selections from the First Conference of the Education Section World Future Society.* Washington, D.C.: World Future Society.

Koehler, V., ed. (1985). *The Educator's Handbook: A Research Perspective.* New York: Longman, Inc.

Kofman, F., and P.M. Senge. (1993). "Communities of Commitment: The Heart of Learning Organizations." *American Management Association*, pp. 5–20.

Kohlberg, L. (1981). *The Philosophy of Moral Development.* New York: Harper and Row.

Kohn, A. (1990). *The Brighter Side of Human Nature: Altruism and Empathy in Everyday Life*. New York: Basic Books.

Kohn, A. (1993). *Punished by Rewards: The Trouble with Gold Stars, Incentive Plans, A's, Praise, and Other Bribes*. New York: Houghton Mifflin.

Kotulak, R. (April 11, 1993). "Research Unraveling Mysteries of the Brain: Unlocking the Mind." *Chicago Tribune*, p. 1.

Lakoff, G., and M. Johnson. (1980). *Metaphors We Live By*. Chicago: University of Chicago Press.

Langer, E. (1989). *Mindfulness*. Reading, Mass: Addison-Wesley.

Lawrence Hall of Science. (1992). *Full Option Science System*. Berkeley, Calif.: Encyclopedia Britannica Education Corporation.

Lazarus, R.S. (1991). *Emotion and Adaptation*. New York: Oxford University Press.

Leadership and the New Science (videotape). (1993). Script by K. McCarey. (Based on *Leadership and the New Science: Learning About Organization from an Orderly Universe*, by M.J. Wheatley, 1992). Carlsbad, Calif.: CRM Films.

LeDoux, J.E. (June 1994). "Emotion, Memory and the Brain." *Scientific American* 270, 6: 50–57.

Legge, J. (1990). *Chaos Theory and Business Planning: How Great Effects Come from Small Causes*. Melbourne, U.C., Australia: Schwartz and Wilkinson.

Letter to the Editor. (June 7, 1996). *USA Today*, p. 3A.

Lieb, B., ed. (March 1993). "Achieving World Class Standards: The Challenge for Educating Teachers." *Proceedings of the OERI Study Group on Educating Teachers for World Class Standards*. Washington, D.C.: U.S. Department of Education.

Lozanov, G. (1978a). *Suggestology and Outlines of Suggestopedy*. New York: Gordon and Breach Science Publishers, Inc.

Lozanov, G. (1978b). *Suggestology and Suggestopedy—Theory and Practice*. Working document for the Expert Working Group, United Nations Educational, Scientific, and Cultural Organization (UNESCO) Vol. ED-78/WS/119.

Macionnis, J.J. (1994). *Sociology*. 4th ed. Englewood Cliffs, N.J.: Prentice-Hall.

Mainzer, K. (1994). *Thinking in Complexity: The Complex Dynamics of Matter, Mind, and Mankind*. New York: Springer-Verlag.

Mandela, N. (1994). *Inaugural Speech*. Republic of South Africa. Online source: http://www.sas.upenn.edu/African_Studies/Articles_Gen/Inaugural_Speech_17984.html.

Marshall, S.P. (January 1995). "The Vision, Meaning, and Language of Educational Transformation." *The School Administrator*, pp. 8–15.

Martin, S. (October 1994). "Music Lessons Enhance Spatial Reasoning Skills." *The APA Monitor* 26, 9: 5.

Martinez, J.L., and R.P. Kesner, eds. (1991). *Learning and Memory: A Biological View*. San Diego, Calif.: Academic Press.

Marzano, R.J. (1992). *A Different Kind of Classroom: Teaching with Dimen- sions of Learning*. Alexandria, Va.: ASCD.

Marzano, R.J., D. Pickering, and J. McTighe. (1993). *Assessing Student Outcomes: Performance Assessment Using the Dimensions of Learning Model*. Alexandria, Va.: ASCD.

Maslow, A.H. (1968). *Toward a Psychology of Being*. 2nd ed. New York: D. Van Nostrand Company.

McClure, R., ed. (February 1993). *Learning and Thinking Styles: Classroom Interaction*. Washington, D.C.: National Education Society.

McLaughlin, C., and G. Davidson. (1994). *Spiritual Politics: Changing the World from the Inside out*. New York: Ballantine Books.

Meadows, D. (June 1982). "Whole Earth Models and Systems." *Co-Evolution Quarterly*, pp. 98–108.

Michaels, M. (1994). *Seven Fundamentals of Complexity*. Savoy, Ill.: People Technologies, The Chaos Network.

Miller, J.P. (March 1992). "Toward A Spiritual Curriculum." *Holistic Education Review* 5, 1: 43.

Miller, J.P. (1993). "Worldviews, Educational Orientations, and Holistic Education." In *The Renewal of Meaning in Education*, edited by R. Miller. Brandon, Vt.: Holistic Education Press.

Miller, N.E. (November 1995). "Clinical-Experimental Interactions in the Development of Neuroscience." *American Psychologist* 50, 11: 901-911.

Miller, R. (1990). *What Are Schools for? Holistic Education in American Culture*. Brandon, Vt.: Holistic Education Press.

Miller, R., ed. (1991). *New Directions in Education: Selections from Holistic Education Review*. Brandon, Vt.: Holistic Education Press.

Morley, D. (February 1993). "Chasing Chaos in Santa Fe." *Manufacturing Systems*, p. 40.

Morley, D. (October 1995). "Nonlinear Social Behavior." *Manufacturing Systems*, p. 16.

Morris, L. (1995). *Managing the Evolving Corporation*. New York: Van Nostrand Reinhold.

Moyers, B. (1993). *Healing and the Mind*. New York: Doubleday. Nadel, L., and J. Wilmer. (1980). "Context and Conditioning: A Place for Space." *Physiological Psychology* 8: 218–228.

Nadel, L., J. Wilmer, and E.M. Kurz. (1984). "Cognitive Maps and Environmental Context." In *Context and Learning*, edited by P. Balsam and A. Tomi. Hillsdale, N.J.: Lawrence Erlbaum.

National Center for Education Statistics. (1995). *The Pocket Condition of Education 1995*. Washington, D.C.: U.S. Department of Education.

Neihardt, J.G. (1961). *Black Elk Speaks: Being. The Life Story of a Holy Man of the Oglala Sioux*. Lincoln: University of Nebraska Press.

Nerburn, K., and L. Mengelkoch, eds. (1991). *Native American Wisdom*. San Rafael, Calif.: The Classic Wisdom Collection, New World Library.

Neville, B. (1989). *Education Psyche: Emotion, Imagination, and the Unconscious in Learning*. North Blackburn, Victoria, Australia: Collins Dove.

Newell, A. (1990). *Unified Theories of Cognition*. Cambridge, Mass.: Harvard University Press.

Nieto, S. (December 1994). "Lessons from Students on Creating a Chance to Dream." *Harvard Educational Review* 64, 4: 392–426.

O'Keefe, J., and L. Nadel. (1978). *The Hippocampus as a Cognitive Map*. Oxford: Clarendon Press.

Oliver, D.W., and K.W. Gershman. (1989). *Education, Modernity, and Fractured Meaning: Toward a Process Theory of Teaching and Learning*. Albany: State University of New York Press.

Olsen, L. (1994). *The Unfinished Journey: Restructuring Schools in a Diverse Society*. San Francisco, Calif.: California Tomorrow.

Ornstein, R. (1991). *The Evolution of Consciousness: The Origins of the Way We Think*. New York: Prentice-Hall.

Pace, G., ed. (1994). "Whole Learning in the Middle School." In *A Learning Journey: Exploring Teaching and Learning in the Middle School Language Arts Classroom*, edited by P.T. Cousin and E. Aragon. Boston: Christopher Gordon Publishers.

Pascale, R.T. (1990). *Managing on the Edge: How the Smartest Companies Use Conflict to Stay Ahead.* New York: Simon and Schuster.

Patterson, J.L. (1993). *Leadership for Tomorrow's Schools.* Alexandria, Va.: ASCD.

Pelletier, K.R. (1994). *Sound Mind, Sound Body: A New Model for Lifelong Health.* New York: Simon and Schuster.

Penrose, R. (1989). *The Emperor's New Mind.* New York: Oxford University Press.

Penrose, R. (1994). *Shadows of the Mind: A Search for the Missing Science of Consciousness.* New York: Oxford University Press.

Perelman, L.J. (1992). *School's Out.* New York: Avon Books.

Perkins, D. (1992). *Smart Schools: From Training Memories to Educating Minds.* New York: The Free Press.

Perkins, D. (1995). *Outsmarting IQ: The Emerging Science of Learnable Intelligence.* New York: The Free Press.

Perrone, V.E., ed. (1991). *Expanding Student Assessment.* Alexandria, Va: ASCD.

Peters, R. (1985). "Notes on the Educational Imagination." (Unpublished review of Eisner, E.W., 1985, *The Educational Imagination—On the Design and Evaluation of School Programs.* 2nd ed. New York: Macmillan Publishing Company). California State University, San Bernandino.

Peterson, C., S. Maier, and M.E.P. Seligman. (1993). *Learned Helplessness: A Theory for the Age of Personal Control.* New York: Oxford University Press.

Phares, J.E. (1976). *Locus of Control in Personality.* Morristown, N.J.: General Learning Press.

Portfolio Submission Guidelines: Student Work Samples. (1995). Park View Middle School. Yucaipa, Calif.

Posner, G.J. (1989). *Field Experience Methods of Reflective Teaching.* White Plains, N.Y.: Longman, Inc.

Posner, G.J. (May 1992) "What Is Reflective Thinking and Why Is It Desirable?" Paper presented at the ASCD Annual Conference, Supporting the Reflective Practitioner. New Orleans, La.

Prigogine, I., and I. Stengers. (1984). *Order Out of Chaos: Man's New Dialogue with Nature.* New York: Bantam Books.

Purkey, W.W. (1970). *Self-Concept and School Achievement.* Englewood Cliffs, N.J.: Prentice-Hall.

Rauscher, F.H., G.L. Shaw, and K.N. Ky. (October 1993). "Music and Spatial Task Performance." *Nature* 365: 611.

Rauscher, F.H., G.L. Shaw, L.J. Levine, K.N. Ky, and E.L. Wright. (1995). "Listening to Mozart Enhances Spatial-Temporal Reasoning: Toward a Neurophysiological Basis." *Neuroscience Letters* 185: 44–47.

Richards, A.C., and A.W. Combs. (1992). "Education and the Humanistic Challenge." *The Humanistic Psychologist* 20, 2 and 3: 372–388.

Robertson, R., and A. Combs, eds. (1995). *Chaos Theory in Psychology and the Life Sciences.* Mahwah, N.J.: Lawrence Erlbaum.

Roehler, L.R., G.G. Duffy, M. Conley, B.A. Herrman, J. Johnson, and S. Michelsen. (April 1987). "Exploring Preservice Teachers' Knowledge Structures." Annual conference of the American Educational Research Association, Washington, D.C.

Rogers, C. (1969). *Freedom to Learn.* Columbus, Ohio: Charles E. Merrill Publishing Company.

Rose, S. (1993). *The Making of Memory.* New York: Anchor Books.

Rosen, R. (June 11, 1995). "In the '90's, Prisons Come Before Schools." *Los Angeles Times,* p. M5.

Roth, K.J. (April 1985). "Conceptual Change Learning and Student Processing of Science Texts." Paper presented at the meeting of the American Educational Research Association, Chicago.

Rottier, L. (October 1995). "If Kids Ruled the World: ICONS." *Educational Leadership* 53, 2: 51–53.

Russell, P. (1979). *The Brain Book.* New York: Penguin Books.

Russell, P. (1995). *The Global Brain Awakens: Our Next Evolutionary Leap.* Palo Alto, Calif: Global Brain, Inc.

Samples, B. (December 1995). "Education as Love." *Holistic Education Review* 8, 4: 4–10.

Sarason, S.B. (1990). *The Predictable Failure of Educational Reform: Can We Change Course Before It's Too Late?* San Francisco: Jossey-Bass.

Sarason, S.B. (1993a). *The Case for Change: Rethinking the Preparation of Educators.* San Francisco: Jossey-Bass.

Sarason, S.B. (1993b). *Letters to a SERIOUS Education President.* Newbury Park, Calif: Corwin Press, Inc.

Scardamalia, M., and C. Bereiter. (1992). "Text-Based and Knowledge-Based Questioning by Children." *Cognition and Instruction* 9, 3: 177–199.

Scheffler, I. (1991). *In Praise of the Cognitive Emotions.* New York: Routledge.

Schein, E.H. (1993). "On Dialogue, Culture, and Organizational Learning." *Organizational Systems* 22, 2: 40–65.

Schon, D.A. (1983). *The Reflective Practitioner.* New York: Basic Books.

Schon, D.A. (1987). *Educating the Reflective Practitioner.* San Francisco: Jossey-Bass.

Schwartz, R. (March 1987). "Our Multiple Selves: Applying Systems Thinking to the Inner Family." *Networker*, pp. 25–83.

Schwartz, R. (November 1988). "When We are Two: Know Thy Selves." *Networker*, pp. 21–29.

Selye, H. (1978). *The Stress of Life.* rev. ed. New York: McGraw-Hill.

Senge, P.M. (1990). *The Fifth Discipline: The Art and Practice of the Learning Organization.* New York: Doubleday Currency.

Shapiro, S.B., and J. Reiff. (1993). "A Framework for Reflective Inquiry on Practice: Beyond Intuition and Experience." *Psychological Reports* 73: 1379–1394.

Sheldrake, R. (1988). *The Presence of the Past. Morphic Resonance and the Habits of Nature.* New York: Times Books.

Sleek, S. (December 1995). "Rallying the Troops Inside our Bodies." *The APA Monitor* 26, 12: 1.

Spielberger, C.D., ed. (1972). *Anxiety: Current Trends in Theory and Research*, Vols. 1 and 2. New York: Academic Press.

Stacey, R.D. (1992). *Managing the Unknowable: Strategic Boundaries Between Order and Chaos in Organizations.* San Francisco: Jossey-Bass.

Stacy, D. (May 1994). "Cosmic Conspiracy: Six Decades of Government UFO Cover-Ups, Part Two." *Omni* 16, 8: 54–87.

Sternberg, R.J. (1988). *The Triarchic Mind: A New Theory of Human Intelligence.* New York: Viking.

Stevenson, H.W. (December 1992). "Learning from Asian Schools." *Scientific American* 267, 6: 70–76.

Sylwester, R. (1995). *A Celebration of Neurons: An Educator's Guide to the Human Brain.* Alexandria, Va.: ASCD.Taylor, W.C. (Reviewer). (November 1994). "Control in an Age of Chaos." *Harvard Business Review* 72, 6: 64–76.

Terry, N. (March 1992). "Where Learning Is the Adventure." *Zip Line* 21: 17–19.

Times Wire Service. (January 2, 1996). "Report Links Gene Variation to Novelty-Seeking Trait." *Los Angeles Times*, p. A13.

Vail, P.B. (1989). *Management as a Performing Art*. San Francisco: Jossey-Bass.

Vela, K. (February 1, 1996). *Letter: The Kids from Outerspace*. Dry Creek Elementary School: Rio Linda, Calif.

Vollmer, J. Local Control Project. (February 1996). P.O. Box 1535, Fairfield, Iowa, 52556.

Vygotsky, L.S. (1978). *Mind in Society*. Cambridge, Mass.: Harvard University Press.

Waldrop, M.M. (1992). *Complexity: The Emerging Science at the Edge of Order and Chaos*. New York: Simon and Schuster.

Wallace, B., and L.E. Fischer. (1987). *Consciousness and Behavior*. Newton, Mass.: Allyn and Bacon.

Wallace, R.K. (1993). *The Physiology of Consciousness*. Fairfield, Iowa: Institute of Science, Technology, and Public Policy and Maharishi International University Press.

Webster's New World Dictionary of the American Language. (1960). Cleveland: The World Publishing Company.

Wheatley, M.J. (1992). *Leadership and the New Science: Learning About Organization from an Orderly Universe*. San Francisco: Berrett-Koehler.

Wheatley, M.J. (September 1995). "Leadership and the New Science." Presentation transcribed as Professional Development Brief No. 3. California State Development Council (CSDC).

Wheatley, M., and F. Capra. (September 1995). "A Diagogue." *The Professional Development Briefs: Fourth Annual Colloguium*. Burlingame, Calif.: California Staff Development Council (CSDC).

Wheatley, M.J., and M. Kellner-Rogers. (1996). *A Simpler Way*. Berrett-Koehler: San Francisco.

Whitehair, J. (December 1994). "Schools on the Move." *It's Elementary* 3, 18: 5.

Wilber, K. (1995). *Sex, Ecology, Spirituality: The Spirit of Evolution*. Boston: Shambhala Publications, Inc.

Wilson, D.L. (May 1995). "Seeking the Neural Correlate of Consciousness." *American Scientist* 83: 269–270.

Wood, G.H. (1992). *Schools That Work: America's Most Innovative Public Education Programs*. New York: Penguin Group.

Woolfolk, A.E. (1995). *Educational Psychology*. 6th ed. Needham Heights, Mass.: Allyn and Bacon.

Index

Page numbers in boldface refer to pages that contain figures.

About the Authors

Renate Nummela Caine is a professor of education at California State University, California. She was an award-winning teacher and has worked at every level of education, from kindergarten to university. She consults on learning, teaching, and education throughout the United States and in other countries.

Geoffrey Caine is a learning consultant. He has taught in the fields of education, law, and management in universities in Australia and the United States. He has extensive experience in business and training, and consults throughout the United States and in other countries.

Renate and Geoffrey Caine can be reached at Caine Learning, P.O. Box 1847, Idyllwild, CA 92549. See below for more contact information:

Telephone: 909-659-0152
Fax: 909-659-0242
E-mail: RNCaine@Wiley.CSUSB.edu
E-mail: Caine@uor.edu
E-mail: gr@pe.net